Spanish

PHRASEBOOK & DICTIONARY

Acknowledgments

Associate Publisher Tali Budlender
Managing Editors Annelies Mertens, Tasmin Waby McNaughtan
Editors Laura Crawford, Jodie Martire, Martine Power, Branislava Vladisavljevic
Series Designer Mark Adams
Managing Layout Designer Chris Girdler, Celia Wood
Layout Designers Frank Deim, Carol Jackson, Jacqui Saunders
Production Support Yvonne Kirk, Glenn van der Knijff
Language Writers Marta López, Cristina Hernández Montero

Thanks

Jane Atkin, Sasha Baskett, Yvonne Bischofberger, Helen Christinis, Brendan Dempsey, Indra Kilfoyle, Nic Lehman, Naomi Parker, Trent Paton, Piers Pickard, Averil Robertson, Joseph Spanti, John Taufa, Juan Winata

Published by Lonely Planet Publications Pty Ltd
ABN 36 005 607 983

5th Edition – March 2012
ISBN 978 1 74220 809 1
Text © Lonely Planet 2012
Cover Image Bruce Bi – Lonely Planet Images

Printed in China 10 9 8 7 6 5 4 3 2 1

Contact lonelyplanet.com/contact

MIX
Paper from
responsible sources
FSC™ C021741
www.fsc.org

Look out for the following icons throughout the book:

'Shortcut' Phrase
Easy-to-remember alternative to the full phrase

Q&A Pair
Question-and-answer pair – we suggest a response to the question asked

Look For
Phrases you may see on signs, menus etc

Listen For
Phrases you may hear from officials, locals etc

Language Tip
An insight into the foreign language

Culture Tip
An insight into the local culture

How to read the phrases:

- Coloured words and phrases throughout the book are phonetic guides to help you pronounce the foreign language.
- Lists of phrases with tinted background are options you can choose to complete the phrase above them.

These abbreviations will help you choose the right words and phrases in this book:

a	adjective	m	masculine	sg	singular
f	feminine	n	noun	v	verb
inf	informal	pl	plural		
lit	literal	pol	polite		

Contents

Spanish

INTRO

español es·pa·*nyol*

Who Speaks Spanish?
Official Language

NORTH & CENTRAL AMERICA
MEXICO
GUATEMALA
HONDURAS
NICARAGUA
EL SALVADOR
COSTA RICA
PANAMA

CARIBBEAN
CUBA
PUERTO RICO
DOMINICAN REPUBLIC

SOUTH AMERICA
ARGENTINA
CHILE · BOLIVIA
PARAGUAY
URUGUAY · PERU
VENEZUELA
COLOMBIA
ECUADOR

EUROPE & AFRICA
SPAIN
EQUATORIAL GUINEA

Widely Understood USA

Why Bother

You'll be seduced by this melodic language and have fun trying to roll your *rr*'s like the locals – not to mention ordering scrumptious tapas or engaging in all the shouting at the *fútbol*.

Distinctive Sounds

The strong and rolled r, harsh and guttural kh and, in European Spanish, 'lisping' th.

Spanish in the World

Over the last 500 years, Spanish in Latin America has evolved differently to the

300 MILLION
speak Spanish as their
first language

100 MILLION
speak Spanish as their
second language

Spanish of Europe. Among other differences, you'll easily recognise Latin Americans by the lack of lisp in their speech – ie *cerveza* (beer) is ther·*ve*·tha in Europe but ser·*ve*·sa across the Atlantic.

Spanish in Spain

Spanish, or Castilian (*castellano* ka·ste·*lya*·no) is primarily the language of Castille (covering the largest territory in Spain). However, Catalan, Galician and Basque are also official languages, and locals in these regions are very proud of their own language.

False Friends

Warning: many Spanish words look like English words but have a different meaning altogether, eg *suburbio* soo·*boor*·byo is a slum district, not a suburb (which is *barrio* ba·ryo in Spanish).

Language Family

Romance (developed from Vulgar Latin spoken by Roman soldiers and merchants during the conquest from the 3rd to the 1st century BC). Close relatives include Portuguese, Italian, French and Romanian.

Must-Know Grammar

Spanish has a formal and informal word for 'you' (*Usted* oo·*ste* and *tú* too respectively). The verbs also have a different ending for each person, like the English 'I do' vs 'he/she do**es**'.

Donations to English

Thanks to Columbus' discovery of the New World in 1492, a large corpus of words from indigenous American languages has entered English via Spanish. You may recognise *canyon, guerrilla, ranch, tornado*...

5 Phrases to Learn Before You Go

1 **What time does it open/close?**
¿A qué hora abren/cierran? a ke o·ra ab·ren/thye·ran

The Spanish tend to observe the siesta (midday break), so opening times may surprise you.

2 **Are these complimentary?**
¿Son gratis? son gra·tees

Tapas (bar snacks) are available pretty much around the clock at Spanish bars. You'll find they're free in some places.

3 **When is admission free?**
¿Cuándo es la entrada gratuita?
kwan·do es la en·tra·da gra·twee·ta

Many museums and galleries in Spain have admission-free times, so check before buying tickets.

4 **Where can we go (salsa) dancing?**
¿Dónde podemos ir a bailar (salsa)?
don·de po·de·mos eer a bai·lar (sal·sa)

Flamenco may be the authentic viewing experience in Spain, but to actively enjoy the music you'll want to do some dancing.

5 **How do you say this in (Catalan/Galician/Basque)?**
¿Cómo se dice ésto en (catalán/gallego/euskera)?
ko·mo se dee·the es·to en (ka·ta·lan/ga·lye·go/e·oos·ke·ra)

Spain has four official languages, and people in these regions will appreciate it if you try to use their local language.

10 Phrases to Sound Like a Local

What's up?	**¿Qué pasa?**	ke *pa*·sa
Great!	**¡Genial!**	khe·*nyal*
How cool!	**¡Qué guay!**	ke gwai
That's fantastic!	**¡Estupendo!**	es·too·*pen*·do
Really?	**¿En serio?**	en *se*·ryo
You don't say!	**¡No me digas!**	no me *dee*·gas
Sure.	**Seguro.**	se·*goo*·ro
OK.	**Vale.**	*va*·le
Of course!	**¡Por supuesto!**	por soo·*pwes*·to
Whatever.	**Lo que sea.**	lo ke *se*·a

ABOUT Spanish

Pronunciation

Spanish pronunciation isn't difficult, as most sounds are similar to the sounds found in English. The relationship between Spanish sounds and their spelling is straightforward and consistent. There are some easy rules to follow and once you learn them you shouldn't have problems being understood. As in most languages, Spanish pronunciation can vary according to region – this book focuses on Castilian Spanish.

Vowel Sounds

SYMBOL	ENGLISH EQUIVALENT	SPANISH EXAMPLE	TRANSLITERATION
a	alms	agua	*a*·gwa
ai	aisle	bailar	bai·*lar*
e	red	número	*noo*·me·ro
ee	bee	día	*dee*·a
ey	hey	seís	seys
o	go	ojo	o·kho
oo	book	gusto	*goo*·sto
ow	cow	autobús	ow·to·*boos*
oy	boy	hoy	oy

Consonant Sounds

SYMBOL	ENGLISH EQUIVALENT	SPANISH EXAMPLE	TRANSLITERATION
b	big	barco	*bar·*ko
ch	chilli	chica	*chee·*ka
d	din	dinero	dee·*ne·*ro
f	fun	fiesta	*fye·*sta
g	go	gato	*ga·*to
k	kick	cabeza, queso	ka·*be·*tha, *ke·*so
kh	as in the Scottish *loch*	jardín, gente	khar·*deen*, *khen·*te
l	loud	lago	*la·*go
ly	million	llamada	lya·*ma·*da
m	man	mañana	ma·*nya·*na
n	no	nuevo	*nwe·*vo
ny	canyon	señora	se·*nyo·*ra
p	pig	padre	*pa·*dre
r	run (but stronger and rolled)	ritmo, burro, mariposa	*reet·*mo, *boo·*ro, ma·*ree·*po·sa
s	so	semana	se·*ma·*na
t	tin	tienda	*tyen·*da
th	thin	Barcelona, manzana	bar·the·*lo·*na, man·*tha·*na
v	soft 'b', between 'v' and 'b'	vaca	*va·*ka
w	win	guardia	*gwar·*dya
y	yes	viaje, ya	*vya·*khe, ya

Reading & Writing

There are some key things to remember about consonants in written Spanish:

» The letter *c* is pronounced with a lisp, eg *cerveza* ther·ve·tha, except when it comes before *a*, *o* and *u* or a consonant. Then, it's pronounced hard like the *k* in 'king'.

» When ending a word, the letter *d* is also pronounced soft, like a th, or is so slight that it hardly gets pronounced at all.

» The letter *j* stands for a harsh and guttural sound, and we use the kh symbol in our pronunciation guides.

» Try to roll your double *r*'s.

» The letter *q* is pronounced hard, like a k.

» The letter *v* sounds more like a b, said with the lips pressed together.

» There are a few letters which don't appear in the English alphabet: *ch*, *ll* and *ñ*. You'll see that these letters have their own entries in the Spanish–English dictionary.

~ SPANISH ALPHABET ~

A	a	a	B	b	be	C	c	the
CH	ch	che	D	d	de	E	e	e
F	f	e·fe	G	g	khe	H	h	a·che
I	i	ee	J	j	*kho·*ta	K	k	ka
L	l	e·le	LL	ll	e·lye	M	m	e·me
N	n	e·ne	Ñ	ñ	e·nye	O	o	o
P	p	pe	Q	q	koo	R	r	e·re
S	s	e·se	T	t	te	U	u	oo
V	v	oo·ve	W	w	*oo·ve do·*ble	X	x	e·kees
Y	y	ee·*grye·*ga	Z	z	*the·*ta			

Word Stress

There is word stress in Spanish, which means you emphasise one syllable in a word over another. Rule of thumb: when a written word ends in *n*, *s* or a vowel, the stress falls on the second-last syllable, eg *lejos* le·khos (far), *casa* ka·sa (house). Otherwise, the final syllable is stressed, eg *hablar* a·blar (talk). If you see an accent mark over a syllable, it cancels out these rules and you just stress that syllable instead, eg *número* noo·me·ro (number).

LANGUAGE TIP

False Friends

Beware of false friends – those words that sound like familiar English, but could land you in a bit of trouble if you use them unwittingly in Spanish. Here are some mistakes that it's a little too easy to make:

el suburbio	el soo·boor·byo slum district, not 'suburb' which is *el barrio*, el ba·ryo
Estoy constipado/a. m/f	es·toy kons·tee·pa·do/a I have a cold, not 'I'm constipated', which is *estoy estreñido/a* m/f es·toy es·tre·nyee·do/a
Estoy embarazada.	es·toy em·ba·ra·tha·da I'm pregnant, not 'I'm embarassed', which is *estoy avergonzado/a* m/f es·toy a·ver·gon·tha·do/a
la injuria	la een·khoo·ree·a insult, not 'injury', which is *la herida*, la e·ree·da
los parientes	los pa·ree·yen·tes relatives, not 'parents', which is *los padres*, los pa·dres
sensible	sen·see·ble sensitive, not 'sensible', which is *prudente*, proo·den·te

ABOUT Spanish

Grammar

This chapter is designed to explain the main grammatical structures you need in order to make your own sentences. Look under each heading for information on functions which these grammatical categories express in a sentence. For example, demonstratives are used for giving instructions, so you'll need them to tell the taxi driver where your hotel is, etc. A glossary of grammatical terms is included at the end of this chapter to help you.

Adjectives & Adverbs

Describing People/Things • Doing Things

When using an adjective to describe a noun, you need to use a different ending depending on whether the noun is masculine or feminine, and singular or plural (see **gender** and **plurals**). Most adjectives use the following four endings:

~ ADJECTIVES ~

	singular		plural	
m	fantástico	fan·*tas*·tee·ko	fantásticos	fan·*tas*·tee·kos
f	fantástica	fan·*tas*·tee·ka	fantásticas	fan·*tas*·tee·kas

a fantastic hotel   un hotel fantástico (lit: a-**m-sg** hotel fantastic-**m-sg**)
oon o·*tel* fan·*tas*·tee·ko

a fantastic meal	una comida fantástica (lit: a-f-sg meal fantastic-f-sg) oo·na ko·*mee*·da fan·*tas*·tee·ka
some fantastic books	unos libros fantásticos (lit: some-m-pl books fantastic-m-pl) oo·nos *lee*·bros fan·*tas*·tee·kos
some fantastic tapas	unas tapas fantásticas (lit: some-f-pl tapas fantastic-f-pl) oo·nas *ta*·pas fan·*tas*·tee·kas

Adjectives generally come after the noun in Spanish. However, adjectives expressing quantity (such as 'much', 'a lot', 'little', 'few', 'many') always precede the noun. See also **demonstratives** and **possessives**.

| **a comfortable hotel** | un hotel cómodo (lit: a-m-sg hotel comfortable-m-sg)
oon o·*tel* ko·mo·do |
| **many tourists** | muchos turistas (lit: many-m-pl tourists)
moo·chos too·rees·tas |

Most adverbs in Spanish are derived from adjectives by adding the ending -*mente* ·*men*·te to the singular feminine form of the adjective (ie the form ending in -*a*), just like you add the ending '-ly' to the adjective in English. In Spanish, adverbs are generally placed after the verb they refer to.

| **a slow train** | un tren lento (lit: a-m-sg train slow-m-sg)
oon tren *len*·to |
| **to speak slowly** | hablar lentamente (lit: to-speak slowly)
ab·*lar* len·ta·*men*·te |

Articles

Naming People/Things

There are four words for the definite article (ie equivalents of 'the' in English) in Spanish, used depending on the gender and the number of the noun (see **gender** and **plurals**). The masculine singular form of the definite article is joined to some prepositions when it's placed after them, so *a el* (to the-m-sg) becomes *al* al and *de el* (of the-m-sg) becomes *del* del. See also **prepositions**.

~ DEFINITE ARTICLES ~

m sg	**the car**	el coche	el ko·che
m pl	**the cars**	los coches	los ko·ches
f sg	**the shop**	la tienda	la tyen·da
f pl	**the shops**	las tiendas	las tyen·das

Similarly, Spanish has four words for the indefinite article (ie 'a/an' in English), depending on the gender and number of the noun.

~ INDEFINITE ARTICLES ~

m sg	**an egg**	un huevo	oon we·vo
m pl	**some eggs**	unos huevos	oo·nos we·vos
f sg	**a house**	una casa	oo·na ka·sa
f pl	**some houses**	unas casas	oo·nas ka·sas

Be

Describing People/Things • Making Statements

Spanish has two words for the English verb 'be': *ser* ser and *estar* es·tar, which are used depending on the context.

~ USE OF *SER* (TO BE) ~

permanent characteristics of persons/things	Liz es muy guapa. leez es mooy *gwa*·pa	Liz is very pretty.
occupations or nationality	Ana es de España. *a*·na es de e·*spa*·nya	Ana is from Spain.
time or location of events	Son las tres. son las tres	It's 3 o'clock.
possession	¿De quién es este bolso? de kyen es *es*·te *bol*·so	Whose bag is this?

~ USE OF *ESTAR* (TO BE) ~

temporary characteristics of persons/things	La sopa está fría. la *so*·pa es·*ta free*·a	The soup is cold.
time or location of persons/things	Estamos en Madrid. es·*ta*·mos en ma·*dreeth*	We're in Madrid.
mood of a person	Estoy contento/a m/f es·toy kon·*ten*·to/a	I'm happy.

~ SER (TO BE) – PRESENT TENSE ~

I	am	yo	soy	yo	soy
you sg inf	**are**	tú	eres	too	e·res
you sg pol	**are**	Usted	es	oo·*ste*	es
he	**is**	él	es	el	es
she	**is**	ella	es	e·lya	es
we	**are**	nosotros m nosotras f	somos	no·*so*·tros no·*so*·tras	*so*·mos
you pl inf	**are**	vosotros m vosotras f	sois	vo·*so*·tros vo·*so*·tras	soys
you pl pol	**are**	Ustedes	son	oo·*ste*·des	son
they	**are**	ellos m ellas f	son	e·lyos e·lyas	son

I	**am**	yo	estoy	yo	es·*toy*
you sg inf	**are**	tú	estás	too	es·*tas*
you sg pol	**are**	Usted	está	oo·*ste*	es·*ta*
he	**is**	él	está	el	es·*ta*
she	**is**	ella	está	e·lya	es·*ta*
we	**are**	nosotros m nosotras f	estamos	no·so·tros no·so·tras	es·*ta*·mos
you pl inf	**are**	vosotros m vosotras f	estáis	vo·so·tros vo·so·tras	es·*tais*
you pl pol	**are**	Ustedes	están	oo·*ste*·des	es·*tan*
they	**are**	ellos m ellas f	están	e·lyos e·lyas	es·*tan*

~ ESTAR (TO BE) – PRESENT TENSE ~

Demonstratives

Giving Instructions • Indicating Location • Pointing Things Out

To point something out, the easiest phrases to use are *es* es (it is), *esto es* es·to es (this is) or *eso es* e·so es (that is).

It's a guide to Seville.	Es una guía de Sevilla. (lit: is a-**f-sg** guide of Seville) es oo·na gee·a de se·*vee*·lya

The Spanish words for 'this' and 'that' vary, depending on whether something is close (ie 'this'), away from you (ie 'that'), or even further away in time or space (ie 'that over there'). Each of these words changes form depending on the gender and number of the noun it refers to. See also **gender** and **plurals**.

~ DEMONSTRATIVES ~

	m sg		m pl	
this (close)	éste	e·ste	éstos	e·stos
that (away)	ése	e·se	ésos	e·sos
that (further away)	aquél	a·kel	aquéllos	a ke·lyos
	f sg		f pl	
this (close)	ésta	e·sta	éstas	e·stas
that (away)	ésa	e·sa	ésas	e·sas
that (further away)	aquélla	a·ke·lya	aquéllas	a·ke·lyas

Gender

Naming People/Things

In Spanish, all nouns (words which denote a thing, person or idea) have either masculine or feminine gender. You can recognise the noun's gender by the article, demonstrative, possessive or any other adjective accompanying the noun, as they all change form to agree with the noun's gender (see **adjectives & adverbs**, **articles**, **demonstratives**, **possessives**). The gender of words is also indicated in the dictionary, but here are some general rules:

» a word is masculine/feminine if it refers to a man/woman
» words ending in -o or -or are generally masculine
» words ending in -a, -d, -z or -ión are usually feminine

The masculine and feminine forms of words are indicated with m and f throughout this book where relevant. See also p138.

Have

Possessing

Possession can be indicated in various ways in Spanish (see also **possessives**). One way is by using the verb *tener* te·*ner* (have). For negative forms with 'have', see **negatives**.

		~ *TENER* (TO HAVE) ~			
I	**have**	yo	tengo	yo	*ten·go*
you sg inf	**have**	tú	tienes	too	*tye·nes*
you sg pol	**have**	Usted	tiene	oo·*ste*	*tye·ne*
he	**has**	él	tiene	el	*tye·ne*
she	**has**	ella	tiene	e·*lya*	*tye·ne*
we	**have**	nosotros m nosotras f	ten-emos	no·so·tros no·so·tras	te·*ne*·mos
you pl inf	**have**	vosotros m vosotras f	tenéis	vo·so·tros vo·so·tras	te·*neys*
you pl pol	**have**	Ustedes	tienen	oo·*ste*·des	*tye*·nen
they	**have**	ellos m ellas f	tienen	e·*lyos* e·*lyas*	*tye*·nen

The word *hay* ai – which is the impersonal form of the verb *haber* ha·*ber* (have) – is used to mean 'there is/are' and in questions for 'is/are there ...?':

Is there hot water?   ¿Hay agua caliente?
(lit: is-there water hot-f-sg)
ai *a*·gwa ka·*lyen*·te

Negatives

Negating

To make a negative statement in Spanish, just add the word *no* no (not) before the main verb of the sentence:

I'm not going to try that.	No voy a probarlo. (lit: not I-go to to-try-it) no voy a pro·*bar*·lo

Contrary to English, Spanish uses double negatives:

I have nothing to declare.	No tengo nada que declarar. (lit: not I-have nothing that to-declare) no *ten*·go *na*·da ke dek·la·*rar*

Personal Pronouns

Making Statements • Naming People/Things

Personal pronouns ('I', 'you' etc) change form in Spanish depending on whether they're the subject or the object of a sentence. It's the same in English, which has 'I' and 'me' as subject and object pronouns (eg 'I see her' and 'She sees me'). Note, however, that the subject pronoun is usually omitted in Spanish as the subject is understood from the corresponding verb form (see **verbs**).

I'm a student.	Soy estudiante. (lit: I-am student-**m&f-sg**) soy es·too·*dyan*·te

ABOUT SPANISH GRAMMAR

~ SUBJECT PRONOUNS ~

I	yo	yo	**we**	nosotros m nosotras f	no·so·tros no·so·tras
you sg inf	tú	too	**you** pl inf	vosotros m vosotras f	vo·so·tros vo·so·tras
you sg pol	Usted	oo·ste	**you** pl pol	Ustedes	oo·ste·des
he **she**	él ella	el e·lya	**they**	ellos m ellas f	e·lyos e·lyas

As the tables show, Spanish has two 'you' forms. With people familiar to you or younger than you, it's usual to use the informal form of 'you', *tú* too, rather than the polite form, *Usted* oo·ste. Phrases in this book use the form that is appropriate to the situation. Where both forms are used, they are indicated by pol and inf. See also the box **addressing people**, p95.

~ OBJECT PRONOUNS ~

me	me	me	**us**	nos	nos
you sg inf	te	te	**you** pl inf	vos	vos
you sg pol	lo/le m la/le f	lo/le la/le	**you** pl pol	los/les m las/les f	los/les las/les
him **it**	lo/le	lo/le	**them**	los/les m las/les f	los/les las/les
her **it**	la/le	la/le			

In this table, the forms separated by a slash are direct/indirect object pronouns.

The direct and indirect object pronouns differ only for the third person ('he', 'she', 'it', 'they') and the polite 'you' forms.

I don't know her.	No la conozco. (lit: not her I-know) no la ko·*noth*·ko
I'm talking to her.	Le hablo. (lit: to-her I-talk) le *a*·blo

The object pronouns generally come before the verb. The indirect object pronoun comes before the direct object pronoun.

I'll show it to you.	Te lo mostraré. (lit: to-you-**sg-inf** it-**m-sg** I-will-show) te lo mos·tra·*re*

Plurals

Naming People/Things

To form plurals in Spanish, add -*s* if the noun ends in a vowel and -*es* if it ends in a consonant. In this book singular and plural forms are shown with **sg** and **pl** respectively where needed.

~ SINGULAR ~			~ PLURAL ~		
bed	cama	*ka*·ma	**beds**	camas	*ka*·mas
woman	mujer	moo·*kher*	**women**	mujeres	moo·*khe*·res

Possessives

Possessing

A common way of indicating possession is by using possessive adjectives before the noun they refer to. Like other adjectives, they agree with the noun in number, and in case of 'our' and 'your' they also agree in gender (see also **gender** and **plurals**).

our daughter	nuestra hija (lit: our-**f-sg** daughter) *nwes*·tra ee·kha

~ POSSESSIVE ADJECTIVES ~

my	mi/mis	mee/ mees	**our**	nuestro/ nuestros m nuestra/ nuestras f	nwes·tro/ nwes·tros nwes·tra/ nwes·tras
your sg inf	tu/tus	too/ toos	**your** pl inf	vuestro/ vuestros m vuestra/ vuestras f	vwes·tro/ vwes·tros vwes·tra/ vwes·tras
your sg pol	su/sus	soo/ soos	**your** pl pol	su/sus	soo/soos
his her its	su/sus	soo/ soos	**their**	su/sus	soo/soos

Note that in the table above, the Spanish possessive adjective forms separated by a slash are used with a singular and plural noun respectively.

my child	mi hijo (lit: my-m-sg child) mee *ee*·kho
my children	mis hijos (lit: my-m-pl children) mees *ee*·khos

Another way to indicate possession is by using possessive pronouns (see the table opposite), which also agree in gender and number with the noun.

The book is mine.	El libro es mío. (lit: the-m-sg book is mine-m-sg) el *lee*·bro es *mee*·o

~ POSSESSIVE PRONOUNS ~

mine	mío/ míos m mía/ mías f	*mee·o/* *mee·os* *mee·a/* *mee·as*	ours	nuestro/ nuestros m nuestra/ nuestras f	*nwes·tro/* *nwes·tros* *nwes·tra/* *nwes·tras*
yours sg inf	tuyo/ tuyos m tuya/ tuyas f	*too·yo/* *too·yos* *too·ya/* *too·yas*	yours pl inf	vuestro/ vuestros m vuestra/ vuestras f	*vwes·tro/* *vwes·tros* *vwes·tra/* *vwes·tras*
yours sg pol	suyo/ suyos m	*soo·yo/* *soo·yos*	yours pl pol	suyo/ suyos m	*soo·yo/* *soo·yos*
his hers its	suya/ suyas f	*soo·ya/* *soo·yas*	theirs	suya/ suyas f	*soo·ya/* *soo·yas*

The four alternatives in this table are used with **m sg**, **m pl**, **f sg** and **f pl** nouns.

Ownership can also be expressed in Spanish using the construction '*de* de (of) + noun', just like in English. See also **have**.

my friend's bag	el bolso de mi amigo (lit: the-m-sg bag of my friend-m-sg) el *bol·*so de mee a·*mee·*go

Prepositions

Giving Instructions • Indicating Location • Pointing Things Out

Like English, Spanish uses prepositions to explain where things are in time or space. Some common prepositions are listed in the table that follows. For more prepositions, see the **dictionary**.

When certain prepositions are followed by a definite article, they are contracted into a single word (see **articles**).

~ PREPOSITIONS ~

after	después de	des·*pwes* de	**from**	de	de
at (time)	a	a	**in (place)**	en	en
before	antes de	*an*·tes de	**to**	a	a

Questions

Asking Questions • Negating

The easiest way of forming 'yes/no' questions in Spanish is to add the phrase *verdad* ver·*da* (literally 'truth') to the end of a statement, similar to 'isn't it?' in English. You can also turn a statement into a question by putting the verb before the subject of the sentence, just like in English.

This is the right stop, isn't it?	¿Ésta es la parada, verdad? (lit: this-**f-sg** is the-**f-sg** stop truth) *es*·ta es la pa·*ra*·da ver·*da*
Is this the right stop?	¿Es ésta la parada? (lit: is this-**f-sg** the-**f-sg** stop) es *es*·ta la pa·*ra*·da

As in English, there are also question words for more specific questions. These words go at the start of the sentence.

~ QUESTION WORDS ~

how	cómo	*ko*·mo	**where**	dónde	*don*·de
what	qué	ke	**who**	quién **sg**	kyen
				quiénes **pl**	*kye*·nes
when	cuándo	*kwan*·do	**why**	por qué	por ke

Verbs

Doing Things

There are three verb categories in Spanish, depending on whether the infinitive ends in *-ar*, *-er* or *-ir*, eg *hablar* ab·lar (talk), *comer* ko·mer (eat), *vivir* vee·veer (live). Tenses are formed by adding various endings for each person to the verb stem (after removing *-ar*, *-er* or *-ir* from the infinitive) or to the infinitive, and for most verbs these endings follow regular patterns. The verb endings for the present, past and future tenses are presented in the tables on the following pages. For negative forms of verbs, see **negatives**.

~ PRESENT TENSE ~

		hablar	comer	vivir
I	yo	hablo	como	vivo
you sg inf	tú	hablas	comes	vives
you sg pol	Usted	habla	come	vive
he/she	él/ella	habla	come	vive
we	nosotros m nosotras f	hablamos	comemos	vivimos
you pl inf	vosotros m vosotras f	habláis	coméis	vivís
you pl pol	Ustedes	hablan	comen	viven
they	ellos m ellas f	hablan	comen	viven

See also **be** and **have**.

~ PAST TENSE ~

		hablar	comer	vivir
I	yo	hablé	comí	viví
you sg inf	tú	hablaste	comiste	viviste
you sg pol	Usted	habló	comió	vivió
he/she	él/ella	habló	comió	vivió
we	nosotros m nosotras f	hablamos	comimos	vivimos
you pl inf	vosotros m vosotras f	hablasteis	comisteis	vivisteis
you pl pol	Ustedes	hablaron	comieron	vivieron
they	ellos m ellas f	hablaron	comieron	vivieron

In case of the future tense, the endings follow the same pattern for all three verb categories, and they are simply added to the infinitive (dictionary form of the verb), not the verb stem:

~ FUTURE TENSE ~

		hablar	comer	vivir
I	yo	hablaré	comeré	viviré
you sg inf	tú	hablarás	comerás	vivirás
you sg pol	Usted	hablará	comerá	vivirá
he/she	él/ella	hablará	comerá	vivirá
we	nosotros m nosotras f	hablaremos	comeremos	viviremos
you pl inf	vosotros m vosotras f	hablaréis	comeréis	viviréis
you pl pol	Ustedes	hablarán	comerán	vivirán
they	ellos m ellas f	hablarán	comerán	vivirán

Word Order

Making Statements

Spanish has a basic word order of subject–verb–object, just like English. However, the subject pronoun is usually omitted in Spanish because the subject is understood from the corresponding verb form (see **verbs**). Both of the following examples are correct, but the second one is more common:

I study business. Yo estudio comercio.
(lit: I I-study business)
yo es·*too*·dyo ko·*mer*·thyo

Estudio comercio. (lit: I-study business)
es·*too*·dyo ko·*mer*·thyo

See also **negatives** and **questions**.

CULTURE TIP **Proverbs in Spain**

Proverbs are big in Spain. The Marqués de Santillana compiled a national collection in the second half of the 15th century, and one of the characters in *Don Quixote*, Sancho Panza, speaks almost entirely in proverbs. The novel's author, Cervantes, described these popular sayings as 'short sentences based on long experience'.

Ser como el perro del hortelano, que ni come las berzas, ni las deja comer al amo.

ser *ko*·mo el *pe*·ro del or·te·*la*·no ke nee *ko*·me las *ber*·thas nee las *de*·kha ko·*mer* al *a*·mo
(lit: to be like the market gardener's dog, who doesn't eat the cabbages and won't let his master eat them either)

~ GRAMMAR GLOSSARY ~

adjective	a word that describes something – 'he was the **greatest** toreador of his time'
adverb	a word that explains how an action is done – 'he turned around **quickly**'
article	the words 'a', 'an' and 'the'
demonstrative	a word that means 'this' or 'that'
direct object	the thing or person in the sentence that has the action directed to it – 'and the bull missed **him**'
gender	classification of *nouns* into classes (like masculine and feminine), requiring other words (eg *adjectives*) to belong to the same class
indirect object	the person or thing in the sentence that is the recipient of the action – 'the public yelled to **him**'
infinitive	dictionary form of a verb – 'to **be** careful'
noun	a thing, person or idea – 'the **fight** was exciting'
number	whether a word is singular or plural – 'and they sent in new **toreadors**'
personal pronoun	a word that means 'I', 'you' etc
possessive adjective	a word that means 'my', 'your' etc
possessive pronoun	a word that means 'mine', 'yours' etc
preposition	a word like 'for' or 'before' in English
subject	the thing or person in the sentence that does the action – '**his cape** fell on the ground'
tense	form of a *verb* that tells you whether the action is in the present, past or future – eg 'run' (present), 'ran' (past), 'will run' (future)
verb	a word that tells you what action happened – 'when the bull **charged** again'
verb stem	part of a *verb* that doesn't change – eg '**mov**e' in '**mov**ing' and '**mov**ed'

Basics

Understanding

KEY PHRASES

Do you speak English?	¿Habla inglés? **pol**	*ab*·la een·*gles*
I (don't) understand.	(No) Entiendo.	(no) en·*tyen*·do
What does ... mean?	¿Qué significa ...?	ke seeg·nee·*fee*·ka ...

There are two words for 'Spanish': *español* es·pa·*nyol* and *castellano* kas·te·*lya*·no. *Español* is used in Spain, whereas *castellano* is more likely to be used by Latin Americans.

Q **Do you speak (English)?**	¿Habla (inglés)? *ab*·la (een·*gles*)
Q **Does anyone speak (English)?**	¿Hay alguien que hable (inglés)? ai al·*gyen* ke *ab*·le een·*gles*
A **I (don't) speak Spanish.**	(No) Hablo español. (no) *ab*·lo es·pa·*nyol*
A **I speak a little (Spanish).**	Hablo un poco de (español). *ab*·lo oon *po*·ko de (es·pa·*nyol*)
I'd like to practise Spanish.	Me gustaría practicar español. me goos·ta·*ree*·a prak·tee·*kar* es·pa·*nyol*
I need an interpreter who speaks (English).	Necesito un intérprete que hable (inglés). ne·the·*see*·to oon in·*ter*·pre·te ke *ab*·le (een·*gles*)

🔊 LISTEN FOR

¿Cómo?	ko·mo	Pardon?
No.	no	No.
Sí.	see	Yes.

Would you like me to teach you some English?	¿Quieres que te enseñe algo de inglés? inf kye·res ke te en·se·nye al·go de een·gles
🅠 Do you understand?	¿Me entiende/entiendes? pol/inf me en·tyen·de/en·tyen·des
🅐 I (don't) understand.	(No) Entiendo. (no) en·tyen·do
How do you pronounce this word?	¿Cómo se pronuncia esta palabra? ko·mo se pro·noon·thya es·ta pa·lab·ra
How do you write 'ciudad'?	¿Cómo se escribe 'ciudad'? ko·mo se es·kree·be thyu·da
What does ... mean?	¿Qué significa ...? ke seeg·nee·fee·ka
Could you repeat that?	¿Puede repetirlo? pwe·de re·pe·teer·lo
Could you please write it down?	¿Puede escribirlo, por favor? pwe·de es·kree·beer·lo por fa·vor
Could you please speak more slowly?	¿Puede hablar más despacio, por favor? pwe·de ab·lar mas des·pa·thyo por fa·vor

✂	Slowly, please!	Más despacio, por favor.	mas des·pa·thyo por fa·vor

Numbers & Amounts

KEY PHRASES

How much?	¿Cuánto?	kwan·to
a little	un poquito	oon po·kee·to
some	algunos/as m/f	al·goo·nos/as

Cardinal Numbers

0	cero	the·ro
1	uno	oo·no
2	dos	dos
3	tres	tres
4	cuatro	kwa·tro
5	cinco	theen·ko
6	seis	seys
7	siete	sye·te
8	ocho	o·cho
9	nueve	nwe·ve
10	diez	dyeth
11	once	on·the
12	doce	do·the
13	trece	tre·the
14	catorce	ka·tor·the
15	quince	keen·the
16	dieciséis	dye·thee·seys
17	diecisiete	dye·thee·sye·te
20	veinte	veyn·te
21	veintiuno	veyn·tee·oo·no

22	veintidós	veyn·tee·*dos*
30	treinta	*treyn*·ta
40	cuarenta	kwa·*ren*·ta
50	cincuenta	theen·*kwen*·ta
60	sesenta	se·*sen*·ta
70	setenta	se·*ten*·ta
80	ochenta	o·*chen*·ta
90	noventa	no·*ven*·ta
100	cien	thyen
101	ciento uno	*thyen*·to oo·no
500	quinientos	kee·*nyen*·tos
1000	mil	mil
1,000,000	un millón	oon mee·*lyon*

Ordinal Numbers

1st	primero/a m/f	pree·*me*·ro/a
2nd	segundo/a m/f	se·*goon*·do/a
3rd	tercero/a m/f	ter·*the*·ro/a

Amounts

How much?	¿Cuánto?	*kwan*·to
a little	un poquito	oon po·*kee*·to
many	muchos/as m/f	*moo*·chos/as
some	algunos/as m/f	al·*goo*·nos/as
more/less	más/menos	mas/*me*·nos
a quarter/half	un cuarto/medio	oon *kwar*·to/*me*·dyo
a third	un tercio	oon *ter*·thyo
all/none	todo/nada	*to*·do/*na*·da

For other amounts, see **self-catering** (p184).

Times & Dates

KEY PHRASES

What time is it?	¿Qué hora es?	ke *o*·ra es
At what time ...?	¿A qué hora ...?	a ke *o*·ra ...
What date?	¿Qué día?	ke *dee*·a

Telling the Time

Q What time is it?	¿Qué hora es? ke *o*·ra es
A It's one o'clock.	Es la una. es la *oo*·na
A It's (10) o'clock.	Son las (diez). son las (dyeth)
Quarter past one.	Es la una y cuarto. es la *oo*·na ee *kwar*·to
Twenty past one.	Es la una y veinte. es la *oo*·na ee *veyn*·te
Half past one.	Es la una y media. es la *oo*·na ee *me*·dya
Twenty to one.	Es la una menos veinte. es la *oo*·na *me*·nos *veyn*·te
Quarter to one.	Es la una menos cuarto. es la *oo*·na *me*·nos *kwar*·to
It's early.	Es temprano. es tem·*pra*·no
It's late.	Es tarde. es *tar*·de

Q At what time?	¿A qué hora? a ke o·ra
A At ...	A las ... a las ...
am	de la mañana de la ma·*nya*·na
pm	de la tarde de la *tar*·de

BASICS · **TIMES & DATES**

The Calendar

Monday	lunes m	*loo*·nes
Tuesday	martes m	*mar*·tes
Wednesday	miércoles m	*myer*·ko·les
Thursday	jueves m	*khwe*·ves
Friday	viernes m	*vyer*·nes
Saturday	sábado m	*sa*·ba·do
Sunday	domingo m	do·*meen*·go

January	enero m	e·*ne*·ro
February	febrero m	fe·*bre*·ro
March	marzo m	*mar*·tho
April	abril m	a·*breel*
May	mayo m	*ma*·yo
June	junio m	*khoo*·nyo
July	julio m	*khoo*·lyo
August	agosto m	a·*gos*·to
September	septiembre m	sep·*tyem*·bre
October	octubre m	ok·*too*·bre
November	noviembre m	no·*vyem*·bre
December	diciembre m	dee·*thyem*·bre

summer	verano m	ve·*ra*·no
autumn	otoño m	o·*to*·nyo
winter	invierno m	een·*vyer*·no
spring	primavera f	pree·ma·*ve*·ra

What date?	¿Qué día? ke *dee*·a
🇶 **What date is it today?**	¿Qué día es hoy? ke *dee*·a es oy
🇦 **It's (18 October).**	Es (el dieciocho de octubre). es (el dye·thee·o·cho de ok·*too*·bre)

Present

now	ahora	a·*o*·ra
right now	ahora mismo	a·*o*·ra *mees*·mo
this afternoon	esta tarde	*es*·ta *tar*·de
this month	este mes	*es*·te mes
this morning	esta manana	*es*·ta ma·*nya*·na
this week	esta semana	*es*·ta se·*ma*·na
this year	este año	*es*·te *a*·nyo
today	hoy	oy
tonight	esta noche	*es*·ta *no*·che

Past

(three) days ago	hace (tres) días	*a*·the (tres) *dya*·as
half an hour ago	hace media hora	*a*·the *me*·dya o·ra
a while ago	hace un rato	*a*·the un *ra*·to
(five) years ago	hace (cinco) años	*a*·the (*theen*·ko) *a*·nyos

day before yesterday	anteayer	an·te·a·*yer*
last month	el mes pasado	el mes pa·*sa*·do
last night	anoche	a·*no*·che
last week	la semana pasada	la se·*ma*·na pa·*sa*·da
last year	el año pasado	el *a*·nyo pa·*sa*·do
since (May)	desde (mayo)	*des*·de (*ma*·yo)
yesterday	ayer	a·*yer*
yesterday afternoon	ayer por la tarde	a·*yer* por la *tar*·de
yesterday evening	ayer por la noche	a·*yer* por la *no*·che
yesterday morning	ayer por la mañana	a·*yer* por la ma·*nya*·na

Future

In (six) days	dentro de (seis) días	*den*·tro de (seys) *dee*·as
in an hour	dentro de una hora	*den*·tro de oo·na *o*·ra
In (five) minutes	dentro de (cinco) minutos	*den*·tro de (*theen*·ko) mee·*noo*·tos
in a month	dentro de un mes	*den*·tro de oon mes
next month	el mes que viene	el mes ke *vye*·ne
next week	la semana que viene	la se·*ma*·na ke *vye*·ne
next year	el año que viene	el *a*·nyo ke *vye*·ne
tomorrow	manana	ma·*nya*·na
tomorrow morning	mañana por la mañana	ma·*nya*·na por la ma·*nya*·na

tomorrow afternoon	mañana por la tarde	ma·*nya*·na por la *tar*·de
tomorrow evening	mañana por la noche	ma·*nya*·na por la *no*·che
day after tomorrow	pasado manana	pa·*sa*·do ma·*nya*·na
until (June)	hasta (junio)	*as*·ta (*khoo*·nyo)

During the Day

afternoon	tarde f	*tar*·de
day	día m	*dee*·a
evening	noche f	*no*·che
midday	mediodía m	me·dyo·*dee*·a
midnight	medianoche f	me·dya·*no*·che
early morning (midnight to 5am)	madrugada f	ma·droo·*ga*·da
morning	mañana f	ma·*nya*·na
night	noche f	*no*·che
sunrise	amanecer m	a·ma·ne·*ther*
sunset	puesta f del sol	*pwes*·ta del sol

Practical

Transport

KEY PHRASES

At what time's the next bus?	¿A qué hora es el próximo autobús?	a ke o·ra es el prok·see·mo ow·to·boos
One ... ticket, please.	Un ... billete, por favor.	oon ... bee·lye·te, por fa·vor
Can you tell me when we get to (Valladolid)?	¿Puede avisarme cuando lleguemos a (Valladolid)?	pwe·de a·vee·sar·me kwan·do lye·ge·mos a (va·lya·do·leeth)
Please take me to this address.	Por favor, lléveme a esta dirección.	por fa·vor lye·ve·me a es·ta dee·rek·thyon
I'd like to hire a car.	Quisiera alquilar un coche.	kee·sye·ra al·kee·lar oon ko·che

Getting Around

At what time does the ... leave/arrive?	¿A qué hora sale/llega el ...? a ke o·ra sa·le/lye·ga el ...	
boat	barco	bar·ko
bus (city)	autobús	ow·to·boos
bus (intercity)	autocar	ow·to·kar
plane	avión	a·vyon
train	tren	tren
tram	tranvía	tran·vee·a

At what time's the first (bus)?	¿A qué hora es el primer (autobús)?
	a ke *o*·ra es el pree·*mer* (ow·to·*boos*)
At what time's the last (train)?	¿A qué hora es el último (tren)?
	a ke *o*·ra es el *ool*·tee·mo (tren)
At what time's the next (boat)?	¿A qué hora es el próximo (barco)?
	a ke *o*·ra es el *prok*·see·mo (*bar*·ko)
How long will it be delayed?	¿Cuánto tiempo se retrasará?
	kwan·to *tyem*·po se re·tra·sa·*ra*
Is this seat free?	¿Está libre este asiento?
	es·*ta* *lee*·bre *es*·te a·*syen*·to

✂ **Is it free?**	¿Está libre?	es·*ta* *lee*·bre

That's my seat.	Ése es mi asiento.
	e·se es mee a·*syen*·to
I'd like to get off at (Aranjuez).	Me gustaría bajarme en (Aranjuez).
	me goos·ta·*ree*·a ba·*khar*·me en (a·ran·*khweth*)
I want to get off here!	¡Quiero bajarme aquí!
	kye·ro ba·*khar*·me a·*kee*
I'd prefer to walk there.	Prefiero ir a pie.
	pre·*fye*·ro eer a pye
Can we get there by public transport?	¿Se puede ir en transporte público?
	se *pwe*·de eer en trans·*por*·te *poo*·blee·ko

Buying Tickets

Do I need to book?	¿Tengo que reservar? *ten*·go ke re·ser·*var*
How much is it?	¿Cuánto cuesta? *kwan*·to *kwes*·ta
Where can I buy a ticket?	¿Dónde puedo comprar un billete? *don*·de *pwe*·do kom·*prar* oon bee·*lye*·te
Is it a direct route?	¿Es un viaje directo? es oon *vya*·khe dee·*rek*·to
Is there a toilet?	¿Hay servicios? ai ser·*vee*·thyos
How long does the trip take?	¿Cuánto se tarda? *kwan*·to se *tar*·da
Can I get a stand-by ticket?	¿Puede ponerme en la lista de espera? *pwe*·de po·*ner*·me en la *lees*·ta de es·*pe*·ra
I'd like an aisle seat.	Quisiera un asiento de pasillo. kee·*sye*·ra oon a·*syen*·to de pa·*see*·lyo
I'd like a window seat.	Quisiera un asiento junto a la ventana. kee·*sye*·ra oon a·*syen*·to *khoon*·to a la ven·*ta*·na
I'd like a (non)smoking seat.	Quisiera un asiento de (no) fumadores. kee·*sye*·ra oon a·*syen*·to de (no) foo·ma·*do*·res

Buying a Ticket

What time is the next ...?

¿A qué hora sale el próximo ...?
a ke *o*·ra sa·le el *prok*·see·mo ...

 boat
barco
bar·ko

 bus
autobús
ow·to·*boos*

 train
tren
tren

One ... ticket, please.

Un billete ..., por favor.
oon bee·*lye*·te ... por fa·*vor*

 one-way
sencillo
sen·*thee*·lyo

 return
de ida y vuelta
de ee·da ee *vwel*·ta

I'd like a/an ... seat.

Quisiera un asiento ...
kee·*sye*·ra oon a·*syen*·to ...

aisle
de pasillo
de pa·*see*·lyo

window
junto a la
ventana
khoon·to a la
ven·*ta*·na

Which platform does it depart from?

¿De cuál andén sale?
de kwal an·*den* sa·le

I'd like to ... my ticket.

Me gustaría ... mi billete.
me goos·ta·*ree*·a ... mee bee·*lye*·te

cancel	cancelar	kan·the·*lar*
change	cambiar	kam·*byar*
collect	recoger	re·ko·*kher*
confirm	confirmer	kon·feer·*mar*

(Two) ... tickets, please.

(Dos) billetes ..., por favor.
(dos) bee·*lye*·tes ... por fa·*vor*

1st-class	de primera clase	de pree·*me*·ra *kla*·se
2nd-class	de segunda clase	de se·*goon*·da *kla*·se
child's	infantil	een·fan·*teel*
return	de ida y vuelta	de ee·da ee *vwel*·ta
student's	de estudiante	de es·too·*dyan*·te

A one-way ticket to (Barcelona).

Un billete sencillo a (Barcelona).
oon bee·*lye*·te sen·*thee*·lyo a (bar·the·*lo*·na)

Luggage

My luggage has been damaged/lost.

Mis maletas han sido dañadas/perdidas.
mees ma·*le*·tas an *see*·do da·*nya*·das/per·*dee*·das

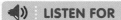 LISTEN FOR

Esta parada es ...	*es*·ta pa·*ra*·da es ... This stop is ...
La próxima parada es ...	la *prok*·see·ma pa·*ra*·da es ... The next stop is ...
Está completo.	es·*ta* kom·*ple*·to It's full.
El ... está retrasado/ cancelado.	el ... es·*ta* re·tra·*sa*·do/ kan·the·*la*·do The ... is delayed/ cancelled.

My luggage has been stolen.	Mis maletas han sido robadas. mees ma·*le*·tas an *see*·do ro·*ba*·das
I'd like a luggage locker.	Quisiera un casillero de consigna. kee·*sye*·ra oon ka·see·*lye*·ro de kon·*seeg*·na

Bus

Which bus goes to (Madrid)?	¿Qué autobús va a (Madrid)? ke ow·to·*boos* va a (ma·*dreeth*)
Where's the bus stop?	¿Dónde está la parada del autobús? *don*·de es·*ta* la pa·*ra*·da del ow·to·*boos*
What's the next stop?	¿Cuál es la próxima parada? kwal es la *prok*·see·ma pa·*ra*·da

Please tell me when we get to (Valladolid).	¿Puede avisarme cuando lleguemos a (Valladolid)? *pwe*·de a·vee·*sar*·me *kwan*·do lye·*ge*·mos a (va·lya·do·*leeth*)
Bus number ...	El autobús número ... el ow·to·*boos noo*·me·ro ...

For bus numbers, see **numbers & amounts**, p34.

Train

What station is this?	¿Cuál es esta estación? kwal es *es*·ta es·ta·*thyon*
What's the next station?	¿Cuál es la próxima estación? kwal es la *prok*·see·ma es·ta·*thyon*
Does this train stop at (Valencia)?	¿Para el tren en (Valencia)? *pa*·ra el tren en (va·*len*·thya)
Do I need to change trains?	¿Tengo que cambiar de tren? *ten*·go ke kam·*byar* de tren
Which carriage is for (Bilbao)?	¿Cuál es el coche para (Bilbao)? kwal es el *ko*·che *pa*·ra (beel·*bow*)

Boat

Are there life jackets?	¿Hay chalecos salvavidas? ai cha·*le*·kos sal·va·*vee*·das
What's the sea like today?	¿Cómo está el mar hoy? *ko*·mo es·*ta* el mar oy
I feel seasick.	Estoy mareado/a. **m/f** es·*toy* ma·re·*a*·do/a

Taxi

I'd like a taxi at (9am).	Quisiera un taxi a (las nueve de la mañana). *kee·sye·ra oon tak·see a (las nwe·ve de la ma·nya·na)*
I'd like a taxi tomorrow.	Quisiera un taxi manana. *kee·sye·ra oon tak·see ma·nya·na*
Where's the taxi stand?	¿Dónde está la parada de taxis? *don·de es·ta la pa·ra·da de tak·sees*

Where's the bus stop?
don·de es·ta la pa·ra·da del ow·to·boos
¿Dónde está la parada del autobús?

Is this taxi free?	¿Está libre este taxi? es·ta lee·bre es·te tak·see
✂ **Is it free?** ¿Está libre? es·ta lee·bre	
How much is the flag fall/ hiring charge?	¿Cuánto es la tasa de alquiler? kwan·to es la ta·sa de al·kee·ler
Please put the meter on.	Por favor, ponga el taxímetro. por fa·vor pon·ga el tak·see·me·tro
How much is it to (the Prado)?	¿Cuánto cuesta ir (al Prado)? kwan·to kwes·ta eer (al pra·do)
Please take me to (this address).	Por favor, lléveme a (esta dirección). por fa·vor lye·ve·me a (es·ta dee·rek·thyon)
✂ **To ...** A ... a ...	
How much is the final fare?	¿Cuánto es en total? kwan·to es en to·tal
Please slow down.	Por favor vaya más despacio. por fa·vor va·ya mas des·pa·thyo
Please wait here.	Por favor espere aquí. por fa·vor es·pe·re a·kee
Stop here!	¡Pare aquí! pa·re a·kee

For other useful phrases, see **directions**, p57.

Car & Motorbike

Where can I hire a ...?	¿Dónde se puede alquilar ...?
	*don·*de se *pwe·*de al·*kee·*lar ...

Does that include insurance/mileage?	¿Incluye el seguro/kilometraje?
	een·*kloo·*ye el se·*goo·*ro/kee·lo·me·*tra·*khe

I'd like to hire a/an ...	Quisiera alquilar ...
	kee·*sye·*ra al·*kee·*lar ...

4WD	un todoterreno	oon to·do·te·*re·*no
automatic car	un coche automático	oon *ko·*che ow·to·*ma·*tee·ko
manual car	un coche manual	oon *ko·*che man·*wal*
motorbike	una moto	*oo·*na *mo·*to

How much for hourly/daily hire?	¿Cuánto cuesta el alquiler por hora/día?
	*kwan·*to *kwes·*ta el al·*kee·*ler por *o·*ra/*dee·*a

How much for weekly hire?	¿Cuánto cuesta el alquiler por semana?
	*kwan·*to *kwes·*ta el al·*kee·*ler por se·*ma·*na

Is this the road to (Seville)?	¿Se va a (Sevilla) por esta carretera?
	se va a (se·*vee·*lya) por es·ta ka·re·*te·*ra

Where's a petrol station?	¿Dónde hay una gasolinera?
	*don·*de ai *oo·*na ga·so·lee·*ne·*ra

PRACTICAL TRANSPORT

LOOK FOR

Acceso	ak·*the*·so	Entrance
Aparcamiento	a·par·ka·*myen*·to	Parking
Ceda el Paso	*the*·da el *pa*·so	Give Way
Desvío	des·*vee*·o	Detour
Dirección Única	dee·rek·*thyon* oo·nee·ka	One Way
Frene	*fre*·ne	Slow Down
Peaje	pe·*a*·khe	Toll
Peligro	pe·*lee*·gro	Danger
Prohibido Aparcar	pro·ee·*bee*·do a·par·*kar*	No Parking
Prohibido el Paso	pro·ee·*bee*·do el *pa*·so	No Entry
Stop	es·*top*	Stop
Vía de Acceso	*vee*·a de ak·*the*·so	Exit Freeway

What's the (city) speed limit?	¿Cuál es el límite de velocidad (en la ciudad)? kwal es el *lee*·mee·te de ve·lo·thee·*da* (en la thyu·*da*)
Please fill it up.	Por favor, lléneme el depósito. por fa·*vor lye*·ne·me el de·*po*·see·to
I'd like (20) litres of ...	Quiero (veinte) litros de ... *kye*·ro (*veyn*·te) *lee*·tros de ...
Please check the oil/water.	Por favor, revise el nivel del aceite/agua. por fa·*vor* re·*vee*·se el nee·*vel* del a·*they*·te/*a*·gwa

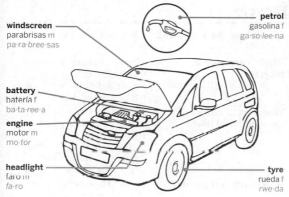

windscreen
parabrisas m
pa·ra·*bree*·sas

petrol
gasolina f
ga·so·*lee*·na

battery
batería f
ba·ta·*ree*·a

engine
motor m
mo·*tor*

headlight
faro m
fa·ro

tyre
rueda f
rwe·da

Please check the tyre pressure.	Por favor, revise la presión de los neumáticos. por fa·*vor* re·*vee*·se la pre·*syon* de los ne·oo·*ma*·tec·kos
(How long) Can I park here?	¿(Por cuánto tiempo) Puedo aparcar aquí? (por *kwan*·to *tyem*·po) *pwe*·do a·par·*kar* a·*kee*
I need a mechanic.	Necesito un/una mecánico/a. m/f ne·the·*see*·to oon/*oo*·na me·*ka*·nee·ko/a
The car has broken down (at Salamanca).	El coche se ha averiado (en Salamanca). el *ko*·che se a a·ve·*rya*·do (en sa·la·*man*·ka)
I had an accident.	He tenido un accidente. e te·*nee*·do oon ak·thee·*den*·te

Bicycle

Can we get there by bike?	¿Se puede ir en bici? se *pwe*·de eer en *bee*·thee
Where can I hire a bicycle?	¿Dónde se puede alquilar una bicicleta? *don*·de se *pwe*·de al·kee·*lar* *oo*·na bee·thee·*kle*·ta
Where can I buy a (secondhand) bike?	¿Dónde se puede comprar una bicicleta (de segunda mano)? *don*·de se *pwe*·de kom·*prar* *oo*·na bee·thee·*kle*·ta (de se·*goon*·da *ma*·no)
How much is it per day?	¿Cuánto cuesta por un día? *kwan*·to *kwes*·ta por oon *dee*·a
How much is it per hour?	¿Cuánto cuesta por una hora? *kwan*·to *kwes*·ta por *oo*·na *o*·ra
I have a puncture.	Se me ha pinchado una rueda. se me a peen·*cha*·do *oo*·na *rwe*·da
I'd like to have my bicycle repaired.	Me gustaría arreglar mi bicicleta. me goo·sta·*ree*·a a·reg·*lar* mee bee·thee·*kle*·ta
Are there cycling paths?	¿Hay carril bicicleta? ai ka·*reel* bee·thee·*kle*·ta
Is there bicycle parking?	¿Hay aparcamiento de bicicletas? ai a·par·ka·*myen*·to de bee·thee·*kle*·tas
Can I take my bike on the train?	¿Puedo llevar mi bicicleta en el tren? *pwe*·do lye·*var* mee bee·thee·*kle*·ta en el tren

Border Crossing

KEY PHRASES

I'm here for ... days.	Estoy aquí por ... días.	es·*toy* a·*kee* por ... *dee*·as
I'm staying at ...	Me estoy alojando en ...	me es·*toy* a·lo·*khan*·do en ...
I have nothing to declare.	No tengo nada que declarar.	no *ten*·go *na*·da ke de·kla·*rar*

Passport Control

I'm here on business.	Estoy aquí de negocios. es·*toy* a·*kee* de ne·*go*·thyos
I'm here on holiday.	Estoy aquí de vacaciones. es·*toy* a·*kee* de va·ka·*thyo*·nes
I'm here in transit.	Estoy aquí en tránsito. es·*toy* a·*kee* en *tran*·see·to
I'm here for ... days.	Estoy aquí por ... días. es·*toy* a·*kee* por ... *dee*·as
I'm here for ... weeks.	Estoy aquí por ... semanas. es·*toy* a·*kee* por ... se·*ma*·nas
I'm here for ... months.	Estoy aquí por ... meses. es·*toy* a·*kee* por ... *me*·ses
I'm going to (Salamanca).	Voy a (Salamanca). voy a (sa·la·*man*·ka)
I'm staying at ...	Me estoy alojando en ... me es·*toy* a·lo·*khan*·do en ...

PRACTICAL BORDER CROSSING

🔊 LISTEN FOR

Su pasaporte, por favor.	soo pa·sa·*por*·te por fa·*vor* Your passport, please.
Su visado, por favor.	soo vee·*sa*·do por fa·*vor* Your visa, please.
¿Está viajando en un grupo?	es·*ta* vya·*khan*·do en oon *groo*·po Are you travelling in a group?
¿Está viajando con familia?	es·*ta* vya·*khan*·do kon fa·*mee*·lya Are you travelling with family?
¿Está viajando solo/a? m/f	es·*ta* vya·*khan*·do *so*·lo/a Are you travelling on your own?

Customs

I have nothing to declare.	No tengo nada que declarar. no *ten*·go *na*·da ke de·kla·*rar*
I have something to declare.	Quisiera declarar algo. kee·*sye*·ra de·kla·*rar al*·go
That's (not) mine.	Eso (no) es mío. *e*·so (no) es *mee*·o
I didn't know I had to declare it.	No sabía que tenía que declararlo. no sa·*bee*·a ke te·*nee*·a ke de·kla·*rar*·lo

For phrases on payments and receipts, see **money & banking**, p91.

Directions

KEY PHRASES

Where's ...?	¿Dónde está ...?	*don*·de es·*ta* ...
What's the address?	¿Cuál es la direc-ción?	kwal es la dee·rek·*thyon*
How far is it?	¿A cuánta distancia está?	a *kwan*·ta dees·*tan*·thya es·*ta*

Excuse me.	Perdón. per·*don*
Could you help me, please?	¿Perdón, puede ayudarme, por favor? per·*don* pwe·de a·yoo·*dar*·me por fa·*vor*
Where's ...?	¿Dónde está ...? *don*·de es·*ta* ...
I'm looking for ...	Busco ... *boos*·ko ...
Which way is ...?	¿Por dónde se va a ...? por *don*·de se va a ...
How can I get there?	¿Cómo se puede ir? *ko*·mo se *pwe*·de eer
How far is it?	¿A cuánta distancia está? a *kwan*·ta dees·*tan*·thya es·*ta*
What's the address?	¿Cuál es la dirección? kwal es la dee·rek·*thyon*

Can you show me (on the map)?	¿Me lo puede indicar (en el mapa)? me lo *pwe*·de een·dee·*kar* (en el *ma*·pa)
It's ...	Está ... es·*ta* ...

behind ...	detrás de ...	de·*tras* de ...
far away	lejos	*le*·khos
here	aquí	a·*kee*
in front of ...	enfrente de ...	en·*fren*·te de ...
left	por la izquierda	por la eeth·*kyer*·da
near	cerca	*ther*·ka
next to ...	al lado de ...	al *la*·do de ...
opposite ...	frente a ...	*fren*·te a ...
right	por la derecha	por la de·*re*·cha
straight ahead	todo recto	*to*·do *rek*·to
there	ahí	a·*ee*

Turn at the corner.	Doble en la esquina. *do*·ble en la es·*kee*·na
Turn at the traffic lights.	Doble en el semáforo. *do*·ble en el se·*ma*·fo·ro
Turn left/right.	Doble a la izquierda/derecha. *do*·ble a la eeth·*kyer*·da/ de·*re*·cha
(two) kilometres	(dos) kilómetros (dos) kee·*lo*·me·tros
(three) metres	(tres) metros (tres) *me*·tros
(six) minutes	(seis) minutos (seys) mee·*noo*·tos

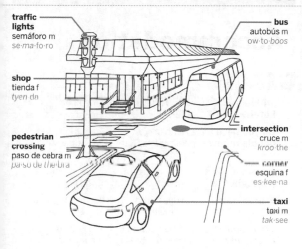

traffic lights
semáforo m
se·*ma*·fo·ro

shop
tienda f
tyen·da

pedestrian crossing
paso de cebra m
pa·so de *the*·bra

bus
autobús m
ow·to·*boos*

intersection
cruce m
kroo·the

corner
esquina f
es·*kee*·na

taxi
taxi m
tak·see

PRACTICAL DIRECTIONS

by bus	por autobús por ow·to·*boos*
by taxi	por taxi por *tak*·see
by train	por tren por tren
on foot	a pie a pye
avenue	avenida f a·ve·*nee*·da
lane	callejón m ka·lye·*khon*
street	calle f *ka*·lye

For locations and compass directions, see the **dictionary**.

Accommodation

KEY PHRASES

Where's a hotel?	¿Dónde hay un hotel?	*don*·de ai on o·tel
Do you have a double room?	¿Tiene una habitación doble?	*tye*·ne *oo*·na a·bee·ta·*thyon* do·ble
How much is it per night?	¿Cuánto cuesta por noche?	*kwan*·to *kwes*·ta por *no*·che
Is breakfast included?	¿El desayuno está incluído?	el de·sa·*yoo*·no es·*ta* een·kloo·ee·do
What time is checkout?	¿A qué hora hay que dejar libre la habitación?	a ke o·ra ai ke de·*khar* lee·bre la a·bee·ta·*thyon*

Finding Accommodation

Where's a ...?	¿Dónde hay ...? *don*·de ai ...	
bed & breakfast	una pensión con desayuno	*oo*·na pen·*syon* kon de·sa·*yoo*·no
camping ground	terreno de cámping	te·*re*·no de *kam*·peeng
guesthouse	una pensión	*oo*·na pen·*syon*
hotel	un hotel	oon o·*tel*
youth hostel	un albergue juvenil	oon al·*ber*·ge khoo·ve·*neel*

Can you recommend somewhere (cheap)?	¿Puede recomendar algún sitio (barato)? *pwe·de re·ko·men·dar al·goon see·tyo (ba·ra·to)*
Can you recommend somewhere (nearby)?	¿Puede recomendar algún sitio (cercano)? *pwe·de re·ko·men·dar al·goon see·tyo (ther·ka·no)*
Can you recommend somewhere (luxurious)?	¿Puede recomendar algún sitio (de lujo)? *pwe·de re·ko·men·dar al·goon see·tyo (de loo·kho)*
What's the address?	¿Cuál es la dirección? *kwal es la dee·rek·thyon*

For more on how to get there, see **directions** (p57).

Booking Ahead & Checking In

I'd like to book a room, please.	Quisiera reservar una habitación. *kee·sye·ra re·ser·var oo·na a·bee·ta·thyon*

✂	**Are there rooms?**	¿Hay habitaciones?	ai a·bee·ta·thyo·nes

I have a reservation.	He hecho una reserva. *e e·cho oo·na re·ser·va*
My name's ...	Me llamo ... *me lya·mo ...*
For (three) nights/weeks.	Por (tres) noches/semanas. *por (tres) no·ches/se·ma·nas*
From (July 2) to (July 6).	Desde (el dos de julio) hasta (el seis de julio). *des·de (el dos de khoo·lyo) as·ta (el seys de khoo·lyo)*

🔊 LISTEN FOR

Lo siento, está completo.	lo *syen*·to es·*ta* kom·*ple*·to	
	I'm sorry, we're full.	
¿Por cuántas noches?	por *kwan*·tas *no*·ches	
	For how many nights?	
Su pasaporte, por favor.	soo pa·sa·*por*·te por fa·*vor*	
	Your passport, please.	

Do I need to pay upfront?	¿Necesito pagar por adelantado? ne·the·*see*·to pa·*gar* por a·de·lan·*ta*·do
Do you offer (long-stay) discounts?	¿Ofrecen descuentos (por larga estancia)? of·*re*·then des·*kwen*·tos (por *lar*·ga es·*tan*·thya)
Is breakfast included?	¿El desayuno está incluído? el de·sa·*yoo*·no es·*ta* een·kloo·*ee*·do
Is there parking?	¿Hay aparcamiento? ai a·par·ka·*myen*·to
How much is it per night/ week?	¿Cuánto cuesta por noche/ semana? *kwan*·to *kwes*·ta por *no*·che/ se·*ma*·na
How much is it per person?	¿Cuánto cuesta por persona? *kwan*·to *kwes*·ta por per·*so*·na
Can I pay by credit card?	¿Puedo pagar con tarjeta de crédito? *pwe*·do pa·*gar* con tar·*khe*·ta de *kre*·dee·to

Finding a Room

Do you have a ... room?

¿Tiene una habitación ...?
tye·ne oo·na a·bee·la·thyon ...

 double
doble
do·ble

 single
individual
een·dee·vee·dwal

 ## How much is it per ...?

¿Cuánto cuesta por ...?
kwan·to kwes·ta por ...

 night
noche
no·che

 person
persona
per·so·na

 ## Is breakfast included?

¿El desyauno está incluído?
el de·sa·yoo·no es·ta een·kloo·ee·do

 ## Can I see the room?

¿Puedo verla?
pwe·do ver·la

I'll take it.
La alquilo.
la al·*kee*·lo

I won't take it.
No la alquilo.
no la al·*kee*·lo

Can I pay by travellers cheque?	¿Puedo pagar con cheques de viajero? *pwe·*do pa·*gar* con *che·*kes de vya·*khe·*ro

For other methods of payment, see **money & banking**, p91.

Do you have a double room?	¿Tiene una habitación doble? *tye·*ne oo·na a·bee·ta·*thyon* do·ble
Do you have a single room?	¿Tiene una habitación individual? *tye·*ne oo·na a·bee·ta·*thyon* een·dee·vee·*dwal*
Do you have a twin room?	¿Tiene una habitación con dos camas? *tye·*ne oo·na a·bee·ta·*thyon* con dos *ka·*mas
Do you have a room with/ without (a) ...?	¿Tiene una habitación con/sin ...? *tye·*ne oo·na a·bee·ta·*thyon* kon/seen ...
Can I see it?	¿Puedo verla? *pwe·*do *ver·*la
It's fine, I'll take it.	Vale, la alquilo. *va·*le la al·*kee·*lo

Requests & Queries

When/Where's breakfast served?	¿Cuándo/Dónde se sirve el desayuno? *kwan·*do/*don·*de se *seer·*ve el de·sa·*yoo·*no
Please wake me at (seven).	Por favor, despiérteme a (las siete). por fa·*vor* des·*pyer·*te·me a (las *sye·*te)

Can I get another ...?	¿Puede darme otro/a ...? m/f *pwe*·de *dar*·me o·*tro*/a ...
Can I use the ...?	¿Puedo usar ...? *pwe*·do oo·*sar* ...

internet	el internet	el *een*·ter·net
kitchen	la cocina	la ko·*thee*·na
laundry	el lavadero	el la·va·*de*·ro
telephone	el teléfono	el te·*le*·fo·no

Is there a/an ...?	¿Hay ...? ai ...

lift (elevator)	ascensor	as·then·*sor*
message board	tablón de anuncios	ta·*blon* de a·*noon*·thyos
safe	una caja fuerte	oo·na ka·kha *fwer*·te
swimming pool	piscina	pees·*thee*·na

Do you arrange tours here?	¿Aquí organizan recorridos? a·*kee* or·ga·nee·*than* re·ko·*ree*·dos
Do you change money here?	¿Aquí cambian dinero? a·*kee* kam·byan dee·*ne*·ro
Is there a message for me?	¿Tiene un mensaje para mí? *tye*·ne oon men·*sa*·khe *pa*·ra mee
I'm locked out of my room.	Cerré la puerta y se me olvidaron las llaves dentro. the·*re* la *pwer*·ta y se me ol·vee·*da*·ron las *lya*·ves *den*·tro

| The (bathroom) door is locked. | La puerta (del baño) está cerrada. la *pwer*·ta (del *ba*·nyo) es·*ta* the·*ra*·da |
| There's no need to change my sheets. | No hace falta cambiar las sábanas. no *a*·the *fal*·ta kam·*byar* las *sa*·ba·nas |

Complaints

| It's too ... | Es demasiado ... es de·ma·*sya*·do ... |

cold	fría f	*free*·a
dark	oscura f	os·*koo*·ra
light/bright	clara f	*kla*·ra
noisy	ruidosa f	rwee·*do*·sa
small	pequeña f	pe·*ke*·nya

| The ... doesn't work. | No funciona ... no foon·*thyo*·na ... |

air-conditioning	el aire acondicionado	el *ai*·re a·kon·dee·thyo·*na*·do
fan	el ventilador	el ven·tee·la·*dor*
heater	la estufa	la es·*too*·fa
toilet	el retrete	el re·*tre*·te
window	la ventana	la ven·*ta*·na

| This ... isn't clean. | Éste/Ésta ... no está limpio/a. m/f *es*·te/*es*·ta ... no es·*ta leem*·pyo/a |
| There's no hot water. | No hay agua caliente. no ai *a*·gwa ka·*lyen*·te |

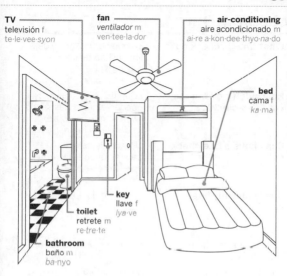

TV
televisión f
te·le·vee·*syon*

fan
ventilador m
ven·tee·la·*dor*

air-conditioning
aire acondicionado m
ai·re a·kon·dee·thyo·*na*·do

bed
cama f
ka·ma

key
llave f
lya·ve

toilet
retrete m
re·*tre*·te

bathroom
baño m
ba·nyo

Answering the Door

Who is it?	¿Quién es? kyen es
Just a moment.	Un momento. oon mo·*men*·to
Come in.	Adelante. a·de·*lan*·te
Can you come back later, please?	¿Puede volver más tarde, por favor? *pwe*·de vol·*ver* mas *tar*·de por fa·*vor*

Checking Out

What time is check out?	¿A qué hora hay que dejar libre la habitación? a ke *o*·ra ai ke de·*khar* *lee*·bre la a·bee·ta·*thyon*
How much extra to stay until (6 o'clock)?	¿Cuánto más cuesta quedarse hasta (las seis)? *kwan*·to mas *kwes*·ta ke·*dar*·se *as*·ta (las seys)
Can I have a late check out?	¿Puedo dejar la habitación más tarde? *pwe*·do de·*khar* la a·bee·ta·*thyon* mas *tar*·de
Can I leave my bags here?	¿Puedo dejar las maletas aquí? *pwe*·do de·*khar* las ma·*le*·tas a·*kee*
There's a mistake in the bill.	Hay un error en la cuenta. ai oon e·*ror* en la *kwen*·ta
I'm leaving now.	Me voy ahora. me voy a·*o*·ra
Can you call a taxi for me (for 11 o'clock)?	¿Me puede pedir un taxi (para las once)? me *pwe*·de pe·*deer* oon *tak*·see (*pa*·ra las *on*·the)
Could I have my deposit, please?	¿Me puede dar mi depósito, por favor? me *pwe*·de dar mee de·*po*·see·to por fa·*vor*

Could I have my passport, please?	¿Me puede dar mi pasaporte, por favor? me *pwe*·de dar mee pa·sa·*por*·te por fa·*vor*
Could I have my valuables, please?	¿Me puede dar mis objetos de valor, por favor? me *pwe*·de dar mees ob·*khe*·tos de va·*lor* por fa·*vor*
I'll be back on (Tuesday).	Volveré el (martes). vol·ve·*re* el (*mar*·tes)
I'll be back in (three) days.	Volveré en (tres) días. vol·ve·*re* en (tres) *dee*·as

Where's a hotel?
don·de ai oon o·*tel*

¿Dónde hay un hotel?

GUY MOBERLY / LONELY PLANET IMAGES ©

I had a great stay, thank you.	He tenido una estancia muy agradable, gracias. e te·*nee*·do *oo*·na es·*tan*·thya mooy a·gra·*da*·ble *gra*·thyas
You've been terrific.	Han sido estupendos. an *see*·do es·too·*pen*·dos
I'll recommend it to my friends.	Se lo recomendaré a mis amigos. se lo re·ko·men·da·*re* a mees a·*mee*·gos

Camping

Where's the nearest camp site?	¿Dónde está el terreno de cámping más cercano? *don*·de es·*ta* el te·*re*·no de *kam*·peeng mas ther·*ka*·no
Can I camp here?	¿Se puede acampar aquí? se *pwe*·de a·kam·*par* a·*kee*
Can I park next to my tent?	¿Se puede aparcar al lado de la tienda? se *pwe*·de a·par·*kar* al *la*·do de la *tyen*·da
Do you have ...?	¿Tiene ...? *tye*·ne ...

electricity	electricidad	e·lek·tree·thee·*da*
shower facilities	duchas	*doo*·chas
a site	un sitio	oon *see*·tyo
tents for hire	tiendas de campaña para alquilar	*tyen*·das de kam·*pa*·nya *pa*·ra al·kee·*lar*

| How much is it per ...? | ¿Cuánto vale por ...? |
| | *kwan·*to *va·*le por ... |

caravan	caravana	ka·ra·*va·*na
person	persona	per·*so·*na
tent	tienda	*tyen·*da
vehicle	vehículo	ve·*ee·*koo·lo

| **Is the water drinkable?** | ¿Se puede beber el agua? |
| | se *pwe·*de be·ber el *a·*gwa |

| **I'm looking for the nearest showers.** | Estoy buscando las duchas más cercanas. |
| | es·*toy* boos·*kan·*do las *doo·*chas mas ther·*ka·*nas |

| **I'm looking for the nearest toilet block.** | Estoy buscando los servicios más cercanos. |
| | es·*toy* boos·*kan·*do los ser·*vee·*thyos mas ther *ka* nos |

| **Could I borrow ...?** | ¿Me puede prestar ...? |
| | me *pwe·*de pres·*tar* ... |

For cooking utensils, see **self-catering** (p186) and the **dictionary**

LOOK FOR

Caballeros	ka·ba·*lye·*ros	Men
Caliente	ka·*lyen·*te	Hot
Dirección Prohibida	dee·rek·*thyon* pro·hee·*bee·*da	No Entry
Frío	*free·*o	Cold
Señoras	se·*nyo·*ras	Women

PRACTICAL ACCOMMODATION

Renting

Do you have a/an ... for rent?
¿Tiene ... para alquilar?
tye·ne ... *pa*·ra al·kee·*lar*

apartment	un piso	oon *pee*·so
cabin	una cabaña	*oo*·na ka·*ba*·nya
house	una casa	*oo*·na *ka*·sa
room	una habitación	*oo*·na a·bee·ta·*thyon*
villa	un chalet	oon cha·*le*

furnished	amueblado/a **m/f** a·mwe·*bla*·do/a
partly furnished	semi amueblado/a **m/f** *se*·mee a·mwe·*bla*·do/a
unfurnished	sin amueblar seen a·mwe·*blar*

Staying with Locals

Can I stay at your place?	¿Me puedo quedar en su/tu casa? **pol/inf** me *pwe*·do ke·*dar* en soo/too *ka*·sa
Thanks for your hospitality.	Gracias por su/tu hospitalidad. **pol/inf** *gra*·thyas por soo/too os·pee·ta·lee·*da*
I have my own mattress.	Tengo mi propio colchón. *ten*·go mee *pro*·pyo kol·*chon*
I have my own sleeping bag.	Tengo mi propio saco de dormir. *ten*·go mee *pro*·pyo *sa*·ko de dor·*meer*

Can I bring anything for the meal?	¿Puedo traer algo para la comida? *pwe·do tra·er al·go pa·ra la ko·mee·da*
Can I use your telephone?	¿Puedo usar su/tu teléfono? **pol/inf** *pwe·do oo·sar soo/too te·le·fo·no*
Can I help?	¿Puedo ayudar? *pwe·do a·yoo·dar*
Can I set/clear the table?	¿Puedo poner/quitar la mesa? *pwe·do po·ner/kee·tar la me·sa*
Can I do the dishes?	¿Puedo lavar los platos? *pwe·do la·var los pla·tos*
Can I take out the rubbish?	¿Puedo sacar la basura? *pwe·do sa·kar la ba·soo·ra*

For compliments to the chef, see **eating out** (p174).

Shopping

KEY PHRASES

I'd like to buy ...	Quisiera comprar ...	kee·sye·ra kom·prar ...
Can I look at it?	¿Puedo verlo?	pwe·do ver·lo
Can I try it on?	¿Me lo puedo probar?	me lo pwe·do pro·bar
How much?	¿Cuánto cuesta?	kwan·to kwes·ta
That's too expensive.	Es muy caro.	es mooy ka·ro

Looking For ...

Where's a (super)market?	¿Dónde está un (super)mercado? *don·de es·ta oon (soo·per·)mer·ka·do*
Where's a camping store?	¿Dónde está una tienda de camping? *don·de es·ta oo·na tyen·da de kam·peeng*
Where can I buy locally produced goods/souvenirs?	¿Dónde puedo comprar recuerdos de la zona? *don·de pwe·do kom·prar re·kwer·dos de la tho·na*
Where can I buy ...?	¿Dónde puedo comprar ...? *don·de pwe·do kom·prar ...*

For more on shops and how to get there, see **directions** (p57) and the **dictionary**.

Making a Purchase

How much is this?	¿Cuánto cuesta esto? *kwan·to kwes·ta es·to*

✂ **How much?** ¿Cuánto cuesta? *kwan·to kwes·ta*

I'd like to buy ...	Quisiera comprar ... *kee·sye·ra kom·prar ...*
I'm just looking.	Sólo estoy mirando. *so·lo es·toy mee·ran·do*
Can I look at it?	¿Puedo verlo? *pwe·do ver·lo*
Do you have any others?	¿Tiene otros? *tye·ne o·tros*
What is this made from?	¿De qué está hecho? *de ke es·ta e·cho*
Do you accept credit/ debit cards?	¿Aceptan tarjetas de crédito/débito? *a·thep·tan tar·khe·tas de kre·dee·to/de·bee·to*
Could I have a bag, please?	¿Podría darme una bolsa, por favor? *po·dree·a dar·me oo·na bol·sa por fa·vor*
Could I have a receipt, please?	¿Podría darme un recibo, por favor? *po·dree·a dar·me oon re·thee·bo por fa·vor*

✂ **Receipt,** El recibo, *el re·thee·bo*
please. por favor. *por fa·vor*

PRACTICAL SHOPPING

🔊 LISTEN FOR

¿En qué le puedo servir?	en ke le *pwe*·do ser·*veer* Can I help you?
No tengo.	no *ten*·go I don't have any.
¿Algo más?	*al*·go mas Anything else?

I don't need a bag, thanks.	No necesito bolsa, gracias. no ne·the·*see*·to *bol*·sa *gra*·thyas
Can you write down the price?	¿Puede escribir el precio? *pwe*·de es·kree·*beer* el *pre*·thyo
Could I have it wrapped?	¿Me lo podría envolver? me lo po·*dree*·a en·vol·*ver*
Does it have a guarantee?	¿Tiene garantía? *tye*·ne ga·ran·*tee*·a
Can I pick it up later?	¿Puedo recogerlo más tarde? *pwe*·do re·ko·*kher*·lo mas *tar*·de
Can I have it sent overseas?	¿Pueden enviarlo por correo a otro país? *pwe*·den en·vee·*ar*·lo por ko·*re*·o a o·tro pa·*ees*
It's faulty.	Es defectuoso. es de·fek·*two*·so
I'd like my change, please.	Quisiera mi cambio, por favor. kee·*sye*·ra mee *kam*·byo por fa·*vor*

Making a Purchase

I'd like to buy ...
Quisiera comprar ...
kee·sye·ra kom·prar ...

How much is it?
¿Cuánto cuesta esto?
kwan·to kwes·ta es·to

OR

Can you write down the price?
¿Puede escribir el precio?
pwe·de es·kree·heer el pre·thyo

Do you accept credit cards?
¿Aceptan tarjetas de crédito?
a·thep·tan tar·khe·tas de kre·dee·to

Could I have a ..., please?
¿Podría darme ..., por favor?
po·dree·a dar·me ... por fa·vor

 receipt
un recibo
oon re·thee·bo

 bag
una bolsa
oo·na bol·sa

🔊 LISTEN FOR

cazador m **de ofertas**	ka·tha·*dor* de o·*fer*·tas	bargain hunter
estafa f	es·*ta*·fa	rip-off
ganga f	*gan*·ga	bargain
rebajas f pl	re·*ba*·khas	specials
ventas f pl	*ven*·tas	sale

I'd like my money back, please.	Quisiera que me devuelva el dinero, por favor. kee·*sye*·ra ke me de·*vwel*·va el dee·*ne*·ro por fa·*vor*
I'd like to return this, please.	Quisiera devolver esto, por favor. kee·*sye*·ra de·vol·*ver* es·to por fa·*vor*

Bargaining

That's too expensive.	Es muy caro. es mooy *ka*·ro
Do you have something cheaper?	¿Tiene algo más barato? *tye*·ne *al*·go mas ba·*ra*·to
Can you lower the price?	¿Podría bajar un poco el precio? po·*dree*·a ba·*khar* oon *po*·ko el *pre*·thyo
I'll give you ...	Le/Te daré ... pol/inf le/te da·*re* ...

Clothes

Can I try it on?	¿Me lo puedo probar? me lo *pwe*·do pro·bar
My size is ...	Uso la talla ... *oo*·so la *ta*·lya ...
It doesn't fit.	No me queda bien. no me *ke*·da byen
small	pequeño/a m/f pe·*ke*·nyo/a
medium	mediano/a m/f me·*dya*·no/a
large	grande m&f *gran*·de

For clothing items, see the **dictionary**. For sizes, see **numbers & amounts** (p34).

I'm just looking.
so·lo es·toy mee·ran·do
Sólo estoy mirando.

Repairs

Can I have my (camera) repaired here?	¿Puede reparar mi (cámara) aquí? *pwe·*de re·pa·*rar* mee (*ka·*ma·ra) a·*kee*
When will my (sun)glasses be ready?	¿Cuándo estarán listas mis gafas (de sol)? *kwan·*do es·ta·*ran lees·*tas mees *ga·*fas (de sol)
When will my shoes be ready?	¿Cuándo estarán listos mis zapatos? *kwan·*do es·ta·*ran lees·*tos mees tha·*pa·*tos

Books & Reading

Is there a/an (English-language) bookshop?	¿Hay una librería (en inglés)? ai *oo·*na lee·bre·*ree·*a (en een·*gles*)
Is there a/an (English-language) section?	¿Hay una sección (en inglés)? ai *oo·*na sek·*thyon* (en een·*gles*)
I (don't) like ...	(No) Me gusta/gustan ... sg/pl (no) me *goos·*ta/*goos·*tan ...
I'm looking for something by (Javier Marías).	Estoy buscando algo de (Javier Marías). es·*toy* boos·*kan·*do *al·*go de (kha·*vyer* ma·*ree·*as)

For more on books and reading, see **interests** (p124).

PRACTICAL

SHOPPING

CULTURE TIP

Hispanic Literature

Spanish-language literature has a long history, dating from the 12th century and written across the Spanish-speaking world. Today's thriving industry includes such authors as Ana María Matute, Isabel Allende, Jorge Luis Borges, Miguel de Unamuno, Carmen Martín Gaite, Juan Goytisolo, Miguel Delibes, 1982 Nobel Prize winner Gabriel García Márquez and the 1989 Nobel Prize winner, Camilo José Cela.

Music & DVD

I heard a band called ...	Escuché a un grupo que se llama ... es·koo·*che* a oon *groo*·po ke se *lya*·ma ...
What's their best recording?	¿Cuál es su mejor disco? kwal es soo me·*khor* dees·ko
Can I listen to this?	¿Puedo escuchar esto? *pwe*·do es·koo·*char* es·to
What region is this DVD for?	¿Para qué región es este DVD? *pa*·ra ke re·*khyon* es es·te de·oo·ve·de
I'd like a CD/DVD.	Quisiera un compact/DVD. kee·*sye*·ra oon kom·pak/de·oo·ve·de
Is this a pirated copy?	¿Es copia pirata? es *ko*·pya pee·*ra*·ta
I'd like some headphones.	Quisiera unos auriculares. kee·*sye*·ra oo·nos ow·ree·koo·*la*·res

Video & Photography

Can you print digital photos?	¿Podría imprimir fotos digitales? po·*dree*·a eem·pree·*meer* *fo*·tos dee·khee·*ta*·les
Can you transfer my photos from camera to CD?	¿Podría pasar las fotos de mi cámara a un compact? po·*dree*·a pa·*sar* las *fo*·tos de mee *ka*·ma·ra a oon *kom*·pak
How much is it to develop this film?	¿Cuánto cuesta revelar este carrete? *kwan*·to *kwes*·ta re·ve·*lar* *es*·te ka·*re*·te
Do you have slide film?	¿Tiene diapositivas? *tye*·ne dee·a·po·see·*tee*·vas
I need a cable to connect my camera to a computer.	Necesito un cable para conectar mi cámara al ordenador. ne·the·*see*·to oon *ka*·ble *pa*·ra ko·nek·*tar* mee *ka*·ma·ra al or·de·na·*dor*
I need a cable to recharge this battery.	Necesito un cable para recargar esta batería. ne·the·*see*·to oon *ka*·ble *pa*·ra re·kar·*gar* *es*·ta ba·te·*ree*·a
Do you have batteries for this camera?	¿Tiene pilas para esta cámara? *tye*·ne *pee*·las *pa*·ra *es*·ta *ka*·ma·ra
Do you have memory cards for this camera?	¿Tiene tarjetas de memoria para esta cámara? *tye*·ne tar·*khe*·tas de me·*mo*·rya *pa*·ra *es*·ta *ka*·ma·ra

CULTURE TIP

The Spanish Lisp

According to a popular legend, one Spanish king – some say Felipe IV, others Ferdinand I – was unable to pronounce the s sound properly and his court, and eventually all of Spain, mimicked his lisp. Of course, the tale is a myth. Indeed, only the letters c and z are pronounced th (when they precede an i or an e), while the letter s remains the same as in English – a selectiveness due to the way Spanish evolved from Latin. So when you hear someone say *gracias gra*·thyas, they are no more lisping than when you say 'thank you' in English.

Do you have (a) ... for this camera?	¿Tiene ... para esta cámara? *tye*·ne ... *pa*·ra es·ta *ka*·ma·ra
I need a B&W film for this camera.	Necesito película en blanco y negro para esta cámara. ne·the·*see*·to pe·*lee*·koo·la en *blan*·ko y *ne*·gro *pa*·ra es·ta *ka*·ma·ra
I need a colour film for this camera.	Necesito película en color para esta cámara. ne·the·*see*·to pe·*lee*·koo·la en ko·*lor pa*·ra es·ta *ka*·ma·ra
I need a (400) speed film for this camera.	Necesito película de sensibilidad (cuatrocientos) para esta cámara. ne·the·*see*·to pe·*lee*·koo·la de sen·see·bee·lee·*da* (*kwa*·tro·*thyen*·tos) *pa*·ra es·ta *ka*·ma·ra
I need a passport photo taken.	Necesito fotos de pasaporte. ne·the·*see*·to *fo*·tos de pa·sa·*por*·te

Communications

KEY PHRASES

Where's the local internet cafe?	¿Dónde hay un cibercafé cercano?	*don*·de ai oon thee·ber·ka·*fe* ther·*ka*·no
I'd like to check my email.	Quisiera revisar mi correo electrónico.	kee·*sye*·ra re·vee·*sar* mee ko·*re*·o e·lek·*tro*·nee·ko
I want to send a parcel.	Quisiera enviar un paquete.	kee·*sye*·ra en·vee·*ar* oon pa·*ke*·te
I'd like a SIM card.	Quisiera una tarjeta SIM.	kee·*sye*·ra oo·na tar·*khe*·ta seem

Post Office

I want to send a parcel.	Quisiera enviar un paquete. kee·*sye*·ra en·vee·*ar* oon pa·*ke*·te
I want to send a postcard.	Quisiera enviar una postal. kee·*sye*·ra en·vee·*ar* oo·na pos·*tal*
I want to buy an envelope.	Quisiera comprar un sobre. kee·*sye*·ra kom·*prar* oon *so*·bre
I want to buy stamps.	Quisiera comprar sellos. kee·*sye*·ra kom·*prar* se·lyos
Please send it by air/ surface mail to ...	Por favor, mándelo por vía aérea/terrestre a ... por fa·*vor* man·de·lo por *vee*·a a·e·re·a/te·*res*·tre a ...

LISTEN FOR

buzón m	boo·*thon*	mail box
código m **postal**	ko·dee·go pos·*tal*	postcode
correo m **certificado**	ko·re·o ther·tee·fee·*ka*·do	registered mail
por vía aérea	por *vee*·a a·e·re·a	airmail
correo m **urgente**	ko·*re*·o oor·*khen*·te	express mail
declaración f **de aduana**	de·kla·ra·*thyon* de a·*dwa*·na	customs declaration
frágil	*fra*·kheel	fragile
internacional	een·ter·na·thyo·*nal*	international
nacional	na·thyo·*nal*	domestic

PRACTICAL COMMUNICATIONS

It contains ...	Contiene ... kon·*tye*·ne ...
Where's the poste restante section?	¿Dónde está la lista de correos? *don*·de es·*ta* la *lees*·ta de ko·re·os
Is there any mail for me?	¿Hay alguna carta para mí? ai al·*goo*·na *kar*·ta pa·ra mee

Phone

Q What's your phone number?	¿Cuál es su/tu número de teléfono? **pol/inf** kwal es soo/too *noo*·me·ro de te·*le*·fo·no
A The number is ...	El número es ... el *noo*·me·ro es ...

Where's the nearest public phone?	¿Dónde hay una cabina telefónica? *don*·de ai *oo*·na ka·*bee*·na te·le·*fo*·nee·ka
Can I look at a phone book?	¿Puedo mirar la guía de teléfonos? *pwe*·do mee·*rar* la *gee*·a de te·*le*·fo·nos
What's the area code for ...?	¿Cuál es el prefijo de la zona de ...? kwal es el pre·*fee*·kho de la *tho*·na de ...
What's the country code for ...?	¿Cuál es el prefijo del país de ...? kwal es el pre·*fee*·kho del pa·*ees* de ...

For telephone numbers, see **numbers & amounts**, page 34.

I want to...	Quiero ... *kye*·ro ...

make a call to (Singapore)	hacer una llamada a (Singapur)	a·*ther* oo·na lya·*ma*·da a (seen·ga·*poor*)
make a local call	hacer una llamada local	a·*ther* oo·na lya·*ma*·da lo·*kal*
a reverse-charge/ collect call	una llamada a cobro revertido	oo·na lya·*ma*·da a *ko*·bro re·ver·*tee*·do
buy a phone card	comprar una tarjeta telefónica	kom·*prar* oo·na tar·*khe*·ta te·le·*fo*·nee·ka

It's engaged.	Está comunicando. es·*ta* ko·moo·nee·*kan*·do

🔊 LISTEN FOR

¿De parte de quién?	de *par*·te de kyen	Who's calling?
¿Con quién quiere hablar?	kon kyen *kye*·re a·*blar*	Who do you want to speak to?
Lo siento, pero ahora no está.	lo *syen*·to *pe*·ro a·*o*·ra no es *ta*	I'm sorry, he/she is not here.
Lo siento, tiene el numero equivocado.	lo *syen*·to *tye*·ne el *noo*·me·ro e·kee·vo·*ka*·do	Sorry, you have got the wrong number.

The connection's bad.	Es mala conexión. es *ma*·la ko·nek·*syon*
Hello. (calling)	Hola. o·la
Hello? (answering)	¿Diga? *dee*·ga
Can I speak to ...?	¿Está ...? es·*ta* ...
It's (Julio) ...	Soy (Julio) ... soy (Julio) ...
I've been cut off.	Me han cortado. me an kor·*ta*·do
Can I leave a message?	¿Puedo dejar un mensaje? *pwe*·do de·*khar* oon men·*sa*·khe
Please tell him/her I called.	Sí, por favor, dile que he llamado. see por fa·*vor dee*·le ke e lya·*ma*·do
I'll call back later.	Ya llamaré más tarde. ya lya·ma·*re* mas *tar*·de

Mobile/Cell Phone

I'd like a/an ...	Quisiera ... kee·*sye*·ra ...	
charger for my phone	un cargador para mi teléfono	oon kar·ga·*dor* *pa*·ra mee te·*le*·fo·no
mobile/cell phone for hire	un móvil para alquilar	oon *mo*·veel *pa*·ra al·kee·*lar*
prepaid phone	una tarjeta prepagada	*oo*·na tar·*khe*·ta pre·pa·*ga*·da
SIM card (for your network)	una tarjeta SIM (para su red)	*oo*·na tar·*khe*·ta seem (*pa*·ra soo red)

What are the rates?	¿Cuál es la tarifa? kwal es la ta·*ree*·fa

The Internet

Where's the local internet cafe?	¿Dónde hay un cibercafé cercano? *don*·de ai oon thee·ber·ka·*fe* ther·*ka*·no
Do you have public internet access here?	¿Tiene acceso público a internet? *tye*·ne ak·*the*·so poo·*blee*·ko a een·ter·net
Is there wireless internet access here?	¿Hay acceso inalámbrico a internet aquí? ai ak·*the*·so een·a·*lam*·bree·ko a een·ter·net a·*kee*

Can I connect my laptop here?	¿Puedo conectar mi ordenador portátil aquí?
	pwe·do ko·nek·tar mee or·de·na·dor por·ta·teel a·kee
Do you have headphones (with a microphone)?	¿Tiene auriculares (con micrófono)?
	tye·ne ow·ree·koo·la·res (kon mee·kro·fo·no)
I'd like to buy a card/ USB for prepaid mobile internet.	Quisiera comprar una tarjeta/USB para internet móvil de prepago.
	kee·sye·ra kom·prar oo·na tar·khe·ta/oo e se be pa·ra een·ter·net mo·veel de pre·pa·go

 LOOK FOR

Here are some Spanish substitutes for common internet-related terms.

charlar	*char·lar*	chat
ciberespacio m	*thee·ber·e·spa·thyo*	cyberspace
correr tabla por la red	*ko·rer ta·bla por la re*	surf
descargar	*des·kar·gar*	download
en línea	*en lee·ne·a*	online
nombre m de usuario	*nom·bre de oo·swa·ryo*	username
página f Web inicial	*pa·khee·na web ee·nee·thyal*	homepage
sistema f de búsqueda	*sees·te·ma de boos·ke·da*	search engine
sitio m Web	*see·tyo web*	website

PRACTICAL COMMUNICATIONS

I'd like to ...		Quisiera ... kee·sye·ra ...
burn a CD	copiar un disco	ko·pyar oon dees·ko
check my email	revisar mi correo electrónico	re·vee·sar mee ko·re·o e·lek·tro·nee·ko
download my photos	descargar mis fotos	des·kar·gar mees fo·tos
use a printer	usar una impresora	oo·sar oo·na eem·pre·so·ra
use a scanner	usar un escáner	oo·sar oon es·ka·ner
use Skype	usar Skype	oo·sar es·kaip

How much per hour/ page?	¿Cuánto cuesta por hora/ página? kwan·to kwes·ta por o·ra/ pa·khee·na
How do I log on?	¿Cómo entro al sistema? ko·mo en·tro al sees·te·ma
It's crashed.	Se ha quedado colgado. se a ke·da·do kol·ga·do
I've finished.	He terminado. e ter·mee·na·do
media player (MP3)	equipo m MP3 e·kee·po e·me·pe·tres
portable hard drive	disco duro m portátil dees·ko doo·ro por·ta·teel
PSP	PSP m pe·e·se·pe
USB flash drive (memory stick)	memoria f USB me·mo·rya oo·e·se·be

Money & Banking

KEY PHRASES

How much is it?	¿Cuánto cuesta esto?	kwan·to kwes·ta es·to
What's the exchange rate?	¿Cuál es el tipo de cambio?	kwal es el tee·po de kam·byo
Where's the nearest ATM?	¿Dónde está el cajero automático más cercano?	don·de es·ta el ka·khe·ro ow·to·ma·tee·ko mas ther·ka·no

Paying the Bill

Q How much is it?	¿Cuánto cuesta esto? kwan·to kwes·ta es·to
A It's (12) euros.	Son (doce) euros. son (do·the) e·oo·ros
A It's free.	Es gratis. es gra·tees
There's a mistake in the bill.	Hay un error en la cuenta. ai oon e·ror en la kwen·ta
Do you accept credit/debit cards?	¿Aceptan tarjetas de crédito/débito? a·thep·tan tar·khe·tas de kre·dee·to/de·bee·to
Do you accept travellers cheques?	¿Aceptan cheques de viajero? a·thep·tan che·kes de vya·khe·ro

I'd like my change, please.	Quisiera mi cambio, por favor.
	kee·*sye*·ra mee *kam*·byo por fa·*vor*
Could I have a receipt, please?	¿Podría darme un recibo, por favor?
	po·*dree*·a *dar*·me oon re·*thee*·bo por fa·*vor*

See also **bargaining** (p78).

Banking

Where can I ...?	¿Dónde puedo ...?
	don·de *pwe*·do ...
I'd like to ...	Me gustaría ...
	me goos·ta·*ree*·a ...

arrange a transfer	hacer una transferencia	ha·*ther* oo·na trans·fe·*ren*·thee·ya
get a cash advance	obtener un adelanto	ob·te·*ner* on a·de·*lan*·to
change money	cambiar dinero	kam·*byar* dee·*ne*·ro
change a travellers cheque	cambiar un cheque de viajero	kam·*byar* oon *che*·ke de vya·*khe*·ro
get change for this note	conseguir cambio para este billete	kon·se·*geer* *kam*·byo *pa*·ra *es*·te bee·*lye*·te
withdraw money	sacar dinero	sa·*kar* dee·*ne*·ro

Where's the nearest ATM?	¿Dónde está el cajero automático más cercano?
	don·de es·*ta* el ka·*khe*·ro ow·to·*ma*·tee·ko mas ther·*ka*·no

🔊 LISTEN FOR

No le quedan fondos.	no le *ke*·dan *fon*·dos You have no money left.
Hay un problema con su cuenta.	ai oon pro·*ble*·ma kon soo *kwen*·ta There's a problem with your account.
¿Puedo ver su identificación, por favor?	*pwe*·do ver soo ee·den·tee·fee·ka·*thyon* por fa·*vor* Can I see your ID, please?
Por favor firme aquí.	por fa·*vor* *feer*·me a·*kee* Please sign here.

Where's the nearest foreign exchange office?	¿Dónde está la oficina de cambio más cercano? *don*·de es·*ta* la o·fee·*thee*·na de *kam*·byo mas ther·*ka*·no
What's the exchange rate?	¿Cuál es el tipo de cambio? kwal es el *tee*·po de *kam*·byo
What's the charge for that?	¿Cuánto hay que pagar por eso? *kwan*·to ai ke pa·*gar* por e·so
The ATM took my card.	El cajero automático se ha tragado mi tarjeta. el ka·*khe*·ro ow·to·*ma*·tee·ko se a tra·*ga*·do mee tar·*khe*·ta
I've forgotten my PIN.	Me he olvidado del NPI. me e ol·vee·*da*·do del e·ne·pe·ee
Has my money arrived yet?	¿Ya ha llegado mi dinero? ya a lye·*ga*·do mee dee·*ne*·ro
How long will it take to arrive?	¿Cuánto tiempo tardará en llegar? *kwan*·to *tyem*·po tar·da·*ra* en lye·*gar*

PRACTICAL BUSINESS

Business

KEY PHRASES

I'm attending a conference.	Asisto a un congreso.	a·sees·to a oon kon·gre·so
I have an appointment with ...	Tengo una cita con ...	ten·go oo·na thee·ta kon ...
Can I have your business card?	¿Puede darme su tarjeta de visita?	pwe·de dar·me soo tar·khe·ta de vee·see·ta

People usually chit-chat for a while before they get down to business. For titles and greetings, see **meeting people** (p106).

I'm attending a ...
Asisto a ...
a·sees·to a ...

conference	un congreso	oon kon·gre·so
course	un curso	oon koor·so
meeting	una reunión	oo·na re·oo·nyon
trade fair	una feria de muestras	oo·na fe·rya de mwes·tras

I'm with my colleagues.	Estoy con mis colegas. m&f es·toy kon mees ko·le·gas
I'm alone.	Estoy solo/a. m/f es·toy so·lo/a
Where's the business district?	¿Dónde está el centro financiero? don·de es·ta el then·tro fee·nan·thye·ro

LANGUAGE TIP Addressing People

To show formality or respect, you should use the polite form of address *Usted* sg pol oo·*ste* or *Ustedes* pl pol oo·*ste*·des in business and with any service providers (be they kiosk attendants or doctors). It's best to take the lead from how people address you, and respond in the same way. For more on polite forms, see **personal pronouns** in the **grammar** chapter, p21.

Where's the conference?	¿Dónde está el congreso? *don*·de es·*ta* el kon·*gre*·so
Where's the meeting?	¿Dónde es la reunión? *don*·de es la re·oo·*nyon*
I have an appointment with ...	Tengo una cita con ... *ten*·go oo·na *thee*·ta kon ...
Q Can I have your business card?	¿Puede darme su tarjeta de visita? *pwe*·de *dar*·me soo tar·*khe*·ta de vee·*see*·ta
A Here's my business card.	Aquí tiene mi tarjeta de visita. a·*kee tye*·ne mee tar·*khe*·ta de vee·*see*·ta
That went very well.	Eso fue muy bien. *e*·so fwe mooy byen
Thank you for your interest/time.	Gracias por su interés/tiempo. *gra*·thyas por soo een·te·*res*/*tyem*·po
Shall we go for a drink/meal?	¿Vamos a tomar/comer algo? *va*·mos a to·*mar*/ko·*mer* al·go
It's on me.	Invito yo. een·*vee*·to yo

Sightseeing

KEY PHRASES

Can we hire a guide?	¿Podemos alquilar un guía?	po·*de*·mos al·kee·*lar* oon *gee*·a
Can I take photographs?	¿Puedo tomar fotos?	*pwe*·do to·*mar fo*·tos
When's the museum open?	¿A qué hora abren el museo?	a ke o·ra *ab*·ren el moo·*se*·o

Requests & Queries

I'd like a/an ...	Quisiera ...	kee·*sye*·ra ...

audio set	un equipo audio	oon e·*kee*·po *ow*·dyo
catalogue	un catálogo	oon ka·*ta*·lo·go
guidebook in English	una guía turística en inglés	*oo*·na *gee*·a too·*rees*·tee·ka en een·*gles*
(local) map	un mapa (de la zona)	oon *ma*·pa (de la *tho*·na)

I'd like to see ...	Me gustaría ver ...	me goos·ta·*ree*·a ver ...

Do you have information on local sights?	¿Tiene información sobre los lugares de interés local? *tye·*ne een·for·ma·*thyon so·*bre los loo·*ga·*res de een·te·*res* lo·*kal*
Do you have information on historical sights?	¿Tiene información sobre los lugares de interés histórico? *tye·*ne een·for·ma·*thyon so·*bre los loo·*ga·*res de een·te·*res* ees·*to·*ree·ko
Do you have information on religious sights?	¿Tiene información sobre los lugares de interés religioso? *tye·*ne een·for·ma·*thyon so·*bre los loo·*ga·*res de een·te·*res* re·lee·*khyo·*so
Can we hire a guide?	¿Podemos alquilar un guía? po·*de·*mos al·kee·*lar* oon *gee·*a
Can I take photographs (of you)?	¿(Le/Te) Puedo tomar fotos? pol/inf (le/te) *pwe·*do to·*mar fo·*tos
I'll send you the photograph.	Le/Te mandaré la foto. pol/inf le/te man·da·*re* la *fo·*to
Could you take a photograph of me?	¿Me puede hacer una foto? me *pwe·*de a·*ther oo·*na *fo·*to
What's that?	¿Qué es eso? ke es *e·*so
How old is it?	¿De qué época es? de ke *e·*po·ka es

Getting In

What time does it open/ close?	¿A qué hora abren/cierran? a ke *o·*ra *ab·*ren/*thye·*ran
What's the admission charge?	¿Cuánto cuesta la entrada? *kwan·*to *kwes·*ta la en·*tra·*da

| **Is there a discount for ...?** | ¿Hay descuentos para ...? |
| | ai des·*kwen*·tos *pa*·ra ... |

children	niños	*nee*·nyos
families	familias	fa·*mee*·lyas
groups	grupos	*groo*·pos
older people	gente mayor	*khen*·te ma·*yor*
students	estudiantes	es·too·*dyan*·tes

Galleries & Museums

When's the gallery open?	¿A qué hora abren la galería?
	a ke *o*·ra *a*·bren la ga·le·*ree*·a
When's the museum open?	¿A qué hora abren el museo?
	a ke *o*·ra *ab*·ren el moo·*se*·o
Q What's in the collection?	¿Qué hay en la colección?
	ke ai en la ko·lek·*thyon*
A It's a/an ... exhibition.	Es una exposición de ...
	es *oo*·na eks·po·see·*thyon* de ...
I like the works of ...	Me gustan las obras de ...
	me *goos*·tan las *o*·bras de ...
It reminds me of ...	Me recuerda a ...
	me re·*kwer*·da a ...
... art	arte m ...
	ar·te ...

graphic	gráfico	*gra*·fee·ko
impressionist	impresionista	eem·pre·syo·*nees*·ta
modernist	modernista	mo·der·*nees*·ta
Renaissance	renacentista	re·na·then·*tees*·ta

🔍 LOOK FOR

Abierto	a·*byer*·to	Open
Cerrado	the·*ra*·do	Closed
Prohibido	pro·ee·*bee*·do	Prohibited

Tours

Are there organised walking tours?	¿Organizan recorridos a pie? or·ga·*nee*·than re·ko·*ree*·dos a pye
I'd like to take cooking/language classes.	Me gustaría ir a clases de cocina/idiomas. me goos·ta·*ree*·a eer a *kla*·ses de ko·*thee*·na/ee·*dyo*·mas

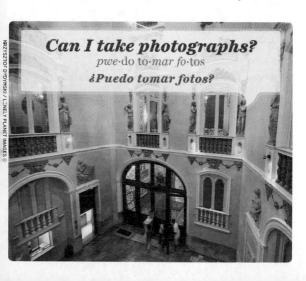

Can I take photographs?
pwe·do to·*mar* fo·tos
¿Puedo tomar fotos?

KRZYSZTOF DYDYNSKI / LONELY PLANET IMAGES ©

| Can you recommend a ...? | ¿Puede recomendar algún/alguna ...? m/f
 pwe·de re·ko·men·dar al·goon/al·goo·na ... |
| When's the next ...? | ¿Cuándo es el/la próximo/a ...? m/f
 kwan·do es el/la prok·see·mo/a ... |

boat trip	paseo m en barca	*pa·se·o en bar·ka*
day trip	excursión f de un día	*eks·koor·syon de oon dee·a*
excursion	excursión f	*eks·koor·syon*
tour	recorrido m	*re·ko·ree·do*

Do I need to take (food) with me?	¿Necesito llevar (comida)? *ne·the·see·to lye·var (ko·mee·da)*
Is (equipment/transport) included?	¿Incluye (equipo/transporte)? *een·kloo·ye (e·kee·po/trans·por·te)*
How long is the tour?	¿Cuánto dura el recorrido? *kwan·to doo·ra el re·ko·ree·do*
What time should I be back?	¿A qué hora tengo que volver? *a ke o·ra ten·go ke vol·ver*
Be back here at ...	Vuelva ... *vwel·va ...*
I've lost my group.	He perdido a mi grupo. *e per·dee·do a mee groo·po*

Senior & Disabled Travellers

KEY PHRASES

I need assistance.	Necesito asistencia.	ne·the·*see*·to a·sees·*ten*·thya
Is there wheelchair access?	¿Hay acceso para la silla de ruedas?	ai ak·*the*·so *pa*·ra la *see*·lya de *rwe*·das
Are there toilets for people with a disablity?	¿Hay aseos para minusválidos?	ai a·*se*·os *pa*·ra mee·noos·*va*·lee·dos

I have a disability.	Soy minusválido/a. m/f soy mee·noos·*va*·lee·do/a
I need assistance.	Necesito asistencia. ne·the·*see*·to a·secs *ten*·thya
Are guide dogs permitted?	¿Se permite la entrada a los perros lazarillos? se per·*mee*·te la en·*tra*·da a los *pe*·ros la·tha·*ree*·lyos
Is there wheelchair access?	¿Hay acceso para la silla de ruedas? ai ak·*the*·so *pa*·ra la *see*·lya de *rwe*·das
Are there parking spaces for people with a disability?	¿Tiene aparcamiento para minusválidos? *tye*·ne a·par·ka·*myen*·to *pa*·ra mee·noos·*va*·lee·dos
Are there rails in the bathroom?	¿Hay pasamanos en el baño? ai pa·sa·*ma*·nos en el *ba*·nyo

LOOK FOR

Acceso para Sillas de Ruedas	ak·*the*·so *pa*·ra *see*·lyas de *rwe*·das	Wheelchair Entrance
Ascensor	a·then·*sor*	Elevator/Lift

Are there toilets for people with a disability?	¿Hay aseos para minusválidos? ai a·*se*·os *pa*·ra mee·noos·*va*·lee·dos
Is there somewhere I can sit down?	¿Hay algun sitio dónde me pueda sentar? ai al·*goon see*·tyo *don*·de me *pwe*·da sen·*tar*
Could you help me cross this street?	¿Me puede ayudar a cruzar la calle? me *pwe*·de a·yoo·*dar* a kroo·*thar* la *ka*·lye
Could you call me a taxi for the disabled?	¿Podría llamar a un taxi para minusválidos? po·*dree*·a lya·*mar* a oon *tak*·see *pa*·ra mee·noos·*va*·lee·dos
crutches	muletas f pl moo·*le*·tas
guide dog	perro m lazarillo *pe*·ro la·tha·*ree*·lyo
ramp	rampa f *ram*·pa
walking frame	andador m an·da·*dor*
walking stick	bastón m bas·*ton*
wheelchair	silla f de ruedas *see*·lya de *rwe*·das

Travel with Children

KEY PHRASES

Are children allowed?	¿Se admiten niños?	se ad·mee·ten nee·nyos
Is there a child discount?	¿Hay descuento para niños?	ai des·kwen·to pa·ra nee·nyos
Is there a baby change room?	¿Hay una sala en la que cambiar el pañal al bebé?	ai oo·na sa·la en la ke kam·byar·le el pa·nyal al be·be

I need a ...   Necesito ...
ne·the·see·to ...

baby/child seat	un asiento de seguridad para bebés/ niños	oon a·syen·to de se·goo·ree·da pa·ra be·bes/ nee·nyos
cot	una cuna	oo·na koo·na
potty	un orinal de niños	oon o·ree·nal de nee·nyos
stroller	un cochecito	oon ko·che·thee·to

Do you sell baby wipes?   ¿Vende toallitas para bebés?
ven·de to·a·lyee·tas pa·ra be·bes

Do you sell disposable nappies/diapers?   ¿Vende pañales de usar y tirar?
ven·de pa·nya·les de oo·sar ee tee·rar

Do you sell milk formula?	¿Vende leche de fórmula? *ven*·de *le*·che de *for*·moo·la
Is there a/an ...?	¿Hay ...? ai ...

baby change room	una sala en la que cambiarle el pañal al bebé	*oo*·na *sa*·la en la ke kam·*byar*·le el pa·*nyal* al be·*be*
child discount	descuento para niños	des·*kwen*·to *pa*·ra *nee*·nyos
child-minding service	servicio de cuidado de niños	ser·*vee*·thyo de kwee·*da*·do de *nee*·nyos
children's menu	menú infantil	me·*noo* een·fan·*teel*
family discount	descuento familiar	des·*kwen*·to fa·mee·*lyar*
highchair	trona	*tro*·na

Do you mind if I breastfeed here?	¿Le molesta que dé de pecho aquí? le mo·*les*·ta ke de de *pe*·cho a·*kee*
Are children allowed?	¿Se admiten niños? se ad·*mee*·ten *nee*·nyos
Is this suitable for (three)-year-old children?	¿Es apto para niños de (tres) años? es *ap*·to *pa*·ra *nee*·nyos de (tres) *a*·nyos

If your child is sick, see **health** (p158).

Social

Meeting People

KEY PHRASES

My name is ...	Me llamo ...	me *lya*·mo ...
I'm from ...	Soy de ...	soy de ...
I work in (education).	Trabajo en (enseñanza).	tra·*ba*·kho en (en·se·*nyan*·tha)
I'm ... years old.	Tengo ... años.	*ten*·go ... *a*·nyos
And you?	¿Y Usted/tú? **pol/inf**	ee oos·*te*/too

Basics

Yes.	Sí. see
No.	No. no
Please.	Por favor. por fa·*vor*
Thank you (very much).	(Muchas) Gracias. (*moo*·chas) *gra*·thyas
You're welcome.	De nada. de *na*·da
Excuse me.	Perdón/Discúlpeme. per·*don*/dees·*kool*·pe·me
Sorry.	Lo siento. lo *syen*·to

Greetings

In Spain people are often quite casual in their social interactions.
It's fine to use the following expressions in both formal and informal
situations.

Hello/Hi.	Hola.
	o·la
Good morning.	Buenos días.
	bwe·nos dee·as
Good afternoon. (until 8pm)	Buenas tardes.
	bwe·nas tar·des
Good evening/night.	Buenas noches.
	bwe·nas no·ches
See you later.	Hasta luego.
	as·ta lwe·go
Goodbye./Bye.	Adiós.
	a·dyos
Q How are you?	¿Qué tal?
	ke tal
A Fine. thanks. And you?	Bien, gracias. ¿Y Usted/tú? pol/inf
	byen gra·thyas ee oos·te/too
Q What's your name?	¿Cómo se llama Usted? pol
	ko·mo se lya·ma oos·te
	¿Cómo te llamas? inf
	ko·mo te lya·mas
A My name is ...	Me llamo ...
	me lya·mo ...
I'm pleased to meet you.	Mucho gusto.
	moo·cho goos·to

I'd like to introduce you to ...	Quisiera presentarle a ... pol
	kee·sye·ra pre·sen·tar·le a ...
	Quisiera presentarte a ... inf
	kee·sye·ra pre·sen·tar·te a ...

| ✂ This is ... | Ésto es... | es·to es ... |

| This is my friend. | Éste/a es mi amigo/a. m/f |
| | es·te/a es mee a·mee·go/a |

Titles & Addressing People

Señor and *Señora* tend to be used in everyday speech. *Doña*, although rare, is used as a mark of respect towards older women, while *Don* is sometimes used to address men. An elderly neighbour, for example, might be called *Doña Lola*. For more on polite forms, see **addressing people** (p95), and **personal pronouns** (p21).

Mr	Señor
	se·nyor
Sir	Don
	don
Miss	Señorita
	se·nyo·ree·ta
Ms/Mrs	Señora
	se·nyo·ra
Madam	Doña
	do·nya

Making Conversation

Spain is known for its distinct regional personalities. A great conversation starter in Spain is to ask someone where they come from. Other good topics are sport, politics, history and travel.

| Do you live here? | ¿Vives aquí? |
| | vee·ves a·kee |

> **LANGUAGE TIP**
>
> **Addressing Friends**
> You may hear friends calling each other *tío* m
> *tee*·o, or *tía* f *tee*·a, but these words are usually
> used when talking about others. They're a bit crass (a little
> like using 'sheila' to describe a girl in Australia). Guys
> use *colega* ko·*le*·ga, and *hombre* om·bre, to address their
> workmates or male friends. In the south, people call their
> friends *pixas pee*·chas or *xoxos cho*·chos.

Where are you going?	¿Adónde vas? a·*don*·de vas	
What are you doing?	¿Qué haces? ke *a*·thes	
Q Are you here on holidays?	¿Estás aquí de vacaciones? es·*tas* a·*kee* de va·ka·*thyo*·nes	
A I'm here for a holiday.	Estoy aquí de vacaciones. es·*toy* a·*kee* de va·ka·*thyo*·nes	
A I'm here on business.	Estoy aquí en viaje de negocios. es·*toy* a·*kee* en *vya*·khe de ne·*go*·thyos	
A I'm here to study.	Estoy aquí estudiando. es·*toy* a·*kee* es·too·*dyan*·do	
That's (beautiful), isn't it?	¿Es (precioso), no? es (pre·*thyo*·so) no	
Q How long are you here for?	¿Cuánto tiempo te vas a quedar? *kwan*·to *tyem*·po te vas a ke·*dar*	
A I'm here for ... weeks/days.	Estoy aquí por ... semanas/días. es·*toy* a·*kee* por ... se·*ma*·nas/*dee*·as	

Nationalities

You'll find that many country names are similar to English, so even if you don't know the Spanish name, it's more than likely you'll be understood. For more countries, see the **dictionary**.

🇶 **Where are you from?**	¿De dónde es Usted? pol de *don*·de es oos·*te* ¿De dónde eres? inf de *don*·de e·res
🅰 **I'm from (Australia).**	Soy de (Australia). soy de (ow·*stra*·lya)
🅰 **I'm from (Canada).**	Soy de (Canadá). soy de (ka·na·*da*)

Age

🇶 **How old are you?**	¿Cuántos años tienes? *kwan*·tos *a*·nyos *tye*·nes
🅰 **I'm ... years old.**	Tengo ... años. *ten*·go ... *a*·nyos
🇶 **How old is your son/ daughter?**	¿Cuántos años tiene tu hijo/hija? *kwan*·tos *a*·nyos *tye*·ne too ee·kho/ee·kha
🅰 **He's/She's ... years old.**	Tiene ... años. *tye*·ne ... *a*·nyos
I'm younger than I look.	Soy más joven de lo que parezco. soy mas *kho*·ven de lo ke pa·*reth*·ko
Too old!	¡Demasiado viejo! de·ma·*sya*·do *vye*·kho

For your age, see **numbers & amounts** (p34).

🔊 LISTEN FOR

¡Cojonudo!	ko·kho·*noo*·do	Great!
¿De veras?	de *ve*·ras	Really?
¡Enhorabuena!	e·no·ra·*bwe*·na	Congratulations!
¡Estupendo!	es·too·*pen*·do	That's fantastic!
¡No me digas!	no me *dee*·gas	You don't say!
¡Qué guay!	ke gwai	How cool!
¿Qué hay?	ke ai	What's up?
¡Qué interesante!	ke een·te·re·*san*·te	How interesting!

SOCIAL   MEETING PEOPLE

Occupations & Study

Q What do you do?	¿A qué te dedicas? a ke te de·*dee*·kas
A I work in (education/ hospitality).	Trabajo en (enseñanza/ hostelería). tra·*ba*·kho en (en·se·*nyan*·tha/ os·te·le·*ree*·a)
A I'm a/an ...	Soy ... soy ...

architect	arquitecto/a m/f	ar·kee·*tek*·to/a
mechanic	mecánico/a m/f	me·*ka*·nee·ko/a
student	estudiante m&f	es·too·*dyan*·te
teacher	profesor/ profesora m/f	pro·fe·*sor*/ pro·fe·*so*·ra

A I'm self-employed.	Soy trabajador/ trabajadora autónomo/a. m/f soy tra·ba·kha·*dor*/ tra·ba·kha·*do*·ra ow·*to*·no·mo/a

A I'm retired.	Estoy jubilado/a. **m/f**	es·*toy* khoo·bee·*la*·do/a
A I'm unemployed.	Estoy en el paro.	es·*toy* en el *pa*·ro
Q What are you studying?	¿Qué estudias?	ke es·*too*·dyas
A I'm studying (languages).	Estudio (idiomas).	es·*too*·dyo (ee·*dyo*·mas)
I'm studying at ...	Estudio en ...	es·*too*·dyo en ...

For more occupations and studies, see the **dictionary**.

Family

Q Do you have (a) ...?	¿Tiene ...? **pol**	*tye*·ne ...
	¿Tienes ...? **inf**	*tye*·nes ...
A I (don't) have (a) ...	(No) Tengo ...	(no) *ten*·go ...

brother	un hermano	oon er·*ma*·no
children	hijos	*ee*·khos
family	una familia	*oo*·na fa·*mee*·lya
partner	una pareja **m&f**	*oo*·na pa·*re*·kha
sister	una hermana	*oo*·na er·*ma*·na

Q Are you married?	¿Estás casado/a? **m/f**	es·*tas* ka·*sa*·do/a
A I'm married.	Estoy casado/a. **m/f**	es·*toy* ka·*sa*·do/a
A I'm single.	Soy soltero/a. **m/f**	soy sol·*te*·ro/a

🅐 I live with someone.	Vivo con alguien. *vee*·vo kon *al*·gyen
🅐 I'm separated.	Estoy separado/a. **m/f** es·*toy* se·pa·*ra*·do/a

Talking with Children

Do you go to school or kindergarten?	¿Vas al colegio o a la guardería? vas al ko·*le*·khyo o a la gwar·de·*ree*·a
What grade are you in?	¿En qué curso estás? en ke *koor*·so es·*tas*
Do you like school?	¿Te gusta el colegio? te *goos*·ta el ko·*le*·khyo
Do you like sport?	¿Te gusta el deporte? te *goos*·ta el de·*por*·te
Do you learn (English)?	¿Aprendes (inglés)? a·*pren*·des (een·*gles*)
I come from very far away.	Vengo de muy lejos. *ven*·go de mooy *le*·khos

Farewells

It's been great meeting you.	Me ha encantado conocerte. me a en·kan·*ta*·do ko·no·*ther*·te
Keep in touch!	¡Nos mantendremos en contacto! nos man·ten·*dre*·mos en kon·*tak*·to
Are you on Facebook?	¿Estás en Facebook? es·*tas* en *feys*·book

LANGUAGE TIP

Spanish Idioms

Even idioms translate across languages. Here are a few golden oldies:

It's like casting pearls before swine.	Es como echar margaritas a los cerdos. (lit: it's like feeding daisies to the pigs)
	es *ko*·mo e·*char* mar·ga·*ree*·tas a los *ther*·dos
When it rains, it pours.	Éramos pocos y parió la abuela. (lit: there were a few of us then granny gave birth)
	e·ra·mos *po*·kos y pa·ree·o la a·*bwe*·la
This is like watching grass grow.	Es más largo que un día sin pan. (lit: it's longer than a day without bread)
	es mas *lar*·go ke oon *dee*·a seen pan

If you ever visit (South Africa), you can stay with me.	Si algún día visitas (Sudáfrica), te puedes quedar conmigo.
	see al·*goon dee*·a vee·*see*·tas (soo·da·free·ka) te *pwe*·des ke·*dar* kon·*mee*·go

🇶 What's your (address)?	¿Cuál es tu (dirección)?
	kwal es too (dee·rek·*thyon*)
🇦 Here's my ...	Ésta es mi ... **m/f**
	es·te/*es*·ta es mee ...
🇦 Here's my address.	Ésta es mi dirección.
	es·ta es mee dee·rek·*thyon*
🇦 Here's my email address.	Ésta es mi dirección de email.
	es·ta es mee dee·rek·*thyon* de *ee*·mayl

For more on addresses, see **directions** (p57).

Basque

Basque (*euskara,* in Basque), is spoken at the western end of the Pyrenees and along the Bay of Biscay – from Bayonne in France to Bilbao in Spain, and inland, almost to Pamplona. Dialects are also spoken, including Bizkaian, Gipuzkoan, High Navarrese, Aezkoan, Salazarese, Lapurdian, Low Navarrese and Suberoan. No one quite knows its origin, but the most likely theory is that Basque is the lone survivor of a language family that once extended across Europe, and was wiped out by the languages of the Celts, Germanic tribes and Romans.

Speaking Spanish in the Basque-speaking towns might be expected from a foreigner, but is not as warmly received as an attempt at one of the most ancient languages of Europe.

Hi!	Kaixo! *kai*·sho
Good morning.	Egun on. e·goon *on*
Good afternoon/evening.	Arratsalde on. a·*ra*·chyal·de *on*
Goodbye.	Agur. a·*goor*
Take care.	Ondo ibili. on·do ee·*beel*·ee
How are you?	Zer moduz? ser mo·*doos*
Fine, thank you.	Ongi, eskerrik asko. on·gee e·*ske*·reek *as*·ko

---

🔊 **LISTEN FOR**

Euskal Herrian beti jai!	e·oos·*kal* e·*ree*·an *be*·tee yai The Basque Country's always partying!
Gora gu 'ta gutarrak!	*go*·ra goo ta *goo*·ta·rak Hurray for us!

Excuse me.	Barkatu. bar·*ka*·too
Please.	Mesedez. me·*se*·des
Thank you.	Eskerrik asko. es·*ke*·reek *as*·ko
You're welcome.	Ez horregatik. es o·*re*·ga·teek
Do you speak English?	Ingelesez ba al dakizu? een·*ge*·le·ses ba al da·*kee*·soo
I know a little Basque.	Euskara apur bat badakit. e·*oos*·ka·ra a·*poor* bat ba·da·*keet*
I don't understand.	Ez dut ulertzen. es toot oo·*ler*·tzen
Could you speak in Castillian, please?	Erdaraz egingo al didazu, mesedez? er·da·ras e·*geen*·go al dee·*da*·soo me·*se*·des
How do you say that in Basque?	Nola esaten da hori euskara? *no*·la e·*sa*·ten da o·ree e·oo·ska·*ra*

CULTURE TIP

Spanish in America

Columbus' arrival in the New World in 1492 launched the era of Spanish expansion in America, one which is also reflected in the language. *Patata*, *tomate*, *cacao* and *chocolate* are just a few examples of words that entered Spanish (and consequently English) from the indigenous American languages. Bear in mind that Spanish has evolved differently in the Americas, and it's a good idea to take Lonely Planet's *Latin American Spanish* phrasebook if that's your destination.

Catalan

Catalan (*català,* in Catalan) is spoken by up to 10 million people in the northeast of Spain, a territory that comprises Catalonia, coastal Valencia and the Balearic Islands (Majorca, Minorca and Ibiza).

Outside Spain, Catalan is also spoken in Andorra, the south of France and the town of Alguer in Sardinia. Many famous creatives have been Catalan speakers: painters like Dalí, Miró and Picasso, architects like Gaudí, and writers like Mercé Rodoreda.

Despite the fact that almost all Catalan speakers from Spain are bilingual, they appreciate it when visitors attempt to communicate, if even in the simplest way, in Catalan.

Hello!	Hola! o·la
Good morning.	Bon dia. bon *dee*·a
Good afternoon.	Bona tarda. *bo*·na *tar*·da
Good evening.	Bon vespre. bon *bes*·pra
Goodbye.	Adéu. a·*the*·oo
How are you?	Com estàs? kom as·*tas*
(Very) Well.	(Molt) Bé. (mol) be
Excuse me.	Perdoni. par·*tho*·nee
Sorry.	Ho sento. oo *sen*·to
Please.	Sisplau. sees·*pla*·oo
Thank you.	Gràcies. *gra*·see·as

🔊 LISTEN FOR

Això rai!	a·*sho* ra·ee	No problem!
Quin tip de riure!	kin tip da ri·a·*oo*·ra	What a laugh!

Yes./No.	Sí./No.
	see/no
Do you speak English?	Parla anglès?
	par·la an·*gles*
Could you speak in Castilian, please?	Pot parlar castellà sisplau?
	pot par·*la* kas·ta·*lya* sees·*pla*·oo
I (don't) understand.	(No) Ho entenc.
	(no) oo an·*teng*
How do you say ...?	Com es diu ...?
	kom az *dee*·oo ...

Galician

Galician (*galego,* in Galician), is an official language of the Autonomous Community of Galicias and is also widely understood in the neighbouring regions of Asturias and Castilla-Léon. It's very similar to Portuguese, as the two languages have roots in Vulgar Latin.

Galicians are likely to revert to Spanish when addressing a stranger, especially a foreigner, but making a small effort to communicate in Galician will always be welcomed.

Hello!	Ola!
	o·la
Good day.	Bon dia.
	bon *dee*·a
Good afternoon/evening.	Boa tarde.
	bo·a *tar*·de

Goodbye.	Adeus. *a·de·oos* Até logo. *a·te lo·go*
Excuse me.	Perdón. per·*don*
Please.	Por favor. por fa·*vor*
Thank you.	Grácias. *gra*·see·as
Many thanks.	Moitas grácias. *moy*·tas *gra*·see·as
That's fine.	De nada. de *na*·da
Yes./No.	Si./Non. see/non
Do you speak English?	Fala inglés? *fa*·la een·*gles*
Could you speak in Castilian, please?	Pode falar en español, por favor? *po*·de fa·*la* en e·spa·*nyol* por fa·*bor*
I (don't) understand.	(Non) Entendo. (non) en·*ten*·do
What's this called in Galician?	Como se chama iso en galego? *ko*·mo se *cha*·ma *ee*·so en ga·*le*·go

Interests

KEY PHRASES

What do you do in your spare time?	¿Qué te gusta hacer en tu tiempo libre?	ke te *goos*·ta a·*ther* en too *tyem*·po *lee*·bre
Do you like (travelling)?	¿Te gusta (viajar)?	te *goos*·ta (vya·*khar*)
I (don't) like ...	(No) Me gusta ...	(no) me *goos*·ta ...

Common Interests

What do you do in your spare time?	¿Qué te gusta hacer en tu tiempo libre? ke te *goos*·ta a·*ther* en too *tyem*·po *lee*·bre
Q Do you like (travelling)?	¿Te gusta (viajar)? te *goos*·ta (vya·*khar*)
A I like (cooking).	Me gusta (cocinar). me *goos*·ta (ko·thee·*nar*)
A I don't like (hiking).	No me gusta (el excursionismo). no me *goos*·ta (el eks·koor·syo·*nees*·mo)
I (don't) like photography.	(No) Me gusta la fotografía. (no) me *goos*·ta la fo·to·gra·*fee*·a
I (don't) like shopping.	(No) Me gusta ir de compras. (no) me *goos*·ta eer de *kom*·pras

For more activities, see **sports** (p142) and the **dictionary**.

Music

Do you like to ...?	¿Te gusta ...? te *goos*·ta ...	
dance	ir a bailar	eer a bai·*lar*
go to concerts	ir a conciertos	eer a kon·*thyer*·tos
listen to music	escuchar música	es·koo·*char* moo·see·ka
play an instrument	tocar algún instrumento	to·kar al·*goon* eens·troo·*men*·to
sing	cantar	*kan*·tar

SOCIAL INTERESTS

What music do you like?
ke *moo*·see·ka te *goos*·ta
¿Qué música te gusta?

Which bands do you like?	¿Qué grupos te gustan? ke *groo*·pos te *goos*·tan
Which singers do you like?	¿Qué cantantes te gustan? ke kan·*tan*·tes te *goos*·tan
What music do you like?	¿Qué música te gusta? ke *moo*·see·ka te *goos*·ta
classical music	música f clásica *moo*·see·ka *kla*·see·ka
jazz	jazz m khath
pop	música f pop *moo*·see·ka pop
rock	música f rock *moo*·see·ka rok
world music	música f étnica *moo*·see·ka *et*·nee·ka

Cinema & Theatre

I feel like going to (a comedy).	Tengo ganas de ir a (una comedia). *ten*·go *ga*·nas de eer a (*oo*·na ko·*me*·dya)
What's showing at the cinema (tonight)?	¿Qué película dan en el cine (esta noche)? ke pe·*lee*·koo·la dan en el *thee*·ne (*es*·ta *no*·che)
Is it in (English)?	¿Es en (inglés)? es en (een·*gles*)
Is it dubbed?	¿Está doblada? es·*ta* dob·*la*·da
Does it have (English) subtitles?	¿Tiene subtítulos (en inglés)? *tye*·ne soob·*tee*·too·los (en een·*gles*)

Have you seen ...?	¿Has visto ...? as vees·to ...
Q Who's in it?	¿Quién actúa? kyen ak·too·a
A It stars ...	Actúa ... ak too·a ...
Are those seats taken?	¿Están ocupados estos asientos? es·tan o·koo·pa·dos es·tos a·syen·tos
Q Did you like the film/play?	¿Te gustó el cine/teatro? te goos·to el thee·ne/te·a·tro
A I thought it was excellent/OK.	Pienso que fue excelente/regular. pyen·so ke fwe eks·the·len·te/re·goo·lar
A I thought it was long.	Pienso que fue largo. pyen·so ke fwe lar·go
I (don't) like ...	(No) Me gusta/gustan ... sg/pl (no) me goos·ta/goos·tan ...

animated films	películas f pl de dibujos animados	pe·lee·koo·las de dee·boo·khos a·nee·ma·dos
comedy	comedia f	ko·me·dya
documentary	documentales m pl	do·koo·men·ta·les
drama	drama m	dra·ma
(Spanish) cinema	cine m (español)	thee·ne (es·pa·nyol)
horror movies	cine m de terror	thee·ne de te·ror
sci-fi	cine m de ciencia ficción	thee·ne de thyen·thya feek·thyon

Off to a show? See **buying tickets** (p44) and **going out** (p130).

SOCIAL INTERESTS

Books & Reading

What kind of books do you read?	¿Qué tipo de libros lees? ke *tee*·po de *lee*·bros *le*·es
On this trip I'm reading ...	En este viaje estoy leyendo ... en *es*·te *vya*·khe es·*toy* le·*yen*·do ...
Have you read ...?	¿Has leído ...? as le·*ee*·do ...
Q Which (Spanish) author do you recommend?	¿Qué autor (español) recomiendas? ke ow·*tor* (es·pa·*nyol*) re·ko·*myen*·das
A I'd recommend ...	Recomiendo a ... re·ko·*myen*·do a ...
Where can I exchange books?	¿Dónde puedo cambiar libros? *don*·de *pwe*·do kam·*byar* *lee*·bros

For more on books and reading, see **shopping** (p80).

Volunteering

I'd like to volunteer my skills.	Me gustaría ofrecer mis conocimientos. me goos·ta·*ree*·a o·fre·*ther* mees ko·no·thee·*myen*·tos
Are there any volunteer programs available in the area?	¿Hay programas de voluntariado en la zona? ai pro·*gra*·mas de vo·loon·ta·*rya*·do en la *tho*·na

Feelings & Opinions

KEY PHRASES

Are you ...?	¿Tienes/Estás ...?	tye·nes/es·tas ...
I'm (not) ...	(No) Tengo/ Estoy ...	(no) ten·go/ es·toy ...
What did you think of it?	¿Qué pensaste de eso?	ke pen·sas·te de e·so
I thought it was ...	Pienso que fue ...	pyen·so ke fwe ...
Did you hear about ...?	¿Has oído que ...?	as o·ee·do ke ...

Feelings

Feelings are described with either nouns or adjectives: the nouns use 'have' in Spanish (eg, 'I have hunger') and the adjectives use 'be' (like in English).

| **Q** Are you ...? | ¿Tienes ...? tye·nes ... |
| **A** I'm (not) ... | (No) Tengo ... (no) ten·go ... |

cold	frío	free·o
hot	calor	ka·lor
hungry	hambre	am·bre
in a hurry	prisa	pree·sa
thirsty	sed	se

| **Q** Are you ...? | ¿Estás ...?
es·*tas* ... |
| **A** I'm (not) ... | (No) Estoy ...
(no) es·*toy* ... |

annoyed	fastidiado/a m/f	fas·tee·*dya*·do/a
embarrassed	avergonzado/a m/f	a·ver·gon·*tha*·do/a
happy	feliz m&f	fe·*leeth*
sad	triste m&f	*trees*·te
tired	cansado/a m/f	kan·*sa*·do/a
well	bien m&f	byen

I'm a little (sad).	Estoy un poco (triste). m&f es·*toy* oon *po*·ko (*trees*·te)
I'm quite (disappointed).	Estoy bastante (decepcionado/a). m/f es·*toy* bas·*tan*·te (de·thep·thyo *na*·do/a)
I feel very (lucky).	Me siento muy (afortunado/a). m/f me *syen*·to mooy (a·for·too·na·do/a)

If you're not feeling well, see **health** (p158).

Opinions

| **Q** Did you like it? | ¿Te gustó?
te goos·*to* |
| **Q** What did you think of it? | ¿Qué pensaste de eso?
ke pen·*sas*·te de *e*·so |

A I thought it was ...	Pienso que fue ...	*pyen·so ke fwe ...*
A It's ...	Es ...	*es ...*

beautiful	bonito/a m/f	bo·*nee*·to/a
bizarre	raro/a m/f	*ra*·ro/a
entertaining	entretenido/a m/f	en·tre·te·*nee*·do/a
excellent	fantástico/a m/f	fan·*tas*·tee·ko/a
horrible	horrible m&f	o·*ree*·ble

I thought it was OK.	Pienso que estaba bien. *pyen·so ke es·ta·ba byen*
He's/She's the best.	Es un trozo de pan. (lit: he's/she's a piece of bread) *es oon tro·tho de pan*
I disagree!	No estoy de acuerdo! *no es·toy de a·kwer·do*
Yes, but ...	Sí, pero ... *see pe·ro ...*
Whatever.	Lo que sea. *lo ke se·a*

Politics & Social Issues

Q Who do you vote for?	¿A quién votas? *a kyen vo·tas*
A I support the ... party.	Apoyo al partido ... *a·po·yo al par·tee·do ...*
Did you hear about ...?	¿Has oído que ...? *as o·ee·do ke ...*
Are you in favour of ...?	¿Estás a favor de ...? *es·tas a fa·vor de ...*

🔊 LISTEN FOR

Claro.	*kla*·ro	Sure.
¡Claro que sí!	*kla*·ro ke see	Of course!
¡De ningún modo!	de neen·*goon* *mo*·do	No way!
Era broma.	e·ra *bro*·ma	Just joking.
Está bien.	es·*ta* byen	It's OK.
Estoy bien.	es·*toy* byen	I'm OK.
Quizás.	kee·*thas*	Maybe.
Sin problema.	seen pro·*ble*·ma	No problem.
Un momento.	oon mo·*men*·to	Just a minute.
Vale.	*va*·le	OK.
¡Ya lo creo!	ya lo *kre*·o	You bet!

How do people feel about ...?	¿Cómo se siente la gente de ...? *ko*·mo se *syen*·te la *khen*·te de ...
the economy	economía f e·ko·no·*mee*·a
health care	seguro m médico se·*goo*·ro *me*·dee·ko
immigration	inmigración f een·mee·gra·*thyon*
war in ...	guerra f en ... *ge*·ra en ...

The Environment

Is there an environmental problem here?	¿Aquí hay un problema con el medio ambiente? a·*kee* ai oon pro·*ble*·ma kon el *me*·dyo am·*byen*·te

Is this (forest) protected?	¿Está este (bosque) protegido? es·ta es·te (bos·ke) pro·te·khee·do
Where can I recycle this?	¿Dónde se puede reciclar esto? don·de se pwe·de re·thee·klar es·to
climate change	cambio m climático kam·byo klee·ma·tee·ko
pollution	contaminación f kon·ta·mee·na·thyon
recycling	reciclaje m re·thee·kla·khe

I'm happy.
es·toy fe·leeth

Estoy feliz.

SOCIAL · **GOING OUT**

Going Out

What's on tonight?	¿Qué hay esta noche?	ke ai es·ta no·che
Where are the clubs?	¿Dónde están las discotecas?	don·de es·tan las dees·ko·te·kas
Would you like to go for a coffee?	¿Quieres que vayamos a tomar un café?	kye·res ke va·ya·mos a to·mar oon ka·fe
What time shall we meet?	¿A qué hora quedamos?	a ke o·ra ke·da·mos
Where will we meet?	¿Dónde quedamos?	don·de ke·da·mos

Where to Go

What's there to do in the evenings?	¿Qué se puede hacer por las noches? ke se pwe·de a·ther por las no·ches
What's on ...?	¿Qué hay ...? ke ai ...

locally	en la zona	en la tho·na
this weekend	este fin de semana	es·te feen de se·ma·na
today	hoy	oy
tonight	esta noche	es·ta no·che

Where are there gay venues?	¿Dónde hay lugares gay? don·de ai loo·ga·res gai

Where are there places to eat?	¿Dónde hay lugares para comer?	don·de ai loo·ga·res pa·ra ko·mer
Where are the clubs?	¿Dónde están las discotecas?	don·de es·tan las dees·ko·te·kas
Where are there pubs?	¿Dónde hay pubs?	don·de ai poobs
Is there a local ... guide?	¿Hay una guía ... de la zona?	ai oo·na gee·a ... de la tho·na

entertainment	del ocio	del o·thyo
film	de cine	de thee·ne
gay	de lugares gay	de loo·ga·res gai
music	de música	de moo·see·ka

I feel like going to a/the ...	Tengo ganas de ir ...	ten·go ga·nas de eer ...

ballet	al ballet	al ba·le
bar	a un bar	a oon bar
cafe	a un café	a oon ka·fe
concert	a un concierto	a oon kon·thyer·to
karaoke bar	a un bar de karaoke	a oon bar de ka·ra·o·ke
movies	al cine	al thee·ne
nightclub	a una discoteca	a oo·na dees·ko·te·ka
party	a una fiesta	a oo·na fyes·ta
restaurant	a un restaurante	a oon res·tow·ran·te
theatre	al teatro	al te·a·tro

Invitations

What are you doing this evening?	¿Qué haces esta noche? ke *a*·thes es·ta *no*·che
What are you up to (right now)?	¿Qué haces (ahora)? ke *a*·thes (a·o·ra)
Would you like to go for a ...?	¿Quieres que vayamos a ...? *kye*·res ke va·*ya*·mos a ...

coffee	tomar un café	to·*mar* oon ka·*fe*
drink	tomar algo	to·*mar* al·go
meal	comer	ko·*mer*
walk	pasear	pa·se·*ar*

I feel like going dancing.	Me apetece ir a bailar. me a·pe·*te*·the eer a bai·*lar*
I feel like going out somewhere.	Me apetece salir. me a·pe·*te*·the sa·*leer*
My round.	Invito yo. een·*vee*·to yo
Do you know a good restaurant?	¿Conoces algún buen restaurante? ko·*no*·thes al·*goon* bwen res·tow·*ran*·te
Do you want to come to the (...) concert with me?	¿Quieres venir conmigo al concierto (de ...)? *kye*·res ve·*neer* kon·*mee*·go al kon·*thyer*·to (de ...)
We're having a party.	Vamos a dar una fiesta. *va*·mos a dar *oo*·na *fyes*·ta
Do you want to come?	¿Por qué no vienes? por ke no *vye*·nes
Are you ready?	¿Estás listo/a? **m/f** es·*tas* lees·to/a

CULTURE TIP   **Movie Subtitles**
Foreign movies are usually dubbed into Spanish, but in bigger cities you'll find that some films have Spanish subtitles. Look out for *v.o.* (*version original* ver·*syon* o·ree·khee·*nal*, 'original version') or *v.o.s.* (*version original subtitulada* ver·*syon* o·ree·khee·*nal* soob·tee·too·*la*·da, 'original version with subtitles') in listings.

Responding to Invitations

Sure!	¡Por supuesto! por soo·*pwes*·to
Yes, I'd love to.	Me encantaría. me en·kan·ta·*ree*·a
Where will we go?	¿A dónde vamos? a *don*·de va·*mos*
That's very kind of you.	Es muy amable por tu parte. es mooy a·*ma*·ble por too *par*·te
No, I'm afraid I can't.	Lo siento pero no puedo. lo *syen*·to *pe*·ro no *pwe*·do
Sorry, I can't sing/dance.	Lo siento, no sé cantar/bailar. lo *syen*·to no se kan·*tar*/bai·*lar*
What about tomorrow?	¿Qué tal mañana? ke tal ma·*nya*·na

🔊 LISTEN FOR

¡Eh, tú!	e *too*	Hey!
¡Escucha (esto)!	es·*koo*·cha (*es*·to)	Listen (to this)!
¡Mira!	*mee*·ra	Look!

Arranging to Meet

Q **What time shall we meet?**	¿A qué hora quedamos? a ke *o*·ra ke·*da*·mos
A **Let's meet at (eight) o'clock.**	Quedamos a las (ocho). ke·*da*·mos a las (*o*·cho)
Q **Where will we meet?**	¿Dónde quedamos? *don*·de ke·*da*·mos
A **Let's meet at the (entrance).**	Quedamos en (la entrada). ke·*da*·mos en (la en·*tra*·da)
I'll pick you up.	Paso a recogerte. *pa*·so a re·ko·*kher*·te
I'll be coming later.	Iré más tarde. ee·*re* mas *tar*·de
Where will you be?	¿Dónde estarás? *don*·de es·ta·*ras*
OK!	¡Hecho! *e*·cho
I'll see you then.	Nos vemos. nos *ve*·mos
See you later/tomorrow.	Hasta luego/mañana. *as*·ta *lwe*·go/ma·*nya*·na
I'm looking forward to it.	Tengo muchas ganas de ir. *ten*·go *moo*·chas *ga*·nas de eer

| Sorry I'm late. | Siento llegar tarde.
syen·to lye·*gar* tar·de |
| Never mind. | No pasa nada.
no *pa*·sa *na*·da |

Nightclubs & Bars

Where can we go (salsa) dancing?	¿Dónde podemos ir a bailar (la salsa)? *don*·de po·*de*·mos eer a bai·*lar* (la *sal*·sa)
Q What type of music do you like?	¿Qué tipo de música prefieres? ke *tee*·po de *moo*·see·ka pre·*tye*·res
A I really like (reggae).	Me encanta (el reggae). me en·*kan*·ta (el *re*·gai)
Come on!	¡Vamos! *va*·mos
This place is great!	¡Este lugar me encanta! *es*·te loo·*gar* me en·*kan*·ta

For more on bars and drinks, see **eating out** (p177).

Drugs

I don't take drugs.	No consumo ningún tipo de drogas. no kon·*soo*·mo neen·*goon* *tee*·po de *dro*·gas
I take ... occasionally.	Tomo ... de vez en cuando. *to*·mo ... de veth en *kwan*·do
Do you want to have a smoke?	¿Nos fumamos un porro? nos foo·*ma*·mos oon *po*·ro
Do you have a light?	¿Tienes fuego? *tye*·nes *fwe*·go

See also **police** (p156).

SOCIAL · GOING OUT

Romance

KEY PHRASES

Would you like to do something?	¿Quieres hacer algo?	kye·res a·ther al·go
I love you.	Te quiero.	te kye·ro
Leave me alone, please	Déjame en paz, por favor.	de·kha·me en path por fa·vor

Asking Someone Out

Don't be surprised if invitations come late in the day. Social life in Spain continues well into the night: sometimes people begin to eat dinner at 10pm and many clubs open at midnight.

Q Would you like to do something (tonight)?

¿Quieres hacer algo (esta noche)?
kye·res a·ther al·go (es·ta no·che)

A Yes, I'd love to.

Me encantaría.
me en·kan·ta·ree·a

A I'm busy.

Estoy ocupado/a. **m/f**
es·toy o·koo·pa·do/a

Pick-up Lines

Would you like a drink?	¿Te apetece una copa? te a·pe·te·the oo·na ko·pa
Do you have a light?	¿Tienes fuego? tye·nes fwe·go

| You're great. | Eres estupendo/a. m/f
e·res es·too·pen·do/a |
| You mustn't come here much, because I would have noticed you sooner. | No debes venir mucho por aquí porque me habría fijado en ti antes.
no de·bes ve·neer moo·cho por a·kee por·ke me a·bree·a fee·kha·do en tee an·tes |

Rejections

I'm here with my boyfriend/girlfriend.	Estoy aquí con mi novio/a. m/f es·toy a·kee kon mee no·vyo/a
Excuse me, I have to go now.	Lo siento, pero me tengo que ir. lo syen·to pe·ro me ten·go ke eer
Leave me alone, please.	Déjame en paz, por favor. de·kha·me en path por fa·vor
Go away!	¡Vete! ve·te
Hey, I'm not interested in talking to you.	Mira tío/a, es que no me interesa hablar contigo. m/f mee·ra tee·o/a es ke no me een·te·re·sa ab·lar kon·tee·go

Getting Closer

| Can I kiss you? | ¿Te puedo besar?
te pwe·do be·sar |
| Do you want to come inside for a drink? | ¿Quieres entrar a tomar algo?
kye·res en·trar a to·mar al·go |

SOCIAL ROMANCE

LANGUAGE TIP

Masculine & Feminine

In this book, masculine forms appear before the feminine forms. If you see a word ending in -o/a, it means the masculine form ends in -o and the feminine form ends in -a (ie you replace the -o ending with the -a ending to make it feminine), eg *hijo/a* ee·kho/a m/f (son/daughter). The same goes for the plural endings -os/as, eg *hijos/as* ee·khos/as m/f (sons/daughters). If you see an *(a)* between brackets at the end of a word, it means you have to add it in order to make that word feminine, eg *español(a)* es·pa·*nyol*/es·pa·*nyo*·la m/f (Spanish). In other cases we spell out the whole word, eg *actor/actriz* ak·*tor*/ak·*treeth* m/f (actor/actress). See also **gender** (p19).

Do you want a massage?	¿Quieres un masaje?
	kye·res oon ma·*sa*·khe
Let's go to bed!	¡Vámonos a la cama!
	va·mo·nos a la *ka*·ma

Sex

Kiss me!	¡Dame un beso!
	da·me oon *be*·so
I want you.	Te deseo.
	te de·*se*·o
I want to make love to you.	Quiero hacerte el amor.
	kye·ro a·*ther*·te el a·*mor*
Do you have a condom?	¿Tienes un condón?
	tye·nes oon kon·*don*
🇶 Do you like this?	¿Esto te gusta?
	es·to te *goos*·ta
🇦 I (don't) like that.	Eso (no) me gusta.
	e·so (no) me *goos*·ta

I think we should stop now.	Pienso que deberíamos parar. *pyen·so ke de·be·ree·a·mos pa·rar*
Oh yeah!	¡Así! *a·see*
That was amazing.	Eso fue increíble. *e·so fwe een·kre·ee·ble*
Can I stay over?	¿Puedo quedarme? *pwe·do ke·dar·me*

Love

Q Do you love me?	¿Me quieres? *me kye·res*
A I love you.	Te quiero. *te kye·ro*
I think we're good together.	Creo que estamos muy bien juntos. *kre·o ke es·ta·mos mooy byen khoon·tos*

SOCIAL ROMANCE

LANGUAGE TIP

Endearments

Here are a few terms of endearment you might use with the one you love.

heart	corazón m&f	*ko·ra·thon*
heaven	cielo m&f	*thye·lo*
little love	amorcito/a m/f	*a·mor·thee·to/a*
my life	mi vida m&f	*mee vee·da*
my love	mi amor m&f	*mee a·mor*
treasure	tesoro m&f	*te·so·ro*

Beliefs & Culture

KEY PHRASES

What's your religion?	¿Cuál es su/tu religión? pol/inf	kwal es soo/too re·lee·khyon
I'm ...	Soy ...	soy ...
I'm sorry, it's against my beliefs.	Lo siento, eso va en contra de mis creencias.	lo syen·to e·so va en kon·tra de mees kre·en·thyas

Religion

Q What's your religion?

¿Cuál es su/tu religión? pol/inf
kwal es soo/too re·lee·khyon

A I'm (not) ...

(No) Soy ...
(no) soy ...

agnostic	agnóstico/a m/f	ag·nos·tee·ko/a
Buddhist	budista m&f	boo·dees·ta
Catholic	católico/a m/f	ka·to·lee·ko/a
Christian	cristiano/a m/f	krees·tya·no/a
Hindu	hindú m&f	een·doo
Jewish	judío/a m/f	khoo·dee·o/a
Muslim	musulmán m	moo·sool·man
	musulmana f	moo·sool·ma·na

I'm (not) religious.

(No) Soy religioso/a. m/f
(no) soy re·lee·khyo·so/a

I (don't) believe in God.	(No) Creo en Dios. (no) kre·o en dyos
I (don't) believe in destiny/fate.	(No) Creo en el destino. (no) kre·o en el des·tee·no
Can I pray here?	¿Puedo rezar aquí? pwe·do re·thar a·kee

Cultural Differences

Is this a local custom?	¿Esto es una costumbre local? es·to es oo·na kos·toom·bre lo·kal
This is fun.	Esto es divertido. es·to es dee·ver·tee·do
This is (very) interesting.	Esto es (muy) interesante. es·to es (mooy) een·te·re·san·te
This is (very) different.	Esto es (muy) diferente. es·to es (mooy) dee·fe·ren·te
I'm not used to this.	No estoy acostumbrado/a a esto. m/f no es·toy a·kos·toom·bra·do/a a es·to
I'm sorry, it's against my beliefs.	Lo siento, eso va en contra de mis creencias. lo syen·to e·so va en kon·tra de mees kre·en·thyas
I'll try it.	Lo probaré. lo pro·ba·re
Sorry, I didn't mean to do/say anything wrong.	Lo siento, lo hice/dije sin querer. lo syen·to lo ee·the/dee·khe seen ke·rer

Sports

SOCIAL SPORTS

KEY PHRASES

What sport do you play?	¿Qué deporte practicas?	ke de·*por*·te prak·*tee*·kas
What's your favourite team?	¿Cuál es tu equipo favorito?	kwal es too e·*kee*·po fa·vo·*ree*·to
What's the score?	¿Cómo van?	*ko*·mo van

Sporting Interests

Q What sport do you play?	¿Qué deporte practicas? ke de·*por*·te prak·*tee*·kas
Q What sport do you follow?	¿A qué deporte eres aficionado/a? m/f a ke de·*por*·te e·res a·fee·thyo·*na*·do/a
A I play/do ...	Practico ... prak·*tee*·ko ...
A I follow ...	Soy aficionado/a al ... m/f soy a·fee·thyo·*na*·do/a al ...

basketball	baloncesto m	ba·lon·*thes*·to
cycling	ciclismo m	thee·*klees*·mo
football (soccer)	fútbol m	*foot*·bol
tennis	tenis m	*te*·nis
volleyball	voleibol m	*vo*·ley·bol

For more sports, see the **dictionary**.

Do you like sport?	¿Te gustan los deportes? te *goos*·tan los de·*por*·tes
I like watching it.	Me gusta mirar. me *goos*·ta mee·*rar*
Who's your favourite sportsperson?	¿Quién es tu deportista favorito/a? m/f kyen es too de·por·*tees*·ta fa·vo·*ree*·to/a
What's your favourite team?	¿Cuál es tu equipo favorito? kwal es too e·*kee*·po fa·vo·*ree*·to

Going to a Game

Would you like to go to a (basketball) game?	¿Te gustaría ir a un partido de (baloncesto)? te goos·ta·*ree*·a eer a oon par·*tee*·do de (ba·lon·*thes*·to)
Who are you supporting?	¿Con qué equipo vas? kon ke e·*kee*·po vas
Who's playing?	¿Quién juega? kyen *khwe*·ga
Who's winning?	¿Quién gana? kyen *ga*·na
That was a (boring) game.	Ese partido fue (aburrido). e·se par·*tee*·do fwe (a·boo·*ree*·do)
That was a (great) game!	¡Ese partido fue (cojonudo)! e·se par·*tee*·do fwe (ko·kho·*noo*·do)
What's the score?	¿Cómo van? *ko*·mo van

CULTURE TIP Local Sports
If you hear the sounds of bat, ball and exertion, it may be *pelotari* (pelota players) enjoying the traditional game of *pelota vasca*, Basque handball. It's also known as *jai-alai* in Basque.

ball	pelota f	pe·*lo*·ta
striker	delantero/a m/f	de·lan·*te*·ro/a
wall	frontón m	fron·*ton*

Playing Sport

🇶 **Do you want to play?**	¿Quieres jugar? kye·res khoo·*gar*
🇦 **Yeah, that'd be great.**	Sí, me encantaría. see me en·kan·ta·*ree*·a
🇦 **Not at the moment, thanks.**	Ahora mismo no, gracias. a·o·ra *mees*·mo no *gra*·thyas
🇦 **I have an injury.**	Tengo una lesión. *ten*·go oo·na le·*syon*
Can I join in?	¿Puedo jugar? *pwe*·do khoo·*gar*
Where's the best place to run around here?	¿Cuál es el mejor sitio para hacer footing por aquí cerca? kwal es el me·*khor see*·tyo pa·ra a·*ther foo*·teen por a·*kee ther*·ka
Where's the nearest gym?	¿Dónde está el gimnasio más cercano? *don*·de es·*ta* el kheem·*na*·syo mas ther·*ka*·no
Do I have to be a member to attend?	¿Hay que ser socio/a para entrar? m/f ai ke ser *so*·thyo/a pa·ra en·*trar*

Where's the nearest swimming pool?	¿Dónde está la piscina más cercana?	*don*·de es·*ta* la pees·*thee*·na mas ther·*ka*·na
Where's the nearest tennis court?	¿Dónde está la pista de tenis más cercana?	*don*·de es·*ta* la *pees*·ta de *te*·nees mas ther·*ka*·na
Where are the change rooms?	¿Dónde están los vestuarios?	*don*·de es·*tan* los ves·*twa*·ryos
What's the charge per ...?	¿Cúanto cobran por ...?	*kwan*·to *ko*·bran por ...

day	día	*dee*·a
game	partida	par·*tee*·da
hour	hora	*o*·ra
visit	visita	vee·*see*·ta

Can I hire a ...?	¿Es posible alquilar una ...?	es po·*see*·ble al·kee·*lar* *oo*·na ...

ball	pelota	pe·*lo*·ta
bicycle	bicicleta	bee·thee·*kle*·ta
court	cancha	*kan*·cha
racquet	raqueta	ra·*ke*·ta

What a goal/pass!	¡Qué gol/pase!	ke gol/*pa*·se
Your/My point.	Tu/Mi punto.	too/mee *poon*·to
Kick it to me!	¡Pásamelo!	*pa*·sa·me·lo

SOCIAL   SPORTS

🔊 LISTEN FOR

fuera de juego	*fwe*·ra de *khwe*·go	offside
penalty m	pe·*nal*·tee	penalty
portero m	por·*te*·ro	goalkeeper
saque m **de esquina**	*sa*·ke de es·*kee*·na	corner
tiro m **libre**	*tee*·ro *lee*·bre	free kick

You're a good player.	Juegas bien. *khwe*·gas byen
Thanks for the game.	Gracias por el partido. *gra*·thyas por el par·*tee*·do

Soccer/Football

Who plays for (Real Madrid)?	¿Quién juega en el (Real Madrid)? kyen *khwe*·ga en el (re·*al* ma·*dreeth*)
What a terrible team!	¡Qué equipo más espantoso! ke e·*kee*·po mas es·pan·*to*·so
He's a great player.	Es un gran jugador. es oon gran khoo·ga·*dor*
He played brilliantly in the match against (Italy).	Jugó de fenomenal en el partido contra (Italia). khoo·*go* de fe·no·me·*nal* en el par·*tee*·do *kon*·tra (ee·*ta*·lya)
Which team is at the top of the league?	¿Qué equipo está en primera posición en la liga? ke e·*kee*·po es·*ta* en pree·*me*·ra po·see·*thyon* en la *lee*·ga

Outdoors

KEY PHRASES

Do we need a guide?	¿Se necesita un guía?	se ne·the·*see*·ta oon *gee*·a
I'm lost.	Estoy perdido/a. m/f	es·*toy* per·*dee*·do/a
What's the weather like?	¿Qué tiempo hace?	ke *tyem*·po *a*·the

Hiking

There's plenty of walking, hiking and mountaineering to do in Spain. A recognised cross-country walking trail is known as *Gran Recorrido (GR)* gran re·ko·*ree*·do, while the shorter walking paths scattered throughout the country are called *Pequeños Recorridos (PR)* pe·*ke*·nyos re·ko·*ree*·dos.

Where can I find out about hiking trails?	¿Dónde hay información sobre caminos rurales de la zona? *don*·de ai een·for·ma·*thyon so*·bre ka·*mee*·nos roo·*ra*·les de la *tho*·na
Do we need a guide?	¿Se necesita un guía? se ne·the·*see*·ta oon *gee*·a
Are there guided treks?	¿Se organizan excursiones guiadas? se or·ga·*nee*·than eks·koor·*syo*·nes gee·*a*·das

Where can I ...?
¿Dónde puedo ...?
don·de pwe·do ...

buy supplies	comprar víveres	kom·*prar* vee·*ver*·es
find someone who knows this area	encontrar a alguien que conozca el área	en·kon·*trar* a *al*·gyen ke ko·*noth*·ka el *a*·re·a
get a map	obtener un mapa	ob·te·*ner* oon *ma*·pa
hire hiking gear	alquilar un equipo para ir de excursion	al·kee·*lar* oon e·*kee*·po *pa*·ra eer de eks·koor·*syon*

How long is the trail?
¿Cuántos kilómetros tiene el camino?
kwan·tos kee·lo·me·tros tye·ne el ka·mee·no

How high is the climb?
¿A qué altura se escala?
a ke al·too·ra se es·ka·la

Do we need to take bedding?
¿Se necesita llevar algo en qué dormir?
se ne·the·see·ta lye·var al·go en ke dor·meer

Do we need to take food/water?
¿Se necesita llevar comida/agua?
se ne·the·see·ta lye·var ko·mee·da/a·gwa

Is the track (well-)marked?
¿Es (bien) marcado el sendero?
es (byen) mar·ka·do el sen·de·ro

Is the track open?
¿Es abierto el sendero?
es a·byer·to el sen·de·ro

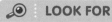

🔍 LOOK FOR

Por Aquí a ...	por a·*kee* a ...	This Way To ...
Prohibido Acampar	pro·ee·*bee*·do a·kam·*par*	No Camping
Terreno de Cámping	te·*re*·no de *kam*·peen	Camping Ground

Is the track scenic?	¿Es pintoresco el sendero? es peen·to·*res*·ko el sen·*de*·ro
Which is the easiest/ shortest route?	¿Cuál es el camino más fácil/corto? kwal es el ka·*mee*·no mas *fa*·theel/*kor*·to
Which is the most interesting route?	¿Cuál es el camino más interesante? kwal es el ka·*mee*·no mas een·te·re·*san*·te
Where's a/the ...?	¿Dónde hay ...? *don*·de ai ...

camping site	un cámping	oon *kam*·peen
village	un pueblo	oon *pwe*·blo
showers	duchas	*doo*·chas
toilets	servicios	ser·*vee*·thyos

Where have you come from?	¿De dónde vienes? de *don*·de *vye*·nes
How long did it take?	¿Cuánto ha tardado? *kwan*·to a tar·*da*·do
Does this path go to ...?	¿Este camino va a ...? *es*·te ka·*mee*·no va a ...
Can we go through here?	¿Se puede pasar por aquí? se *pwe*·de pa·*sar* por a·*kee*

SOCIAL OUTDOORS

¡Prohibido Nadar! pro·ee·*bee*·do na·*dar* No Swimming!

Is the water OK to drink?	¿Se puede beber el agua? se *pwe*·de be·*ber* el *a*·gwa
Is it safe?	¿Es seguro? es se·*goo*·ro
Is there a hut there?	¿Hay una cabaña allí? ai *oo*·na ka·*ba*·nya a·*lyee*
When does it get dark?	¿A qué hora oscurece? a ke *o*·ra os·koo·*re*·the
I'm lost.	Estoy perdido/a. m/f es·*toy* per·*dee*·do/a

At the Beach

Where's the best beach?	¿Dónde está la playa mejor? *don*·de es·*ta* la *pla*·ya me·*khor*
Where's the nearest beach?	¿Dónde está la playa más cercana? *don*·de es·*ta* la *pla*·ya mas ther·*ka*·na
Is it safe to dive/swim here?	¿Es seguro bucear/nadar aquí? es se·*goo*·ro boo·the·*ar*/na·*dar* a·*kee*
What time is high/low tide?	¿A qué hora es la marea alta/baja? a ke *o*·ra es la ma·*re*·a *al*·ta/*ba*·kha
How much to rent a chair?	¿Cuánto por alquilar una silla? *kwan*·to por al·kee·*lar* *oo*·na *see*·lya

| How much to rent an umbrella? (for sun) | ¿Cuánto por alquilar un parasol? |
| | kwan·to por al·kee·lar oon pa·ra·sol |

Weather

| **Q** What's the weather like? | ¿Qué tiempo hace? |
| | ke tyem·po a·the |

| **A** Today it's ... | Hoy hace ... |
| | oy a·the ... |

cold	frío	free·o
freezing	un frío que pela	oon free·o ke pe·la
hot	mucho calor	moo·cho ka·lor
sunny	sol	sol
warm	calor	ka·lor
windy	viento	vyen·to

| **A** (Today) It's raining. | (Hoy) Está lloviendo. |
| | (oy) es·ta lyo·vyen·do |

| **A** (Today) It's snowing. | (Hoy) Está nevando. |
| | (oy) es·ta ne·van·do |

| **Q** What's the weather forecast? | ¿Cuál es el pronóstico del tiempo? |
| | kwal es el pro·nos·tee·ko del tyem·po |

| **A** (Tomorrow) It will be raining. | (Mañana) Lloverá. |
| | (ma·nya·na) lyo·ve·ra |

| Where can I buy a rain jacket? | ¿Dónde puedo comprar un impermeable? |
| | don·de pwe·do kom·prar oon eem·per·me·a·ble |

Where can I buy sunblock?	¿Dónde puedo comprar crema solar? *don·de pwe·do kom·prar kre·ma so·lar*
Where can I buy an umbrella? (for rain)	¿Dónde puedo comprar un paraguas? *don·de pwe·do kom·prar oon pa·ra·gwas*
hail	granizo m *gra·nee·tho*
storm	tormenta f *tor·men·ta*
sun	sol m *sol*

Flora & Fauna

What ... is that?	¿Qué ... es ése/ésa? m/f *ke ... es e·se/e·sa*

animal	animal m	*a·nee·mal*
bird	pájaro m	*pa·kha·ro*
flower	flor f	*flor*
plant	planta f	*plan·ta*
tree	árbol m	*ar·bol*

Can you eat the fruit?	¿Se puede comer la fruta? *se pwe·de ko·mer la froo·ta*
Is it endangered?	¿Está en peligro de extinción? *es·ta en pe·lee·gro de eks·teen·thyon*
Is it common?	¿Es común? *es ko·moon*

For geographical and agricultural terms, and names of animals and plants, see the **dictionary**.

Safe Travel

Emergencies

KEY PHRASES

Help!	¡Socorro!	so·ko·ro
There's been an accident.	Ha habido un accidente.	a a·bee·do oon ak·thee·den·te
It's an emergency!	¡Es una emergencia!	es oo·na e·mer·khen·thee·ya

Help!	¡Socorro! so·ko·ro
Stop!	¡Pare! pa·re
Go away!	¡Váyase! va·ya·se
Leave me alone!	¡Déjame en paz! de·kha·me en path
Thief!	¡Ladrón! lad·ron
Fire!	¡Fuego! fwe·go
It's an emergency!	¡Es una emergencia! es oo·na e·mer·khen·thee·ya
There's been an accident.	Ha habido un accidente. a a·bee·do oon ak·thee·den·te
Do you have a first-aid kit?	¿Tiene un botiquín de primeros auxilios? tye·ne oon bo·tee·keen de pree·me·ros owk·see·lyos

🔊 LISTEN FOR

¡Es peligroso!	es pe·lee·*gro*·so	It's dangerous!

Call the police!	¡Llame a la policía! *lya*·me a la po·lee·*thee*·a
Call a doctor!	¡Llame a un médico! *lya*·me a oon *me*·dee·ko
Call an ambulance!	¡Llame a una ambulancia! *lya*·me a oo·na am boo *lan* thya
Could you help me, please?	¿Me puede ayudar, por favor? me *pwe*·de a·yoo·*dar* por fa·*vor*
I have to use the telephone.	Necesito usar el teléfono. ne·the·*see*·to oo·*sar* el te·le·fo·no
I'm lost.	Estoy perdido/a. m/f es·*toy* per·dee·do/a
Where are the toilets?	¿Dónde están los servicios? *don*·de es·*tan* los ser·*vee*·thyos

Police

KEY PHRASES

Where's the police station?	¿Dónde está la comisaría?	*don*·de es·*ta* la ko·mee·sa·*ree*·a
I want to contact my embassy/ consulate.	Quiero ponerme en contacto con mi embajada/ consulado.	*kye*·ro po·*ner*·me en kon·*tak*·to kon mee em·ba·*kha*·da/ kon·soo·*la*·do
My bag was stolen.	Mi bolso fue robado.	mee *bol*·so fwe ro·*ba*·do

In an emergency, call the police. They will then put you through to other emergency services (fire brigade and ambulance). For more on making a call, see **communications** (p85).

Where's the police station?	¿Dónde está la comisaría? *don*·de es·*ta* la ko·mee·sa·*ree*·a
I want to report an offence.	Quiero denunciar un delito. *kye*·ro de·noon·*thyar* oon de·*lee*·to
I've been robbed.	Me han robado. me an ro·*ba*·do
I've been raped.	He sido violado/a. **m/f** e *see*·do vee·o·*la*·do/a
It was him/her.	Fue él/ella. fwe el/*e*·lya
My (money) was stolen.	Mi (dinero) fue robado. mee (dee·*ne*·ro) fwe ro·*ba*·do
My (bag/handbag) was stolen.	Mi (bolso) fue robado. mee (*bol*·so) fwe ro·*ba*·do

My (bags/suitcases) were stolen.	Mis (maletas) fueron robadas. mee (ma·*le*·tas) fwe·*ron* ro·*ba*·das
I've lost (my passport).	He perdido (mi pasaporte). e per·*dee*·do (mee pa·sa·*por*·te)
What am I accused of?	¿De qué me acusan? de ke me a·*ku*·san
I didn't realise I was doing anything wrong.	No sabía que estaba haciendo algo mal. no sa·*bee*·a ke es·*ta*·ba a·*thyen*·do al·go mal
I'm innocent.	Soy inocente. soy ee·no·*then*·te
I want to contact my embassy/consulate.	Quiero ponerme en contacto con mi embajada/consulado. *kye*·ro po·*ner*·me en kon·*tak*·to kon mee em·ba·*kha*·da/kon·soo·*la*·do
Can I call a lawyer?	¿Puedo llamar a un abogado? *pwe*·do lya·*mar* a oon a·bo·*ga*·do
I need a lawyer who speaks (English).	Necesito un abogado que hable (inglés). ne·the·*see*·to oon a·bo·*ga*·do ke *a*·ble (een·*gles*)
Can I have a copy, please?	¿Puede darme una copia, por favor? *pwe*·de *dar*·me oo·na *ko*·pya por fa·*vor*
This drug is for personal use.	Esta droga es para uso personal. es·ta *dro*·ga es *pa*·ra oo·so per·so·*nal*
I have a prescription for this drug.	Tengo receta para esta droga. *ten*·go re·*the*·ta *pa*·ra es·ta *dro*·ga

Health

KEY PHRASES

Where's the nearest hospital?	¿Dónde está el hospital más cercano?	*don*·de es·*ta* el os·*pee*·tal mas ther·*ka*·no
I'm sick.	Estoy enfermo/a. m/f	es·*toy* en·*fer*·mo/a
I need a doctor.	Necesito un doctor.	ne·the·*see*·to oon dok·*tor*
I'm on regular medication for ...	Estoy bajo medicación para ...	es·*toy* ba·kho me·dee·ka·*thyon* *pa*·ra ...
I'm allergic to ...	Soy alérgico/a a... m/f	soy a·*ler*·khee·ko/a a ...

Doctor

Where's the nearest ...?   ¿Dónde está ... más cercano/a? m/f
don·de es·*ta* ... mas ther·*ka*·no/a

chemist	la farmacia f	la far·*ma*·thya
dentist	el dentista m	el den·*tees*·ta
doctor	el médico m	el *me*·dee·ko
hospital	el hospital m	el os·pee·*tal*
medical centre	el consultorio m	el kon·sool·*to*·ryo
optometrist	el oculista m	el o·koo·*lees*·ta

CULTURE TIP	**Etiquette Tip**

A polite way to respond to someone sneezing is by saying *¡Salud!* sa·*loo* (health) or *¡Jesús!* khe·*soos* (lit: 'Jesus').

I need a doctor (who speaks English).	Necesito un doctor (que hable inglés). ne·the·*see*·to oon dok·*tor* (ke a·ble een·*gles*)
Could I see a female doctor?	¿Puede examinarme una doctora? *pwe*·de ek·sa·mee·*nar* me *oo*·na dok·*to*·ra
I've run out of my medication.	Se me terminaron los medicamentos. se me ter·mee·*na*·ron los me·dee·ka·*men*·tos
This is my usual medicine.	Éste es mi medicamento habitual. *es*·te es mee me·dee·ka·*men*·to a·bee·too·*al*
I don't want a blood transfusion.	No quiero que me hagan una transfusión de sangre. no *kye*·ro ke me a·gan *oo*·na trans·foo·*syon* de *san*·gre
Please use a new syringe.	Por favor, use una jeringa nueva. por fa·*vor* *oo*·se *oo*·na khe·*reen*·ga *nwe*·va
I need new contact lenses.	Necesito lentes de contacto nuevas. ne·the·*see*·to *len*·tes de kon·*tak*·to *nwe*·vas
I need new glasses.	Necesito gafas nuevas. ne·the·*see*·to *ga*·fas *nwe*·vas

| I've been vaccinated for ... | Estoy vacunado/a contra ... m/f es·*toy* va·koo·*na*·do/a *kon*·tra ... |
| He's/She's been vaccinated for ... | Está vacunado/a contra ... m/f es·*ta* va·koo·*na*·do/a *kon*·tra ... |

tetanus	el tétano	el *te*·ta·no
typhoid	la tifus	la *tee*·foos
hepatitis A/B/C	la hepatitis A/B/C	la e·pa·*tee*·tees a/be/the
... fever	la fiebre ...	la *fye*·bre ...

For women's medical issues, see **women's health** (p162).

Symptoms & Conditions

I'm sick.	Estoy enfermo/a. m/f es·*toy* en·*fer*·mo/a
I have ...	Tengo ... *ten*·go ...
I've recently had ...	Hace poco he tenido ... a·the *po*·ko e te·*nee*·do ...
I'm on regular medication for ...	Estoy bajo medicación para ... es·*toy* ba·kho me·dee·ka·*thyon* pa·ra ...
It hurts here.	Me duele aquí. me *dwe*·le a·*kee*
I've been injured.	He sido herido/a. m/f e *see*·do e·*ree*·do/a
I've been vomiting.	He estado vomitando. e es·*ta*·do vo·mee·*tan*·do

🔊 LISTEN FOR

¿Qué le pasa?	ke le *pa*·sa What's the problem?
¿Dónde le duele?	*don*·de le *dwe*·le Where does it hurt?
¿Tiene fiebre?	*tye*·ne *fye*·bre Do you have a temperature?
¿Desde cuándo se siente así?	*des*·de *kwan*·do se *syen*·te a·*see* How long have you been like this?
¿Ha tenido esto antes?	a te·*nee*·do *es*·to *an*·tes Have you had this before?

I can't sleep.	No puedo dormir. no *pwe*·do dor·*meer*
I have a rash.	Tengo una erupción cutánea. *ten*·go *oo*·na e·roop·*thyon* koo·*ta*·ne·a
I have an infection.	Tengo una infección. *ten*·go *oo*·na in·fek·*thyon*
I feel ...	Me siento ... me *syen*·to ...

better	mejor m&f	me·*khor*
depressed	deprimido/a m/f	de·pree·*mee*·do/a
dizzy	mareado/a m/f	ma·re·*a*·do/a
shivery	destemplado/a m/f	des·tem·*pla*·do/a
weak	débil m&f	*de*·beel
worse	peor m&f	pe·*or*

asthma	asma m *as*·ma
diarrhoea	diarrea f dee·a·*re*·a
fever	fiebre f *fye*·bre
headache	dolor m de cabeza do·*lor* de ka·*be*·tha
sprain	torcedura f tor·the·*doo*·ra

For more symptoms & conditions, see the **dictionary**.

Women's Health

(I think) I'm pregnant.	(Creo que) Estoy embarazada. (*kre*·o ke) es·*toy* em·ba·ra·*tha*·da
I haven't had my period for ... weeks.	Hace ... semanas que no me viene la regla. *a*·the ... se·*ma*·nas ke no me *vye*·ne la *reg*·la
I'm on the Pill.	Tomo la píldora. *to*·mo la *peel*·do·ra
I've noticed a lump here.	He notado un bulto aquí. e no·*ta*·do oon *bool*·to a·*kee*
I have period pain.	Tengo dolor menstrual. *ten*·go do·*lor* mens·*troo*·al
contraception	anticonceptivos m pl an·tee·kon·thep·*tee*·vos
pregnancy test	prueba f de embarazo *prwe*·ba de em·ba·*ra*·tho
the morning-after pill	píldora f del día siguiente *peel*·do·ra del *dee*·a see·*gyen*·te

 **LISTEN FOR**

¿Usted bebe?	oos·*te be*·be Do you drink?
¿Usted fuma?	oos·*te foo*·ma Do you smoke?
¿Usted toma drogas?	oos·*te to*·ma *dro*·gas Do you take drugs?
¿Tiene Usted alergias?	*tye*·ne oos·*te* a·*ler*·khyas Are you allergic to anything?
¿Se encuentra bajo medicación?	se en·*kwen*·tra *ba*·kho me·dee·ka·*thyon* Are you on medication?

Allergies

I'm allergic to ...	Soy alérgico/a ... **m/f** soy a·*ler*·khee·ko/a ...
He/She is allergic to ...	Es alérgico/a ... **m/f** es a·*ler*·khee·ko/a ...

antibiotics	a los antibióticos	a los an·tee·*byo*·tee·kos
anti-inflam-matories	a los anti-inflamatorios	a los an·tee·een·fla·ma·*to*·ryos
aspirin	a la aspirina	a la as·pee·*ree*·na
bees	a las abejas	a las a·*be*·khas
codeine	a la codeina	a la ko·de·*ee*·na
penicillin	a la penicilina	a la pe·nee·thee·*lee*·na
pollen	al polen	al *po*·len

I have a skin allergy.	Tengo una alergia en la piel. *ten*·go *oo*·na a·*ler*·khya en la pyel

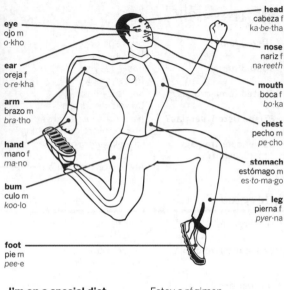

eye
ojo m
o·kho

ear
oreja f
o·re·kha

arm
brazo m
bra·tho

hand
mano f
ma·no

bum
culo m
koo·lo

foot
pie m
pee·e

head
cabeza f
ka·be·tha

nose
nariz f
na·reeth

mouth
boca f
bo·ka

chest
pecho m
pe·cho

stomach
estómago m
es·to·ma·go

leg
pierna f
pyer·na

I'm on a special diet.	Estoy a régimen especial. es·*toy* a re·*khee·*men es·pe·*thyal*
antihistamines	antihistamínicos m pl *an·*tee·ees·ta·*mee·*nee·kos
inhaler	inhalador m een·a·la·*dor*
sulphur-based drugs	drogas con base de azufre f pl *dro·*gas kon *ba·*se de a·*thoo·*fre

For food-related allergies, see **vegetarian & special meals** (p187).

Parts of the Body

My ... hurts.	Me duele ... me *dwe*·le ...
I can't move my ...	No puedo mover ... no *pwe*·do mo·*ver* ...
I have a cramp in my ...	Tengo calambres en ... *ten*·go ka·*lam*·bres en ...
My ... is swollen.	Mi ... está hinchado. mee ... es·*ta* een·*cha*·do

For more parts of the body, see the **dictionary**.

Chemist

I need something for ...	Necesito algo para ... ne·the·*see*·to *al*·go *pa*·ra ...
I have a prescription.	Tengo receta médica. *ten*·go re·*the*·ta *me*·dee·ka
Do I need a prescription for ...?	¿Necesito receta para ...? ne·the·*see*·to re·*the*·ta *pa*·ra ...
How many times a day?	¿Cuántas veces al día? *kwan*·tas *ve*·thes al *dee*·a

For pharmaceutical items, see the **dictionary**.

 LISTEN FOR

¿Ha tomado esto antes?	a to·*ma*·do *es*·to *an*·tes Have you taken this before?
Dos veces al día (con la comida).	dos *ve*·thes al *dee*·a (kon la ko·*mee*·da) Twice a day (with food).

SAFE TRAVEL

HEALTH

LISTEN FOR

Abra.	*a·*bra	Open wide.
No se mueva.	no se *mwe·*va	Don't move.
¡Enjuague!	en·*khwa·*ge	Rinse!

Dentist

I have a broken tooth.	Se me ha roto un diente. se me a *ro·*to oon *dyen·*te
I have a toothache.	Me duele una muela. me *dwe·*le *oo·*na *mwe·*la
I've lost a filling.	Se me ha caído un empaste. se me a ka·*ee·*do oon em·*pas·*te
My orthodontic braces broke/fell off.	Se me rompió/cayó el aparato dental. se me rom·*pyo/*ka·*yo el a·pa·*ra·*to den·*tal*
My gums hurt.	Me duelen las encías. me *dwe·*len las en·*thee·*as
I don't want it extracted.	No quiero que me lo saquen. no *kye·*ro ke me lo *sa·*ken
I need an anaesthetic.	Necesito una anestesia. ne·the·*see·*to *oo·*ne a·nes·*te·*sya
I need a filling.	Necesito un empaste ne·the·*see·*to oon em·*pas·*te

Food

Eating Out

KEY PHRASES

Can you recommend a restaurant?	¿Puede recomendar un restaurante?	*pwe*·de re·ko·men·*dar* oon res·tow·*ran*·te
I'd like a table for two, please.	Quisiera una mesa para dos, por favor.	kee·*sye*·ra oo·na *me*·sa *pa*·ra dos por fa·*vor*
I'd like the menu, please.	Quisiera el menu, por favor.	kee·*sye*·ra el me·*noo* por fa·*vor*
I'd like ...	Quisiera ...	kee·*sye*·ra ...
Please bring the bill.	Por favor nos trae la cuenta.	por fa·*vor* nos *tra*·e la *kwen*·ta

Basics

The main meal in Spain, 'lunchtime' is called *la hora de comer* la o·ra de ko·*mer*. It's served between 1.30pm and 4.30pm.

breakfast	desayuno m de·sa·*yoo*·no
lunch	comida f ko·*mee*·da
dinner	cena f *the*·na
snack	tentempié m ten·tem·*pye*
eat/drink	comer/beber ko·*mer*/be·*ber*

I'd like ...	Quisiera ...
	kee·*sye*·ra ...

I'm starving!	¡Estoy hambriento/a! m/f
	es·*toy* am·*bryen*·to/a

Enjoy your meal!	¡Buen provecho!
	bwen pro·*ve*·cho

Finding a Place to Eat

Can you recommend a ...?	¿Puede recomendar un/una ...? m/f
	pwe·de re·ko·men·*dar* oon/*oo*·na ...

bar	bar m	bar
cafe	café m	ka·*fe*
coffee bar	cafetería f	ka·fe·te·*ree*·a
restaurant	restaurante m	res·tow·*ran*·te

Are you still serving food?	¿Siguen sirviendo comida?
	see·gen seer·*vyen*·do ko·*mee*·da

How long is the wait?	¿Cuánto hay que esperar?
	kwan·to ai ke es·pe·*rar*

Where would you go for a cheap meal?	¿Adónde se va para comer barato?
	a·*don*·de se va *pa*·ra ko·*mer* ba·*ra*·to

Where would you go for local specialities?	¿Adónde se va para comer comida típica?
	a·*don*·de se va *pa*·ra ko·*mer* ko·*mee*·da *tee*·pee·ka

FOOD EATING OUT

🔊 LISTEN FOR

Lo siento, hemos cerrado.	lo *syen*·to *e*·mos the·*ra*·do
	Sorry, we're closed.
No tenemos mesa.	no te·*ne*·mos *me*·sa
	We have no free tables.
Un momento.	oon mo·*men*·to
	One moment.

I'd like to reserve a table for (two) people.	Quisiera reservar una mesa para (dos) personas. kee·*sye*·ra re·ser·*var* oo·na *me*·sa pa·ra (dos) per·so·nas.
I'd like to reserve a table for (eight) o'clock.	Quisiera reservar una mesa para las (ocho). kee·*sye*·ra re·ser·*var* oo·na *me*·sa pa·ra las (*o*·cho)

At the Restaurant

I'd like the (non)smoking section, please.	Quisiera el área de (no) fumadores, por favor. kee·*sye*·ra el *a*·re·a de (no) foo·ma·*do*·res por fa·*vor*
I'd like a table for (two), please.	Quisiera una mesa para (dos), por favor. kee·*sye*·ra oo·na *me*·sa pa·ra (dos) por fa·*vor*
✂ **For two, please.**	Para dos, por favor. pa·ra dos por fa·*vor*
I'd like the drink list, please.	Quisiera la lista de bebidas, por favor. kee·*sye*·ra la *lees*·ta de be·*bee*·das por fa·*vor*

Eating Out

Can I see the menu, please?

¿Puedo ver el menú, por favor?
pwe·do ver el me·noo por fa·vor

What would you recommend for ...?

¿Qué me recomendaría para ...?
ke me re·ko·men·da·ree·a pa·ra ...

 the main meal
el plato principal
el pla·to preen·thee·pal

 dessert
postre
pos·tre

 drinks
bebidas
be·bee·das

Can you bring me some ..., please?

Por favor me trae ...
por fa·vor me tra·e ...

I'd like the bill, please.

Quisiera la cuenta, por favor.
kee·sye·ra la kwen·ta por fa·vor

FOOD EATING OUT

I'd like the menu, please.	Quisiera el menú, por favor.	kee·*sye*·ra el me·*noo* por fa·*vor*

 The menu, please. | El menú, por favor. | el me·*noo* por fa·*vor*

Do you have children's meals?	¿Tienen comidas para niños?	*tye*·nen ko·*mee*·das *pa*·ra *nee*·nyos
Do you have a menu in English?	¿Tienen un menú en inglés?	*tye*·nen oon me·*noo* en een·*gles*
Is service included in the bill?	¿La cuenta incluye servicio?	la *kwen*·ta een·*kloo*·ye ser·*vee*·thyo
What would you recommend?	¿Qué recomienda?	ke re·ko·*myen*·da
Can you tell me which traditional foods I should try?	¿Que platos típicos debería probar?	ke *pla*·tos *tee*·pee·kos de·be·*ree*·a pro·*bar*

🔊 **LISTEN FOR**

¿Le gusta ...?	le *goos*·ta ... Do you like ...?
Recomiendo ...	re·ko·*myen*·do ... I suggest the ...
¿Cómo lo quiere preparado?	*ko*·mo lo *kye*·re pre·pa·*ra*·do How would you like that cooked?

I'll have what they're having.	Tomaré lo mismo que ellos. to·ma·*re* lo *mees*·mo ke e·lyos
Does it take long to prepare?	¿Tarda mucho en prepararse? *tar*·da *moo*·cho en pre·pa·*rar*·se
What's in that dish?	¿Que lleva ese plato? ke *lye*·va e·se *pla*·to
Are these complimentary?	¿Éstos son gratis? es·tos son *gra*·tees
We're just having drinks.	Sólo queremos tomar algo. so·lo ke·*re*·mos to·*mar* al·go

✂ **Just drinks.** Sólo bebidas. so·lo be·*bee*·das

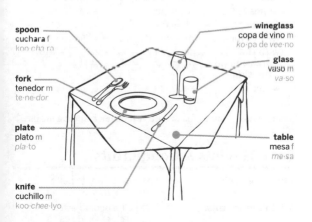

spoon
cuchara f
koo·*cha*·ra

wineglass
copa de vino m
ko·pa de *vee*·no

glass
vaso m
va·so

fork
tenedor m
te·ne·*dor*

plate
plato m
pla·to

table
mesa f
me·sa

knife
cuchillo m
koo·*chee*·lyo

Requests

Please bring a glass.	Por favor nos trae un vaso.	por fa·*vor* nos *tra*·se oon *va*·so
Please bring a serviette.	Por favor nos trae una servilleta.	por fa·*vor* nos *tra*·se oo·na ser·vee·*lye*·ta
I'd like it ...	Lo quiero ...	lo *kye*·ro ...
I don't want it ...	No lo quiero ...	no lo *kye*·ro ...

deep fried	frito en aceite abundante	*free*·to en a·*they*·te a·boon·*dan*·te
medium	no muy hecho	no mooy e·*cho*
rare	vuelta y vuelta	*vwel*·ta ee *vwel*·ta
re-heated	recalentado	re·ka·len·*ta*·do
steamed	al vapor	al va·*por*
well-done	muy hecho	mooy e·*cho*
with the dressing on the side	con el aliño aparte	kon el a·*lee*·nyo a·*par*·te
without ...	sin ...	seen ...

For other specific meal requests, see **vegetarian & special meals** (p187).

Compliments & Complaints

I love this dish.	Me encanta este plato.	me en·*kan*·ta es·te *pla*·to
I didn't order this.	Yo no he pedido esto.	yo no e pe·*dee*·do es·to

🔍 LOOK FOR

Aperitivos	a·pe·ree·*tee*·vos	Appetisers
Cervezas	ther·*ve*·thas	Beers
Caldos	*kal*·dos	Soups
De Entrada	de en·*tra*·da	Entrees
Ensaladas	en·sa·*la*·das	Salads
Postres	*pos*·tres	Desserts
Refrescos	re·*fres*·kos	Soft Drinks
Segundos Platos	se·*goon*·dos *pla*·tos	Main Courses

FOOD

EATING OUT

That was delicious!	¡Estaba buenísimo! es·*ta*·ba bwe·*nee*·see·mo
My compliments to the chef.	Mi enhorabuena al cocinero. mee en·o·ra·*bwe*·na al ko·thee·*ne*·ro
I'm full.	Estoy lleno/a. m/f es·*toy* *lye*·no/a
This is burnt.	Esto está quemado. es·to es·*ta* ke·*ma*·do
This is (too) cold.	Esto está (demasiado) frío. es·to es·*ta* (de·ma·*sya*·do) *free*·o
This is superb.	Esto está exquisito. es·to es·*ta* eks·kee·*see*·to
We love the local cuisine.	Nos encanta la comida típica de la zona. nos en·*kan*·ta la ko·*mee*·da *tee*·pee·ka de la *tho*·na

Paying the Bill

Please bring the bill.	Por favor nos trae la cuenta.
	por fa·*vor* nos *tra*·e la *kwen*·ta

✂ **Bill, please.**	La cuenta, por favor.	la *kwen*·ta por fa·*vor*

There's a mistake in the bill.	Hay un error en la cuenta.
	ai oon e·*ror* en la *kwen*·ta

For methods of payment, see **money & banking** (p91).

Nonalcoholic Drinks

I don't drink alcohol.	No bebo alcohol.
	no *be*·bo al·*kol*
(cup of) coffee ...	(taza de) café ...
	(*ta*·tha de) ka·*fe* ...
(cup of) tea ...	(taza de) té ...
	(*ta*·tha de) te ...
with milk	con leche
	kon *le*·che
without sugar	sin azúcar
	seen a·*thoo*·kar
soft drink	refresco m
	re·*fres*·ko
(boiled) water	agua (hervida)
	a·gwa (er·*vee*·da)
(sparkling) mineral water	agua mineral (con gas)
	a·gwa mee·ne·*ral* (kon gas)

Alcoholic Drinks

... beer		cerveza f ... ther·ve·tha ...
draught	de barril	de ba·*ril*
dark	negra	*neg*·ra
light	rubia	*roo*·bee·a
nonalcoholic	sin alcohol	sin al·*kol*
small bottle of beer (250 ml)		botellín m bo·te·*lyin*
litre bottle of beer		litrona f lee·*tro*·na
bottle of beer (300 ml)		mediana f me·*dya*·na

What would you recommend?
ke re·ko·*myen*·da
¿Qué recomienda?

FOOD EATING OUT

a glass/pint of beer	una caña/pinta de cerveza *oo*·na *ka*·nya/*peen*·ta de ther·*ve*·tha
a jug of beer	una jarra de cerveza *oo*·na *kha*·ra de ther·*ve*·tha
brandy	coñac m *ko*·nyak
Champagne	champán m cham·*pan*
cocktail	combinado m kom·bee·*na*·do
sangria (red-wine punch)	sangría f san·*gree*·a
a shot of (rum)	un chupito de (ron) oon choo·*pee*·to de (ron)
a shot of (gin)	un chupito de (ginebra) oon choo·*pee*·to de (khee·*ne*·bra)
a shot of (whisky)	un chupito de (güisqui) oon choo·*pee*·to de (*gwees*·kee)
a bottle/glass of ... wine	una botella/copa de vino ... *oo*·na bo·*te*·lya/*ko*·pa de *vee*·no ...

dessert	dulce	*dool*·the
red	tinto	*teen*·to
rose	rosado	ro·*sa*·do
sparkling	espumoso	es·poo·*mo*·so
white	blanco	*blan*·ko

CULTURE TIP

Tapas

Tapas are scrumptious cooked bar snacks, available pretty much around the clock at bars and some clubs. You'll find they're free in some places, laid out in the bar for you to choose from. Other venues will rotate the dishes.

banderilla f/	ban·de·*ree*·lya/	small tapa
moruno m/	mo·*roo*·no/	serving on bread or
pinchito m	peen·*chee*·to	a toothpick
ración f	ra·*thyon*	large tapa serving
montadito m	mon·ta·*dee*·to	bread-topped tapa
pan tumaca m	pan too·*ma*·ka	tapa of toasted bread rubbed with tomatoes and garlic, served with oil
queso m **en aceite**	*ke*·so en a·*they*·te	cheese in olive oil, served as a tapa

FOOD   EATING OUT

In the Bar

Excuse me!	¡Oiga! *oy*·ga
I'm next.	Ahora voy yo. a·o·ra voy yo
Q What would you like?	¿Qué quieres tomar? ke *kye*·res to·*mar*
A I'll have ...	Para mí ... *pa*·ra mee ...
Same again, please.	Otra de lo mismo. o·tra de lo *mees*·mo
No ice, thanks.	Sin hielo, gracias. seen *ye*·lo *gra*·thyas
I'll buy you a drink.	Te invito a una copa. te een·*vee*·to a *oo*·na *ko*·pa

🔊 LISTEN FOR

¿Dónde le gustaría sentarse?	don·de le gus·ta·*ree*·a sen·*tar*·se Where would you like to sit?
¿En qué le puedo servir?	en ke le *pwe*·do ser·*veer* What can I get for you?
¡Aquí tiene!	a·*kee* *tye*·ne Here you go!

It's my round.	Es mi ronda. es mee *ron*·da
You can get the next one.	La próxima la pagas tú. la *prok*·see·ma la *pa*·gas too
Do you serve meals here?	¿Sirven comidas aquí? *seer*·ven ko·*mee*·das a·*kee*

Drinking Up

Cheers!	¡Salud! sa·*loo*
Thanks, but I don't feel like it.	Lo siento, pero no me apetece. lo *syen*·to *pe*·ro no me a·pe·*te*·the
No thanks, I'm driving.	No gracias, tengo que conducir. no *gra*·thyas *ten*·go ke kon·doo·*theer*
This is hitting the spot.	Me lo estoy pasando muy bien. me lo es·*toy* pa·*san*·do mooy byen

> **CULTURE TIP**
>
> **Minis**
> Many Spanish bars provide massive plastic beakers of beer to cater for young revellers. It's cut with water and average tasting – but cheap and free flowing! These fountains of froth are called *minis*.

I feel fantastic!	¡Me siento fenomenal! me *syen*·to fe·no·me·*nal*
I'm feeling drunk.	Esto me está subiendo mucho. es·to me es·*ta* soo·*byen*·do *moo*·cho
I think I've had one too many.	Creo que he tomado demasiado. *kre*·o ke e to·*ma*·do de·ma·*sya*·do
I'm tired, I'd better go home.	Estoy cansado/a, mejor me voy a casa. m/f es·*toy* kan·*sa*·do/a me·*khor* me voy a *ka*·sa
I don't think you should drive.	No creo que deberías conducir. no *kre*·o ke de·be·*ree*·as kon·doo·*theer*
Can you call a taxi for me?	¿Me puedes pedir un taxi? me *pwe*·des pe·*deer* oon *tak*·see

FOOD EATING OUT

Self-Catering

KEY PHRASES

What's the local speciality?	¿Cuál es la especialidad de la zona?	kwal es la es·pe·thya·lee·*da* de la *tho*·na
Where can I find the ... section?	¿Dónde está la sección de ...?	*don*·de es·*ta* la sek·*thyon* de ...
I'd like ...	Póngame ...	*pon*·ga·me ...

Buying Food

Where can I find the ... section?	¿Dónde está la sección de ...? *don*·de es·*ta* la sek·*thyon* de ...

dairy	productos lácteos	pro·*dook*·tos *lak*·te·os
frozen goods	productos congelados	pro·*dook*·tos kon·khe·*la*·dos
fruit and vegetable	frutas y verduras	*froo*·tas ee ver·*doo*·ras
meat	carne	*kar*·ne

Where's the health-food section/store?	¿Dónde esta la sección/ tienda de comida dietética? *don*·de es·*ta* la sek·*thyon*/ *tyen*·da de ko·*mee*·da dye·*te*·tee·ka
What's that?	¿Qué es eso? ke es *e*·so

🔊 LISTEN FOR

¿En qué le puedo servir?	en ke le *pwe*·do ser·*veer* Can I help you?
¿Qué querías?	ke ke·*ree*·as What would you like?
No tengo.	no *ten*·go I don't have any.
No queda más.	no *ke*·da mas There's none left.

Can I taste it?	¿Puedo probarlo/a? m/f *pwe*·do pro·*bar*·lo/a
What's the local speciality?	¿Cuál es la especialidad de la zona? kwal es la es·pe·thya·lee·*da* de la *tho*·na
How much?	¿Cuánto? *kwan*·to
How many?	¿Cuántos/as? m/f *kwan*·tos/as
How much is (a kilo of cheese)?	¿Cuánto vale (un kilo de queso)? *kwan*·to *va*·le (oon *kee*·lo de *ke*·so)
Do you have anything cheaper?	¿Tiene algo más barato? *tye*·ne *al*·go mas ba·*ra*·to
Do you have any other kinds?	¿Tiene otros tipos? *tye*·ne *ot*·ros *tee*·pos
Do you sell locally produced food?	¿Se venden comestibles de la zona? se *ven*·den ko·mes·*tee*·bles de la *tho*·na

Do you sell organic produce?	¿Se venden productos agrícolas biológicos? se *ven*·den pro·*dook*·tos a·*gree*·ko·las bee·o·*lo*·khee·kos
I'd like ...	Póngame ... *pon*·ga·me ...

(three) pieces	(tres) piezas	(tres) *pye*·thas
(six) slices	(seis) lonchas	(seys) *lon*·chas
(two) kilos	(dos) kilos	(dos) *kee*·los
(200) grams	(doscientos) gramos	(dos·*thyen*·tos) *gra*·mos

half a dozen	una media docena *oo*·na *me*·dya do·*the*·na
half a kilo	un medio kilo oon *me*·dyo *kee*·lo
a kilo	un kilo oon *kee*·lo
a bottle (of ...)	una botella (de ...) *oo*·na bo·*te*·lya (de ...)
a jar	una jarra *oo*·na *kha*·ra
a packet	un paquete oon pa·*ke*·te
(just) a little	(sólo) un poquito (*so*·lo) oon po·*kee*·to
many	muchos/as **m/f** *moo*·chos/as
(a bit) more	(un poco) más (oon *po*·ko) mas
some	algunos/as **m/f** al·*goo*·nos/as

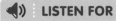
🔊 LISTEN FOR

Eso es (un manchego).	e·so es (oon man·*che*·go) That's (a manchego).
Eso es (cinco euros).	e·so es (*theen*·ko e·oo·ros) That's (five euros).
¿Algo más?	*al*·go mas Anything else?

less	menos *me*·nos
that one	ése e·se
this	esto es·to
Enough!	¡Basta! *ba*·sta

For food items, see the **menu decoder** (p190) and the **dictionary**.

Cooking

cooked	cocido/a m/f ko·*thee*·do/a
dried	seco/a m/f *se*·ko/a
fresh	fresco/a m/f *fres*·ko/a
frozen	congelado/a m/f kon·khe·*la*·do/a
raw	crudo/a m/f *kroo*·do/a
smoked	ahumado/a m/f a·oo·*ma*·do/a

FOOD · SELF-CATERING

Could I please borrow a/an ...?	¿Me puede prestar un/una ...? m/f me *pwe*·de pres·*tar* oon/*oo*·na ...
Where's a/an ...?	¿Dónde hay un/una ...? m/f *don*·de ai oon/*oo*·na ...

bottle opener	abrebotellas m	a·bre·bo·*te*·lyas
can opener	abrelatas m	a·bre·*la*·tas
chopping board	tabla f para cortar	*tab*·la *pa*·ra kor·*tar*
corkscrew	sacacorchos m	sa·ka·*kor*·chos
cup	taza f	*ta*·tha
fork	tenedor m	te·ne·*dor*
frying pan	sartén f	sar·*ten*
glass	vaso m	*va*·so
knife	cuchillo m	koo·*chee*·lyo
plate	plato m	*pla*·to
saucepan	cazo m	*ka*·tho
spoon	cuchara f	koo·*cha*·ra
toaster	tostadora f	tos·ta·*do*·ra

For more cooking terminology, see the **dictionary**.

Vegetarian & Special Meals

KEY PHRASES

Do you have vegetarian food?	¿Tienen comida vegetariana?	tye·nen ko·mee·da ve·khe·ta·rya·na
Could you prepare a meal without ...?	¿Me puede preparar una comida sin ...?	me pwe·de pre·pa·rar oo·na ko·mee·da seen ...
I'm allergic to ...	Soy alérgico/a a ... m/f	soy a·ler·khee·ko/a a ...

Special Diets & Allergies

I'm vegetarian.	Soy vegetariano/a. m/f soy ve·khe·ta·rya·no/a
I'm on a special diet.	Estoy a régimen especial. es·toy a re·khee·men es·pe·thyal
I'm allergic to ...	Soy alérgico/a ... m/f soy a·ler·khee·ko/a ...

dairy produce	a los productos lácteos	a los pro·dook·tos lak·te·os
honey	al miel	al myel
MSG	al glutamato monosódico	al gloo·ta·rna·to mo·no·so·dee·ko
nuts	a las nueces	a las nwe·thes
seafood	a los mariscos	a los ma·rees·kos
shellfish	a los crustáceos	a los kroos·ta·thyos

Ordering Food

Is there a (vegetarian) restaurant near here?	¿Hay un restaurante (vegetariano) por aquí? *ai oon res·tow·ran·te (ve·khe·ta·rya·no) por a·kee*
Do you have vegetarian food?	¿Tienen comida vegetariana? *tye·nen ko·mee·da ve·khe·ta·rya·na*
Do you have halal food?	¿Tienen comida halal? *tye·nen ko·mee·da a·lal*
Do you have kosher food?	¿Tienen comida kosher? *tye·nen ko·mee·da ko·sher*
Do you have vegan food?	¿Tienen comida vegetariana estricta? *tye·nen ko·mee·da ve·khe·ta·rya·na es·trik·ta*
I don't eat red meat.	No como carne roja. *no ko·mo kar·ne ro·kha*
Is it cooked in/with butter?	¿Esta cocinado en/con mantequilla? *es·ta ko·thee·na·do en/kon man·te·kee·lya*
Could you prepare a meal without ...?	¿Me puede preparar una comida sin ...? *me pwe·de pre·pa·rar oo·na ko·mee·da seen ...*

eggs	huevo	*we·vo*
fish	pescado	*pes·ka·do*
meat/fish stock	caldo de carne/ pescado	*kal·do de kar·ne/ pes·ka·do*
pork	cerdo	*ther·do*
poultry	aves	*a·ves*

LISTEN FOR

¿Puede comer ...?	pwe·de ko·mer ...	
	Can you eat ...?	
Le preguntaré al cocinero.	le pre·goon·ta·re al ko·thee·ne·ro	
	I'll check with the cook.	
Todo lleva (carne).	to·do lye·va (kar·ne)	
	It all has (meat) in it.	

Is this ...?   ¿Esto es ...?
                  es·to es ...

free of animal produce	sin productos de animales	seen pro·dook·tos de a·nce·ma·les
free-range	de corral	de ko·ral
genetically modified	transgénico	trans·khe·nee·ko
gluten-free	sin gluten	seen gloo·ten
low in sugar	bajo en azúcar	ba·kho en a·lhoo·kar
low-fat	bajo en grasas	ba·kho en gra·sas
organic	orgánico	or·ga·nee·ko
salt-free	sin sal	seen sal

FOOD

VEGETARIAN & SPECIAL MEALS

A

Menu
~ DECODER ~
léxico culinario

This miniguide to Spanish cuisine lists dishes and ingredients in Spanish alphabetical order (see **alphabet**, p12). Spanish nouns have their gender indicated by ⓜ or ⓕ. If it's a plural noun, you'll also see pl.

MENU DECODER

~ A ~

acebuche ⓜ a·the·*boo*·che wild olive
acedía ⓕ a·the·*dee*·a plaice/flounder
aceite ⓜ a·*they*·te oil
— de girasol de khee·ra·*sol* sunflower oil
— de oliva de o·*lee*·va olive oil
— de oliva virgen extra de o·*lee*·va *veer*·khen *eks*·tra extra virgin olive oil
aceituna ⓕ a·they·*too*·na olive
— negra *ne*·gra black olive
— verde *ver*·de green olive
ácido/a ⓜ/ⓕ a·*thee*·do/a tart (flavour)
adobo ⓜ a·*do*·bo marinade
agrios ⓜ pl a·gryos citrus fruits
aguacate ⓜ a·gwa·*ka*·te avocado
aguaturma ⓕ a·gwa·*toor*·ma Jerusalem artichoke
ajiaco ⓜ a·*khya*·ko spicy potato dish
ajoaceite ⓜ a·kho·a·*they*·te garlic & oil sauce • garlic mayonnaise
ajoharina ⓕ a·kho·a·*ree*·na potatoes stewed in garlic sauce
(al) ajoarriero (al) a·kho·a·*rye*·ro 'mule-driver's garlic' – anything cooked in a sauce of onions, garlic & chilli

ala ⓕ a·la (chicken) wing
alajú ⓜ a·la·*khoo* honey & almond cake
albaricoque ⓜ al·ba·ree·*ko*·ke apricot
— seco *se*·ko dried apricot
albóndigas ⓕ pl al·*bon*·dee·gas meatballs
— de pescado de pes·*ka*·do fish balls
alcachofas ⓕ pl al·ka·*cho*·fas artichokes
— guisadas a la española gee·sa·das a la es·pa·*nyo*·la artichokes in wine
— rellenas re·*lye*·nas stuffed artichokes
alcaparra ⓕ al·ka·*pa*·ra caper
alioli ⓜ a·lee·o·*lee* garlic mayonnaise
almejas ⓕ pl al·*me*·khas clams – superb eaten raw
— a la marinera a la ma·ree·*ne*·ra clams in white wine
— al horno al *or*·no baked clams
almendrado ⓜ al·men·*dra*·do almond cake or biscuit • chocolate covered ice cream bar
almendras ⓕ pl al·*men*·dras almonds
alubia ⓕ a·*loo*·bya haricot bean

anacardo ⓜ a·na·kar·do cashew nut
anchoas ① pl an·cho·as anchovies – mostly eaten fresh, grilled or fried
angelote ⓜ an·khe·lo·te monkfish
anguila ① an·gee·la adult eel
angulas ① pl an·goo·las baby eels – prized as a delicacy, they resemble vermicelli
— **en all i pebre** en al ee pe·bre baby eels with pepper & garlic
apio ⓜ a·pyo celery
arándano ⓜ a·ran·da·no blueberry
arenque ⓜ a·ren·ke herring
— **ahumado** a·oo·ma·do kipper
arroz ⓜ a·roth rice
— **a la Alcireña** a la al thee·re·nya baked rice dish
— **abanda (de València)** a·ban·da (de va·len·thya) fish paella
— **con leche** kon le·che rice pudding
— **con pollo** kon po·lyo chicken & rice
— **integral** een·te·gral brown rice
— **marinera** ma·ree·ne·ra seafood & rice
— **salvaje** sal·va·khe wild rice
asadillo ⓜ a·sa·dee·lyo roasted red capsicums
asados ⓜ pl a·sa·dos roast meats
atún ⓜ a·toon tuna – often served marinated & raw
— **al horno** al or·no baked tuna
avellana ① a·ve·lya·na hazelnut
aves ① pl a·ves poultry
azúcar ⓜ a·thoo·kar sugar

~ **B** ~

bacalao ⓜ ba·ka·low cod – usually salted & dried
— **a la vizcaína** a la veeth·ka·ee·na cod with chillies & capsicums
— **del convento** del kon·ven·to cod with potatoes & spinach in broth
bacón ⓜ ba·kon bacon
barbo ⓜ bar·bo red mullet

barra ① ba·ra long stick of bread
batata ① ba·ta·ta sweet potato
beicon ⓜ bey·kon streaky bacon rashers
berberechos ⓜ pl ber·be·re·chos cockles
— **en vinagre** en vee·na·gre cockles in vinegar
berenjenas ① pl be·ren·khe·nas eggplants
— **a la mallorquina** a la ma·lyor·kee·na eggplants with garlic mayonnaise
— **con setas** kon se·tas eggplants with mushrooms
berza ① ber·tha cabbage
— **a la andaluza** a la an·da·loo·tha cabbage & meat hotpot
besugo ⓜ be·soo·go red bream
— **a la Donostiarra** a la do·nos·tya·ra barbecued red bream with garlic & paprika
— **estilo San Sebastián** es·tee·lo san se·bas·tyan barbecued red bream with garlic & paprika
bienmesabe ⓜ byen·me·sa·be sponge cake, egg & almond confection
bisbe ⓜ bees·be black & white blood sausage
bistec ⓜ bees·tek steak
— **con patatas** kon pa·ta·tas steak with chips
bizcocha ① **manchega** beeth·ko·cha man·che·ga cake soaked in milk, sugar, vanilla & cinnamon
bizcocho ⓜ beeth·ko·cho sponge cake
— **de almendra** de al·men·dra almond cake
— **de avellana** de a·ve·lya·na hazelnut cake
bizcochos ⓜ pl **borrachos** beeth·ko·chos bo·ra·chos cake soaked in liqueur
bocadillo ⓜ bo·ka·dee·lyo bread roll with a filling

bocas ① pl **de la isla** *bo*-kas de la
ees-la large crab claws
bogavante ⓜ bo-ga-*van*-te lobster
bollo ⓜ *bo*-lyo crusty bread roll
bonito ⓜ bo-*nee*-to white fleshy tuna
boquerón ⓜ bo-ke-*ron* whitebait
boquerones ⓜ pl bo-ke-*ro*-nes
anchovies marinated in wine vinegar
— fritos *free*-tos fried anchovies
brama ① *bra*-ma sea bream
brócoli ⓜ *bro*-ko-lee broccoli
budín **de atún** boo-*deen* de
a-*toon* baked tuna pudding
bull **de atún** bool de a-*toon*
rabbit with garlic & tuna boiled with
potatoes
buñuelitos ⓜ pl boo-*nywe*-*lee*-tos
small cheese or ham fritters
— de San José de san kho-*se* lemon
& vanilla crepes
buñuelo ⓜ boo-*nywe*-lo fried pastry
burrida ① **de ratjada** boo-*ree*-da de
rat-*kha*-da fish soup with almonds
butifarra ① **(blanca)** boo-tee-*fa*-ra
(*blan*-ka) cured pork sausage
— con setas kon se-tas Catalan
sausage with mushrooms

~ **C** ~

caballa ① ka-*ba*-lya mackerel
cabra ① *ka*-bra goat
cabracho ⓜ ka-*bra*-cho scorpion
fish • mullet
cacahuete ⓜ ka-ka-*we*-te peanut
cachelos ⓜ pl ka-*che*-los potatoes
with spicy sausage & pork
cádiz ⓜ *ka*-deeth fresh goats' milk
cheese
calabacín ⓜ ka-la-ba-*theen* zucchini
calabaza ① ka-la-*ba*-tha pumpkin
calamares ⓜ pl ka-la-*ma*-res
calamari – popular fried or stuffed
— fritos a la romana *free*-tos a la
ro-*ma*-na squid rings fried in batter
— rellenos re-*lye*-nos stuffed squid

calçots ⓜ pl kal-*sots* spring onion-
like vegetables chargrilled and eaten
with a **romesco** dipping sauce
caldeirada ① kal-dey-*ra*-da salted
cod & potatoes in a paprika sauce •
fish soup
caldereta ① kal-de-*re*-ta stew
— asturiana as-too-*rya*-na fish stew
— de cordero de kor-*de*-ro lamb
stew
caldillo **de perro** kal-*dee*-lyo de
pe-ro 'puppy dog soup' – stew of
onions, fresh fish & orange juice
caldo ⓜ *kal*-do broth • clear soup •
stock
— al estilo del Mar Menor al
es-*tee*-lo del mar me-*nor* fish stew
from the Mar Menor
— gallego ga-*lye*-go broth with
haricot beans, ham & sausage
callos ⓜ pl *ka*-lyos tripe
camarones fritos ⓜ pl ka-ma-*ro*-nes
free-tos deep-fried prawns
canagroc ka-na-*grok* mushroom
cañaillas ① pl **de la Isla**
ka-*nyay*-lyas de la ees-la boiled sea
snails
canelones ⓜ pl ka-na-*lo*-nes squares
of pasta for making cannelloni
— con espinaca kon es-pee-*na*-ka
cannelloni with spinach, anchovies
& bechamel
— con pescado kon pes-*ka*-do
cannelloni with cod, eggs &
mushrooms
canapés ⓜ pl **de fiambres**
ka-na-*pes* de fee-*am*-bres mini hors
d'oeuvres with ham, anchovies or
cheese
cangrejo ⓜ kan-*gre*-kho
large-clawed crab usually eaten
steamed or boiled
cantalupo ⓜ kan-ta-*loo*-po
cantaloupe
canutillos ⓜ pl ka-noo-*tee*-lyos
cream biscuits

capones ⓜ pl **de Villalba** ka·po·nes de vee·*lyal*·ba Christmas dish of chicken marinated in brandy
caracoles ⓜ ka·ra·ko·les snails
caramelos ⓜ pl ka·ra·me·los caramels • confection
cardos ⓜ pl **fritos** kar·dos *free*·tos fried thistles
carne ⓕ *kar*·ne meat
— de membrillo de mem·*bree*·lyo quince 'cheese'
— molida mo·*lee*·da minced meat
cassolada ⓕ ka·so·*la*·da potato & vegetable stew with bacon & ribs
castaña ⓕ kas·*ta*·nya chestnut
caviar ⓜ ka·*vyar* caviar
caza ⓕ ka·tha game
cazón ⓜ ka·*thon* dogfish or shark with a sweet scallop-like flavour
cazuelitas ⓕ pl **de langostinos San Rafael** ka·thwe·*lee*·tas de lan·gos·*tee*·nos san ra·fa·*el* baked rice with seafood
cebolla ⓕ the·*bo*·lya onion
cecina ⓕ the·*thee*·na cured meat
cerdo ⓜ *ther*·do pork
cereales ⓜ pl the·re·a·les cereal
cereza ⓕ the·*re*·tha cherry
— silvestre seel·*ves*·tre wild cherry
ciervo ⓜ *thyer*·vo deer
cigala ⓕ thee·*ga*·la crayfish
ciruela ⓕ thee·*rwe*·la plum
— pasa *pa*·sa prune
civet ⓜ **de llebre** see·*vet* de *le*·bre hare stew
cochifrito ⓜ **de cordero** ko·chee·*free*·to de kor·*de*·ro lamb fried with garlic & lemon
cochinillo ⓜ ko·chee·*nee*·lyo suckling pig
— asado a·*sa*·do roast suckling pig
— de pelotas de pe·*lo*·tas meatball stew
coco ⓜ *ko*·ko coconut
codornices ⓕ pl **a la plancha** ko·dor·*nee*·thes a la *plan*·cha grilled quail

codorniz ⓕ ko·dor·*neeth* quail
— con pimientos kon pee·*myen*·tos capsicums stuffed with quail
col ⓕ kol cabbage
— lombarda lom·*bar*·da red cabbage
coles ⓕ pl **de bruselas** ko·les de broo·*se*·las Brussels sprouts
coliflor ⓕ ko·lee·*flor* cauliflower
conejo ⓜ ko·*ne*·kho rabbit
— de monte de *mon*·te wild rabbit
coquina ⓕ ko·*kee*·na large clam
corazón ⓜ ko·ra·*thon* heart
cordero ⓜ kor·*de*·ro lamb
— al chilindrón al chee·leen·*dron* lamb in tomato & capsicum sauce
— con almendras kon al·*men*·dras lamb in almond sauce
costillas ⓕ pl kos·*tee*·lyas ribs
crema ⓕ *kre*·ma cream
— catalana ka·ta·*la*·na creme brulee
— de espinacas de es·pee·*na*·kas cream of spinach soup
— de naranja de na·*ran*·kha orange cream dessert
— de San José de san kho·*se* egg custard flavoured with cinnamon
— de verduras de ver·*doo*·ras cream of vegetable soup
crocante ⓜ kro·*kan*·te ice cream with chopped nuts & chocolate

~ CH ~

chalote ⓜ cha·*lo*·te shallot
champiñones ⓜ pl cham·pee·*nyo*·nes cultivated white mushrooms
chanquetes ⓜ pl chan·*ke*·tes whitebait • baby anchovies
(al) chilindrón (al) chee·leen·*dron* cooked in a tomato & red pepper sauce
chipirón ⓜ chee·pee·*ron* baby squid – very popular in the Basque Country

D

chocolate ⓜ cho·ko·*la*·te chocolate
— caliente ka·lee·*en*·te thick hot chocolate
chocos ⓜ pl *cho*·kos squid
chorizo ⓜ cho·*ree*·tho spicy red cooked sausage, similar to salami
— de Pamplona de pam·*plo*·na fine-textured, hard chorizo
— de Salamanca de sa·la·*man*·ka chunky chorizo from Salamanca
chuletas ⓕ pl choo·*le*·tas chops · cutlets
— al sarmiento al sar·*myen*·to chops prepared over wood from vines
— de buey de bwey ox chops
— de cerdo a la aragonesa de *ther*·do a la a·ra·go·*ne*·sa baked pork chops with wine & onion
churros ⓜ *choo*·ros fried doughnut strips bought from street-sellers or in cafes

~ **D** ~

de soja de *so*·kha of/with soya
despojos ⓜ pl des·*po*·khos offal
dorada ⓕ **a la sal** do·*ra*·da a la sal salted sea bream
dulce ⓜ *dool*·the sweet
— de batata de ba·*ta*·ta sweet potato pudding from Málaga
dulces ⓜ pl *dool*·thes sweets
— de las monjas *dool*·thes de las *mon*·khas confectionery made by nuns & sold in convents or cake shops

~ **E** ~

embutidos ⓜ pl em·boo·*tee*·dos generic name for cured sausages
empanada ⓕ em·pa·*na*·da savoury pie
— de carne de *kar*·ne spicy meat pie
— de espinaca de es·pee·*na*·ka spinach pie
empanadilla ⓕ em·pa·na·*dee*·lya small pie, either sweet or savoury

empanado ⓜ em·pa·*na*·do coated in bread crumbs
emparedado ⓜ em·pa·re·*da*·do sandwich
— de jamón y espárragos de kha·*mon* ee es·*pa*·ra·gos fried ham & asparagus rolls
empiñonado ⓜ em·pee·nyo·*na*·do small marzipan-filled pastry with pinenuts
en salsa verde en *sal*·sa *ver*·de in a parsley & garlic sauce
encurtidos ⓜ pl en·koor·*tee*·dos pickles
ensaimada ⓕ **mallorquina** en·sai·*ma*·da ma·lyor·*kee*·na spiral-shaped bun made with lard
ensalada ⓕ en·sa·*la*·da salad
— de frutas de *froo*·tas fruit salad
— de patatas de pa·*ta*·tas potato salad
— del tiempo del *tyem*·po seasonal salad
— mixta *meeks*·ta mixed salad
escaldadillas ⓕ pl es·kal·da·*dee*·lyas dough soaked in orange juice & fried
escalivada ⓕ es·ka·lee·*va*·da roasted red capsicums in olive oil
escalopes ⓜ pl **de ternera rellenos** es·ka·*lo*·pes de ter·*ne*·ra re·*lye*·nos deep fried veal cutlets stuffed with egg & cheese
espaguetis ⓜ pl es·pa·*ge*·tees spaghetti
espárragos ⓜ pl es·*pa*·ra·gos asparagus
— con dos salsas kon dos *sal*·sas asparagus & tomato or paprika mayonnaise
— en vinagreta en vee·na·*gre*·ta asparagus in vinaigrette
espinacas ⓕ pl es·pee·*na*·kas spinach
— a la catalana a la ka·ta·*la*·na spinach with pinenuts & raisins

esqueixada ① es·kee·sha·da cod dressed with olives, tomato & onion

etxeko kopa e·che·ko ko·pa ice cream dessert

~ F ~

fabada ① **asturiana** fa·ba·da as·too·rya·na stew made with pork, blood sausage & white beans

faisán ⓜ fai·san pheasant

faves ① pl **a la catalana** fa·ves a la ka·ta·la·na broad beans with ham

fiambres ⓜ pl fee·am·bres cold meats

— surtidos soor·tee·dos selection of cold meats

fideos ⓜ pl fee·de·os pasta noodles

fideua ① fee·de·wa rice or noodles with fish & shellfish

fideus ⓜ pl **a la cassola** fee·de·oos a la ka·so·la Catalan noodle dish

filete ⓜ fee·le·te steak • any boneless slice of meat

— a la parrilla a la pa·ree·lya grilled beef steak

— de ternera de ter·ne·ra veal steak

filloas ① pl fee·lyo·as Galician pancakes filled with cream

flan ⓜ flan creme caramel

flaó ① fla·o sweet cheese flan

flor manchega ① flor man·che·ga deep-fried sweet wafers

frambuesa ① fram·bwe·sa raspberry

frangellos ⓜ pl fran·khe·lyos sweet made from cornmeal, milk & honey

fresa ① fre·sa strawberry

fricandó ⓜ **de langostinos** free·kan·do de lan·gos·tee·nos shrimp in almond sauce

frite ⓜ free·te lamb stew, served on festive occasions

fritos ⓜ pl free·tos fritters

— con miel kon myel honey-roasted fritters

fritura ① free·too·ra mixed fried fish

fruta ① froo·ta fruit

— variada va·ree·a·da selection of fresh fruit

frutas ① pl **en almíbar** froo·tas en al·mee·bar fruit in syrup

frutos ⓜ pl **secos** froo·tos se·kos nuts & dried fruit

fuet ① foo·et thin pork sausage

~ G ~

gachas ① pl **manchegas** ga·chas man·che·gas flavoured porridge

galleta ① ga·lye·ta biscuit

gambas ① pl gam·bas prawns

— a la plancha a la plan·cha grilled prawns

— en gabardina en ga·bar·dee·na prawns in batter

Gamonedo ⓜ ga·mo·ne·do sharp-tasting cheese, smoked & cured

garbanzos ⓜ pl gar·ban·thos chickpeas

— con cebolla kon the·bo·lya chickpeas in onion sauce

— tostados tos·ta·dos roasted chickpeas (sold as a snack)

garbure ① gar·boo·re green vegetable soup • pork & ham dish

garúm ⓜ ga·room olive & anchovy dip

Gata-Hurdes ga·ta·oor·des cheese

gazpacho ⓜ gath·pa·cho cold tomato soup

— andaluz an·da·looz cold tomato soup with chopped salad vegetables

— pastoril pas·to·reel rabbit stew with tomato & garlic

gazpachos ⓜ pl **manchegos** gath·pa·chos man·che·gos game & vegetable hotpot

Gaztazarra ⓜ gath·ta·tha·ra cheese

gitano ⓜ khee·ta·no Andalusian chickpea & tripe stew

H

gofio ⓜ go·fyo toasted cornmeal or barley

granadilla ⓕ gra·na·dee·lya passion fruit

grano ⓜ gra·no grain

— largo lar·go long-grain (rice)

gratinado ⓜ **de berenjenas** gra·tee·na·do de be·ren·khe·nas eggplant gratin

Grazalema ⓕ gra·tha·le·ma semi-cured sheep's milk cheese

guindilla ⓕ geen·dee·lya mild green chilli

guisado ⓜ gee·sa·do stew

— de cordero de kor·de·ro lamb ragout

— de ternera de ter·ne·ra veal ragout

guisante ⓜ gee·san·te pea

— seco se·ko split pea

— mollar mo·lyar snow pea

guisantes ⓜ pl **con jamón a la española** gee·san·tes kon kha·mon a la es·pa·nyo·la pea & ham dish

guisat ⓜ **de marisco** gee·sat de ma·rees·ko stew made with seafood

guiso ⓜ **de conejo estilo canario** gee·so de ko·ne·kho es·tee·lo ka·na·ryo rabbit stew

guiso ⓜ **de rabo de toro** gee·so de ra·bo de to·ro stewed bull's tail with potatoes

~ **H** ~

habas ⓕ pl a·bas broad beans

— a la granadina a la gra·na·dee·na broad beans with eggs & ham

— fritas free·tas fried broad beans (sold as a snack)

habichuela ⓕ a·bee·chwe·la white bean

hamburguesa ⓕ am·boor·ge·sa hamburger

harina ⓕ a·ree·na flour

— integral een·te·gral wholemeal flour

helado ⓜ e·la·do ice cream

hígado ⓜ ee·ga·do liver

higo ⓜ ee·go fig

— seco se·ko dried fig

hogaza ⓕ o·ga·tha dense, thick-crusted bread

hoja ⓕ **de parra** o·kha de pa·ra vine leaf

hojaldres ⓜ pl o·khal·dres small flaky pastries covered in sugar

hojas ⓕ pl **verdes** o·khas ver·des green vegetables

hornazo ⓜ or·na·tho bread stuffed with sausage

hortalizas ⓕ pl or·ta·lee·thas vegetables

huevo ⓜ we·vo egg

— cocido ko·thee·do boiled egg

— de chocolate de cho·ko·la·te chocolate egg

— frito free·to fried egg

huevos ⓜ pl we·vos egg dishes

— a la flamenca a la fla·men·ka baked vegetables with egg & ham

— al estilo Sóller al es·tee·lo so·lyer fried eggs served with a milk & vegetable sauce

— en salsa agria en sal·sa a·grya boiled eggs in wine & vinegar

— escalfados es·kal·fa·dos poached eggs

— revueltos re·vwel·tos scrambled eggs

~ **J** ~

jabalí ⓜ kha·ba·lee wild boar

— con salsa de castaños kon sal·sa de kas·ta·nyos wild boar in chestnut sauce

jamón ⓜ kha·mon ham

— cocido ko·thee·do cooked ham

— ibérico ee·ber·ik·o ham from the Iberian pig, said to be the best in Spain

— serrano se·ra·no cured mountain ham

jengibre ⓜ khen·gee·bre ginger
jerez (al) khe·reth (al) in a sherry sauce
judía ⓕ khoo·dee·a fresh green bean • dried kidney bean
judías ⓕ pl **del tío Lucas** khoo·dee·as del tee·o loo·kas bean stew with garlic & bacon
judías ⓕ pl **verdes a la castellana** khoo·dee·as ver·des a la kas·te·lya·na fried capsicums, garlic & green beans
judiones ⓜ pl **de la granja** kho·dee·o·nes de la gran·kha pork & bean stew

~ K ~

kiskilla kees·kee·lya shrimp (also spelled **quisquilla**)

~ L ~

langosta ⓕ lan·gos·ta lobster
— a la ibicenca a la ee·bee·then·ka lobster with stuffed squid
langostinos ⓜ pl lan·gos·tee·nos king prawns
— a la plancha a la plan·cha grilled king prawns
lavanco ⓜ la·van·ko wild duck
lechuga ⓕ le·choo·ga lettuce
legumbres ⓕ pl le·goom·bres pulses • vegetables • vegetable dishes
— secas se·kas dried pulses
leguminosas ⓕ pl le·goo·mee·no·sas legumes
lengua ⓕ len·gwa tongue
— a la aragonesa a la a·ra·go·ne·sa tongue in tomato & capsicum sauce
lenguado ⓜ len·gwa·do sole
— al chacolí con hongos al cha·ko·lee kon on·gos sole with white wine & mushrooms
lenguados ⓜ pl **al plato** len·gwa·dos al pla·to sole & mushroom casserole

lenguas ⓕ pl **con salsa de almendras** len·gwas kon sal·sa de al·men·dras tongue in almond sauce
lentejas ⓕ pl len·te·khas lentils
liebre ⓕ lye·bre hare
— con castañas kon kas·ta·nyas hare with chestnuts
— estofada es·to·fa·da stewed hare
lima ⓕ lee·ma lime
limón ⓜ lee·mon lemon
lomo ⓜ lo·mo fillet • loin • sirloin
— curado koo·ra·do cured pork sausage
— de cerdo de ther·do loin of pork
longaniza ⓕ lon·ga·nee·tha chorizo, long & skinny sausage
lubina ⓕ loo·bee·na sea bass
— a la marinera a la ma·ree·ne·ra sea bass in parsley sauce
lucio ⓜ loo·thyo pike

~ LL ~

llagostí ⓜ **a l'allioll** lyan·gos·tee a la·lyee·o·lee grilled prawns in garlic mayonnaise
llenguado ⓜ **a la nyoca** lyen·gwa·do a la nyo·ka sole with pine nuts & raisins

~ M ~

macedonia ⓕ **de frutas** ma·the·do·nya de froo·tas fruit salad
macedonia ⓕ **de verduras** ma·the·do·nya de ver·doo·ras mixed vegetables
magdalena ⓕ ma·da·le·na small fairy cake to dunk in coffee
magras ⓕ pl ma·gras fried eggs, ham, cheese & tomato
maíz ⓜ ma·eeth maize • corn
— tierno tyer·no sweetcorn
mandarina ⓕ man·da·ree·na tangerine • mandarin
mango ⓜ man·go mango
manitas ⓕ pl **de cerdo** ma·nee·tas de ther·do pig's trotters

K

MENU DECODER

manitas ① pl **de cordero** ma·nee·tas de kor·de·ro leg of lamb

manteca ① man·te·ka lard

mantecado ⓜ man·te·ka·do a soft lard biscuit • dairy ice cream

mantequilla ① man·te·kee·lya butter

— sin sal seen sal unsalted butter

manzana ① man·tha·na apple

manzanas ① **asadas** man·tha·nas a·sa·das baked apples

margarina ① mar·ga·ree·na margarine

marinera (a la) ma·ree·ne·ra (a la) cooked or served in a white wine sauce

mariscos ⓜ ma·rees·kos shellfish • seafood

marmitako mar·mee·ta·ko fresh tuna & potato casserole

marrano ⓜ ma·ra·no pork

mar y cel ⓜ mar es sel dish of sausages, rabbit, shrimp & angler fish

masa ① ma·sa pastry (dough)

mayonesa ① ma·yo·ne·sa mayonnaise

medallones ⓜ pl **de merluza** me·da·lyo·nes de mer·loo·tha hake steaks

mejillones ⓜ pl me·khee·lyo·nes mussels

— al vino blanco al vee·no blan·ko mussels in white wine

— con salsa kon sal·sa mussels with tomato sauce

mel ① **i mató** mel ee ma·to dessert of curd cheese with honey

melocotón ⓜ me·lo·ko·ton peach

melocotones ⓜ pl **al vino** me·lo·ko·to·nes al vee·no peaches in red wine

melón ⓜ me·lon melon

membrillo ⓜ mem·bree·lyo quince

menestra ① me·nes·tra mixed vegetable stew

— de pollo de po·lyo chicken & vegetable stew

merengue ⓜ me·ren·ge meringue

merluza ① mer·loo·tha hake

mermelada ① mer·me·la·da marmalade

mero ⓜ me·ro halibut • grouper • sea bass

miel ① myel honey

— de azahar de a·tha·ar orange blossom honey

— de caña de ka·nya treacle

migas ① pl mee·gas fried cubes of bread with capsicums

— a la aragonesa a la a·ra·go·ne·sa fried bread with bacon rashers in tomato sauce

— mulatas moo·la·tas cubes of bread soaked in chocolate & fried

mojarra ① mo·kha·ra type of sea bream

moje ⓜ **manchego** mo·khe man·che·go cold broth with black olives

mojete ⓜ mo·khe·te dipping sauce for bread, made from potatoes, garlic, tomatoes & paprika

— murciano moor·thya·no fish & capsicum dish

mojo ⓜ mo·kho spicy capsicum sauce

mollejas ① pl mo·lye·khas sweetbreads

mollete ⓜ mo·lye·te soft round bap roll

monas ① pl **de pascua** mo·nas de pas·kwa Easter cakes • figures made of chocolate

mongetes ① pl **seques i butifarra** mon·zhe·tes se·kes ee boo·tee·fa·ra haricot beans with roasted pork sausage

mora ① mo·ra blackberry

moraga ① **de sardina** mo·ra·ga de sar·dee·na fresh anchovies on a spit

morcilla ① mor·thee·lya black pudding, often stewed with beans & vegetables

mortadela ① mor·ta·de·la mortadella sausage

morteruelo ⓜ mor·te·rwe·lo pate dish containing offal, game & spices

mostachones ⓜ pl mos·ta·cho·nes small cakes for dipping in coffee or hot chocolate (also spelled **mostatxones**)

mostaza ① mos·ta·tha mustard

— en grano en gra·no mustard seed

múgil ⓜ moo·kheel grey mullet

mujol ⓜ **guisado** moo·khol gee·sa·do red mullet

mus ⓜ **de chocolate** moos de cho·ko·la·te chocolate mousse

muslo ⓜ moos·lo (chicken) leg & thigh

N

nabo ⓜ na·bo root vegetable • turnip

naranja ① na·ran·kha orange

nata ① na·ta cream

— agria a·grya sour cream

— montada mon·ta·da whipped cream

natillas ① pl na·tee·lyas creamy custard dessert

— de chocolate de cho·ko·la·te chocolate custard

navaja ① na·va·kha razor clam

nécora ① ne·ko·ra small crab

nueces ① pl new·thes nuts

nuez ① nweth nut

— de América de a·me·ree·ka pecan nut

— de nogal de no·gal walnut

~ Ñ ~

ñora ① nyo·ra sweet red capsicum (usually dried)

~ O ~

oca ① o·ka goose

olla ① o·lya meat & vegetable stew • cooking pot

oreja ① **de mar** o·re·kha de mar abalone

ostiones ⓜ pl **a la gaditana** os·tyo·nes a la ga·dee·ta·na Cádiz oysters with garlic, parsley & bread crumbs

ostra ① os·tra oyster

oveja ① o·ve·kha mutton

~ P ~

pá ⓜ **amb oli** pa amb o·lee toasted bread with garlic & olive oil

pacana ① pa·ka·na pecan

paella ① pa·e·lya rice dish which has many regional variations

— marinera ma·ree·ne·ra paella with fish & seafood

— zamorana tha·mo·ra·na paella with meat

palitos ⓜ pl **de queso** pa·lee·tos de ke·so cheese straws

palmera ① pal·me·ra leaf-shaped flaky pastry, often coated in chocolate

palomitas ① pl pa·lo·mee·tas popcorn

pan ⓜ pan bread

— aceite a·they·te flat round bread

— árabe a·ra·be pita bread

— de Alá de a·la 'Allah's Bread' – dessert

— de boda de bo·da sculpted bread traditionally made for weddings

— de centeno de then·te·no rye bread

— duro doo·ro stale bread, used for toasting & eating with olive oil

— integral een·te·gral wholemeal bread

panaché ⓜ pa·na·che mixed vegetable stew

panallets ⓜ pl pa·na·lyets marzipan sweets

panceta ① pan·the·ta salt-cured, streaky bacon

P

panchineta ⓕ pan·chee·ne·ta almond tart

panecillo ⓜ pa·ne·thee·lyo small bread roll

panojas ⓕ pl **malagueñas** pa·no·khas ma·la·ge·nyas sardine dish

papas ⓕ pl **arrugadas** pa·pas a·roo·ga·das potatoes boiled in their jackets

pargo ⓜ par·go sea bream

parrillada ⓕ pa·ree·lya·da grilled meat

— de mariscos de ma·rees·kos seafood grill

pastel ⓜ pas·tel cake

— de boda de bo·da wedding cake

— de chocolate de cho·ko·la·te chocolate cake

— de cierva de thyer·va meat pie

— de cumpleaños de koom·ple·a·nyos birthday cake

pastelitos ⓜ pl **de miel** pas·te·lee·tos de myel honey fritters

pataco ⓜ pa·ta·ko tuna & potato stew

patatas ⓕ pl pa·ta·tas potatoes

— a la riojana a la ree·o·kha·na potatoes with chorizo & paprika

— alioli a·lee·o·lee potatoes in garlic mayonnaise

— bravas bra·vas potatoes in spicy tomato sauce

— con chorizo kon cho·ree·tho potatoes with chorizo

— estofadas es·to·fa·das boiled potatoes

pato ⓜ pa·to duck

— a la sevillana a la se·vee·lya·na duck with orange sauce

— alcaparrada al·ka·pa·ra·da duck with capers & almonds

pavo ⓜ pa·vo turkey

pececillos ⓜ pl pe·the·thee·lyos small fish

pechina ⓕ pe·chee·na scallop

pecho ⓜ pe·cho breast of lamb

pechuga ⓕ pe·choo·ga breast of poultry

pepinillo ⓜ pe·pee·nee·lyo gherkin

pepino ⓜ pe·pee·no cucumber

pepitoria ⓕ pe·pee·to·rya sauce made with egg & almond

pepitos ⓜ pl pe·pee·tos chocolate eclair cakes filled with custard

pera ⓕ pe·ra pear

La Peral ⓕ la pe·ral soft cheese

perca ⓕ per·ka perch

perdices ⓕ pl per·dee·thes partridges

— a la manchega a la man·che·ga partridge in red wine & capsicums

— con chocolate kon cho·ko·la·te partridge with chocolate

perdiz ⓕ per·deeth partridge

peregrina ⓕ pe·re·gree·na scallop

pericana ⓕ pe·ree·ka·na dish of olives, cod oil, capsicums & garlic

perrito ⓜ **caliente** pe·ree·to ka·lee·en·te hot dog

pescada ⓕ **á galega** pes·ka·da a ga·le·ga hake fried in olive oil & served with garlic & paprika sauce

pescadilla ⓕ pes·ka·dee·lya whiting • young hake

pescaditos ⓜ pl **rebozados** pes·ka·dee·tos re·bo·tha·dos small fish fried in batter

pescado ⓜ pes·ka·do fish

— a l'all cremat a lal kre·mat fish in burnt garlic

pescaíto ⓜ **frito** pes·ka·ee·to free·to tiny fried fish

pestiños ⓜ pl pes·tee·nyos honey-coated aniseed pastries, fried with filling

pez ⓕ **espada** peth es·pa·da swordfish

— frito free·to fried swordfish steaks on a skewer

picada ⓕ pee·ka·da mixture of garlic, parsley, toasted almonds & nuts, often used to thicken sauces

picadillo ⓜ pee·ka·*dee*·lyo salad consisting of diced vegetables
— **de atún** de a·*toon* salad made with diced tuna & capsicums
— **de ternera** de ter·*ne*·ra minced veal

pichón ⓜ pee·*chon* pigeon

pichones ⓜ pl **asados** pee cho·nes a·*sa*·dos roast pigeons

pilotes ⓕ pl pee·*lo*·tes Catalan meatballs

pimiento ⓜ pee·*myen*·to capsicum
— **amarillo** a·ma·*ree*·lyo yellow capsicum
— **rojo** ro·kho red capsicum
— **verde** ver·de green capsicum

pimientos ⓜ pl pee·*myen*·tos capsicums (the ones from El Bierzo are especially good)
— **a la riojana** a la ree·o·*kha*·na roast red capsicum fried in oil & garlic
— **al chilindrón** al chee·leen·*dron* capsicum casserole

piña ⓕ pee·nya pineapple

pinchito ⓜ **moruno** peen·*chee*·to mo·roo·no lamb & chicken kebabs

piñón ⓜ pee·*nyon* pinenut

pinta ⓕ peen·ta pinto bean

pintada ⓕ peen·*ta*·da guinea fowl

piquillo ⓜ pee·kee·lyo sweet & spicy capsicums

pistacho ⓜ pees·*ta*·cho pistachio nut

pisto ⓜ **manchego** pees·to man·che·go zucchini with capsicum & tomato, fried or stewed

plátano ⓜ pla·ta·no banana

pochas ⓕ pl po·chas beans
— **a la riojana** a la ree·o·*kha*·na beans with chorizo in spicy paprika sauce
— **con almejas** kon al·*me*·khas beans with clams

pollo ⓜ po·lyo chicken
— **asado** a·*sa*·do roast chicken
— **con samfaina** kon sam·*fai*·na chicken with mixed vegetables

— **en escabeche** en es·ka·be·che marinated chicken
— **en salsa de ajo** en *sal*·sa de a·kho chicken in garlic sauce
— **granadina** gra·na·*dee*·na chicken with wine & ham
— **y langosta** ee lan·gos·ta chicken with craylish

polvorón ⓜ pol·vo·*ron* almond shortbread, often eaten at Christmas

pomelo ⓜ po·me·lo grapefruit

postre ⓜ pos·tre dessert
— **de naranja** de na *ran*·kha cream-filled oranges

potaje ⓜ po·*ta*·khe broth
— **castellano** kas·te·*lya*·no broth with beans & sausages
— **de garbanzos** de gar·*ban*·thos broth with chickpeas
— **de lentejas** de len·*te*·khas lentil broth

pote ⓜ **gallego** po·te ga·*lye*·go stew

potito ⓜ po·*tee*·to jar of baby food

pringada ⓕ preen·*ga*·da bread dipped in sauce • a marinated sandwich

productos ⓜ pl **biológicos** pro·*dook*·tos bee·o·*lo*·khee·kos organic produce

productos ⓜ pl **del mar** pro·*dook*·tos del mar seafood products

productos ⓜ pl **lácteos** pro·*dook*·tos lak·te·os dairy products

puchero ⓜ poo·*che*·ro casserole

pudin ⓜ poo·din pudding

puerco ⓜ pwer·ko pork

puerro ⓜ pwe·ro leek

pulpo ⓜ pool·po octopus
— ⓜ **a feira** pool·po a fey·ra spicy boiled octopus

punta ⓕ **de diamante** poon·ta de dya·*man*·te confection from Valencia

porrusalda ⓕ po·roo·*sal*·da cod & potato stew

Q

~ Q ~

queso Ⓜ *ke*·so cheese
— azul a·*thool* blue cheese
— crema *kre*·ma cream cheese
quisquilla Ⓕ kees·*kee*·lya shrimp
(also spelled **kiskilla**)

~ R ~

rábano Ⓜ *ra*·ba·no radish
rabas Ⓕ **en salsa verde** *ra*·bas en
sal·sa *ver*·de squid in green sauce
rabassola Ⓕ ra·ba·*so*·la mushroom
rape Ⓜ *ra*·pe monkfish
— a la gallega a la ga·*lye*·ga
monkfish with potatoes & garlic sauce
— a la Monistrol a la mo·nees·*trol*
monkfish with bechamel sauce
redondo Ⓜ re·*don*·do round (of
beef)
— al horno al *or*·no roast beef
regañaos Ⓜ pl re·ga·*nya*·os
pastry stuffed with sardines & red
capsicum
relleno Ⓜ re·*lye*·no stuffing
remolacha Ⓕ re·mo·*la*·cha
beetroot
reo Ⓜ *re*·o sea trout
repollo Ⓜ re·*po*·lyo cabbage
repostería Ⓕ re·pos·te·*ree*·a
confectionery
requesón Ⓜ re·ke·*son* cottage
cheese
riñón Ⓜ ree·*nyon* kidney
róbalo Ⓜ *ro*·ba·lo haddock • sea
bass
rodaballo Ⓜ ro·da·*ba*·lyo turbot •
brill
romero Ⓜ ro·*me*·ro rosemary
romesco Ⓜ ro·*mes*·ko sweet red
capsicum, almond & garlic sauce
rosca Ⓕ **de carne** *ros*·ka de *kar*·ne
meatloaf wrapped in bacon
rosco Ⓜ *ros*·ko small sweet bun
rossejat Ⓜ ro·se·*dyat* rice with fish
& shellfish

rovellons Ⓜ pl **a la plancha**
ro·ve·*lyons* a la *plan*·cha garlic
mushrooms
ruibarbo Ⓜ roo·ee·*bar*·bo rhubarb

~ S ~

salchicha Ⓕ sal·*chee*·cha pork
sausage
salchichón Ⓜ sal·chee·*chon* cured &
peppery white sausage
salmón Ⓜ sal·*mon* salmon
— a la ribereña a la ree·be·*re*·nya
salmon in a cider sauce
— ahumado a·oo·*ma*·do smoked
salmon
salmonete Ⓜ sal·mo·*ne*·te red
mullet
salmorejo Ⓜ sal·mo·*re*·kho thick
gazpacho soup made from tomato,
bread, olive oil, vinegar, garlic & green
capsicum
— de Córdoba de *kor*·do·ba
gazpacho soup made with more
vinegar than usual
salpicón Ⓜ sal·pee·*kon* fish or meat
salad
salsa Ⓕ *sal*·sa sauce
— alioli a·lee·o·*le* garlic & olive oil
vinaigrette • garlic mayonnaise
— de holandesa de o·lan·*de*·sa
hollandaise sauce
— de mayonesa de ma·yo·*ne*·sa
mayonnaise sauce
— de tomate de to·*ma*·te tomato
sauce
— inglesa een·*gle*·sa Worcestershire
sauce
— tártara *tar*·ta·ra tartar sauce
— verde *ver*·de parsley & garlic
sauce
samfaina Ⓕ sam·*fai*·na grilled
vegetable sauce
sancocho Ⓜ san·*ko*·cho fish dish
served with potatoes
sandía Ⓕ san·*dee*·a watermelon

sándwich ⓜ *san·weech* sandwich
— mixto *meeks·to* toasted ham & cheese sandwich
sanocho ⓜ **canario** *sa·no·cho ka·na·ryo* baked monkfish with potatoes
sardinas ⓕ *sar·dee·nas* sardines
— a la parrilla *a la pa·ree·lya* sardines grilled
— en cazuela *en ka·thwe·la* sardines served in a clay pot
sargo ⓜ *sar·go* bream
sepia ⓕ *se·pya* cuttlefish
sesos ⓜ pl *se·sos* brains
setas ⓕ pl *se·tas* wild mushrooms
— a la kashera *a la ka·she·ra* sauteed wild mushrooms
— rellenas *re·lye·nas* mushrooms stuffed
sofrit pagés ⓜ *so·freet pa·zhes* vegetable stew
sofrito ⓜ *so·free·to* fried tomato sauce
soja ⓕ *so·kha* soya bean
soldaditos ⓜ pl **de Pavía** *sol·da·dee·tos de pa·vee·a* cod fritters
solomillo ⓜ *so·lo·mee·lyo* fillet
sopa ⓕ *so·pa* soup
— del día *del dee·a* soup of the day
sopas ⓕ pl **de leche** *so·pas de le·che* pieces of bread soaked in milk & cinnamon
sopas ⓕ pl **engañadas** *so·pas en·ga·nya·das* soup made from capsicum, onion shoots, vinegar, figs & grapes
sorbete ⓜ *sor·be·te* sorbet
sorroputún ⓜ *so·ro·poo·toon* tuna casserole
suizo ⓜ *swee·tho* sugared bun
sukaldi *soo·kal·dee* beef stew
suquet ⓜ *soo·ket* clams in almond sauce
suquet de peix ⓜ *soo·ket de peysh* fish stew

suspiros ⓜ pl **de monja** *soos·pee·ros de mon·kha* 'nun's sighs' – custard sweets

~ **T** ~

tallarines ⓜ pl *ta·lya·ree·nes* pasta noodles
tarta ⓕ *tar·ta* cake • tart
— de almendra *de al·men·dra* almond tart
— de manzana *de man·tha·na* apple tart
tartaleta ⓕ *tar·ta·le·ta* tartlet
tartaletas ⓕ pl **de huevos revueltos** *tar·ta·le·tas de we·vos re·vwel·tos* scrambled egg tartlets
ternera ⓕ *ter·ne·ra* veal
— a la sevillana *a la se·vee·lya·na* veal served with wine & olives
— en cazuela con berenjenas *en ka·thwe·la kon be·ren·khe·nas* veal & eggplant casserole
tocino ⓜ *to·thee·no* salted pork • bacon
— del cielo *del thye·lo* creamy dessert made with egg yolk & sugar, with a caramel topping
tocrudo *to·kroo·do* 'everything raw' – salad of meat, garlic, onion & green capsicum
tomate ⓜ *to·ma·te* tomatoes
— (de) pera *(de) pe·ra* plum tomato
— frito *free·to* tinned tomato sauce
tomates ⓜ pl *to·ma·tes*
— enteros y pelados *en·te·ros ee pe·la·dos* tinned whole tomatoes
— rellenos de atún *re·lye·nos de a·toon* tomatoes stuffed with tuna
toro ⓜ *to·ro* bull meat
torrefacto ⓜ *to·re·fak·to* dark-roasted coffee beans
torrija ⓕ *to·ree·kha* French toast
torta ⓕ *tor·ta* pie • tart • flat bread
— de aceite *de a·they·te* sweet, flat cake or biscuit made with oil

— **pascualina** pas·kwa·*lee*·na spinach & egg pie, eaten at Easter
tortilla ① tor·*tee*·lya omelette
— **española** es·pa·*nyo*·la potato & onion omelette
— **francesa** fran·*the*·sa plain omelette
tortillas ① pl **de camarones** tor·*tee*·lyas de ka·ma·*ro*·nes shrimp fritters
tortita ① tor·*tee*·ta waffle
tostada ① tos·*ta*·da toasted bread
tocino ⓜ to·*thee*·no bacon
tripas ① pl *tree*·pas intestines • guts
trucha ① *troo*·cha trout
— **a la marinera** a la ma·ree·*ne*·ra trout in a white wine sauce
truchas ① pl *troo*·chas trout
— **a la navarra** a la na·*va*·ra trout with ham
— **con vino y romero** kon *vee*·no ee ro·*me*·ro trout with red wine & rosemary
trufa ① *troo*·fa truffle
— **tarta** *tar*·ta chocolate truffle cake
tumbet (de peix) ⓜ toom·*bet* (de peysh) vegetable souffle, sometimes containing fish
turrón ⓜ too·*ron* Spanish nougat

~ **U** ~

uva ① *oo*·va grape
— **de corinto** de ko·*reen*·to currant
— **pasa** *pa*·sa raisin
— **sultana** sool·*ta*·na sultana

~ **V** ~

vacuno ⓜ va·*koo*·no beef
venado ⓜ ve·*na*·do venison
verduras ① ver·*doo*·ras vegetables
vieira ① vee·*ey*·ra scallop
villagodio ⓜ vee·lya·*go*·dyo large steak
vinagre ⓜ vee·*na*·gre vinegar
visita ① vee·*see*·ta almond cake

~ **Y** ~

yemas ① pl *ye*·mas small round cakes • egg whites
yogur ⓜ yo·*goor* yoghurt

~ **Z** ~

zanahoria ① tha·na·*o*·rya carrot
zarangollo ⓜ tha·ran·*go*·lyo fried zucchini
zarzamora ① thar·tha·*mo*·ra blackberry
zarzuela ① **de mariscos** thar·*thwe*·la de ma·*rees*·kos spicy shellfish stew
zarzuela ① **de pescado** thar·*thwe*·la de pes·*ka*·do fish in almond sauce
zurrukutano ⓜ thoo·roo·koo·*ta*·no cod & green capsicum soup

Dictionary

ENGLISH *to* SPANISH

inglés– español

Nouns in the dictionary have their gender indicated by ⓜ or ⓕ.
If it's a plural noun, you'll also see pl. Where a word that could be
either a noun or a verb has no gender indicated, it's a verb.

A

(to be) able poder po·*der*
aboard a bordo a·*bor*·do
abortion aborto ⓜ a·*bor*·to
about sobre so·*bre*
above arriba a·*rree*·ba
abroad en el extranjero en el
eks·tran·*khe*·ro
accept aceptar a·thep·*tar*
accident accidente ⓜ ak·thee·*den*·te
accommodation alojamiento ⓜ
a·lo·kha·*myen*·to
across a través a tra·*ves*
activist activista ⓜ&ⓕ ak·tee·vees·ta
acupuncture acupuntura ⓕ
a·koo·poon·*too*·ra
adaptor adaptador ⓜ a·dap·ta·*dor*
address dirección ⓕ dee·rek·*thyon*
administration administración ⓕ
ad·mee·nees·tra·*thyon*
admission price precio ⓜ de entrada
pre·thyo de en·*tra*·da
admit admitir ad·mee·*teer*
adult adulto ⓜ a·*dool*·to
advertisement anuncio ⓜ
a·*noon*·thyo
advice consejo ⓜ kon·*se*·kho
aerobics aeróbic ⓜ ai·ro·beek

Africa África ⓕ a·*free*·ka
after después de des·*pwes* de
aftershave bálsamo de aftershave
bal·sa·mo de *ahf*·ter·sha·eev
again otra vez o·tra veth
age edad ⓕ e·*da*
aggressive agresivo/a ⓜ/ⓕ
a·gre·*see*·vo/a
agree estar de acuerdo es·*tar* de
a·*kwer*·do
agriculture agricultura ⓕ
a·gree·kul·*too*·ra
AIDS SIDA ⓜ *see*·da
air aire ⓜ ai·re
air mail por vía aérea por *vee*·a
a·*e*·re·a
air-conditioned con aire acondicionado kon ai·re a·kon·dee·thyo·*na*·do
air-conditioning aire ⓜ acondicionado ai·re a·kon·dee·thyo·*na*·do
airline aerolínea ⓕ ai·ro·*lee*·nya
airport aeropuerto ⓜ ai·ro·*pwer*·to
airport tax tasa ⓕ del aeropuerto
ta·sa del ai·ro·*pwer*·to
alarm clock despertador ⓜ
des·per·ta·*dor*
alcohol alcohol ⓜ al·*kol*
all todo *to*·do
allergy alergia ⓕ a·*ler*·khya

B

allow permitir per·mee·*teer*
almonds almendras ① pl al·*men*·dras
almost casi *ka*·see
alone solo/a ⓜ/① *so*·lo/a
already ya ya
also también tam·*byen*
altar altar ⓜ al·*tar*
altitude altura ① al·*too*·ra
always siempre *syem*·pre
amateur amateur ⓜ&① a·ma·*ter*
ambassador embajador/embajadora
ⓜ/① em·ba·kha·*dor*/em·ba·kha·*do*·ra
among entre *en*·tre
anarchist anarquista ⓜ&①
a·nar·*kees*·ta
ancient antiguo/a ⓜ/① an·*tee*·gwo/a
and y ee
angry enfadado/a ⓜ/① en·fa·*da*·do/a
animal animal ⓜ a·nee·*mal*
ankle tobillo ⓜ to·*bee*·lyo
answer respuesta ① res·*pwes*·ta
answering machine contestador ⓜ automático kon·tes·ta·*dor*
ow·to·*ma*·tee·ko
ant hormiga ① or·*mee*·ga
anthology antología ①
an·to·lo·*khee*·a
antibiotics antibióticos ⓜ pl
an·tee·*byo*·tee·kos
antinuclear antinuclear
an·tee·noo·kle·*ar*
antique antigüedad ① an·tee·gwe·*da*
antiseptic antiséptico ⓜ
an·tee·*sep*·tee·ko
any alguno/a ⓜ/① al·*goo*·no/a
appendix apéndice ⓜ a·*pen*·dee·the
apple manzana ① man·*tha*·na
appointment cita ① *thee*·ta
apricot albaricoque ⓜ al·ba·ree·*ko*·ke
archaeological arqueológico/a ⓜ/①
ar·keo·lo·*khee*·ko/a
architect arquitecto/a ⓜ/①
ar·kee·*tek*·to/a
architecture arquitectura ①
ar·kee·tek·*too*·ra
argue discutir dees·koo·*teer*

arm brazo ⓜ *bra*·tho
army ejército ⓜ e·*kher*·thee·to
arrest detener de·te·*ner*
arrivals llegadas ① pl lye·*ga*·das
arrive llegar lye·*gar*
art arte ⓜ *ar*·te
art gallery museo ⓜ de arte
moo·se·o de *ar*·te
artichoke alcachofa ① al·ka·*cho*·fa
artist artista ⓜ&① ar·*tees*·ta
ashtray cenicero ⓜ the·nee·*the*·ro
Asia Asia ① *a*·sya
ask (a question) preguntar
pre·goon·*tar*
ask (for something) pedir pe·*deer*
aspirin aspirina ① as·pee·*ree*·na
assault asalto ⓜ a·*sal*·to
asthma asma ⓜ *as*·ma
athletics atletismo ⓜ at·le·*tees*·mo
atmosphere atmósfera ①
at·*mos*·fe·ra
aubergine berenjena ① be·ren·*khe*·na
aunt tía ① *tee*·a
Australia Australia ① ow·*stra*·lya
Australian Rules football fútbol ⓜ
australiano *foot*·bol ow·stra·*lya*·no
automatic teller machine cajero ⓜ
automático ka·*khe*·ro ow·to·*ma*·tee·ko
autumn otoño ⓜ o·*to*·nyo
avenue avenida ① a·ve·*nee*·da
avocado aguacate ⓜ a·gwa·*ka*·te

B

B&W (film) blanco y negro *blan*·ko
ee *ne*·gro
baby bebé ⓜ be·*be*
baby food comida ① de bebé
ko·*mee*·da de be·*be*
baby powder talco ⓜ *tal*·ko
babysitter canguro ⓜ kan·*goo*·ro
back (of body) espalda ① es·*pal*·da
back (of chair) respaldo ⓜ res·*pal*·do
backpack mochila ① mo·*chee*·la
bacon tocino ⓜ to·*thee*·no
bad malo/a ⓜ/① *ma*·lo/a
bag bolso ⓜ *bol*·so

baggage equipaje ⓜ e·kee·pa·khe
baggage allowance ⓜ límite de equipaje lee·mee·te de e·kee·pa·khe
baggage claim recogida ⓕ de equipajes re·ko·khee·da de e·kee·pa·khes
bakery panadería ⓕ pa·na·de·ree·a
balance (account) saldo ⓜ sal·do
balcony balcón ⓜ bal·kon
ball pelota ⓕ pe·lo·ta
ballet ballet ⓜ ba·le
banana plátano ⓜ pla·ta·no
band grupo ⓜ groo·po
bandage vendaje ⓜ ven·da·khe
band-aids tiritas ⓕ pl tee·ree·tas
bank banco ⓜ ban·ko
bank account cuenta ⓕ bancaria kwen·ta ban·ka·rya
banknotes billetes ⓜ pl (de banco) bee·lye·tes (de ban·ko)
baptism bautizo ⓜ bow·tee·tho
bar bar ⓜ bar
bar (with music) pub ⓜ poob
bar work trabajo ⓜ de camarero/a ⓜ/ⓕ tra·ba·kho de ka·ma·re·ro/a
basket canasta ⓕ ka·nas·ta
basketball baloncesto ⓜ ba·lon·thes·to
bath bañera ⓕ ba·nye·ra
bathing suit bañador ⓜ ba·nya·dor
bathroom baño ⓜ ba·nyo
battery (car) batería ⓕ ba·te·ree·a
battery (small) pila ⓕ pee·la
be ser ser · estar es·tar
beach playa ⓕ pla·ya
bean sprouts brotes ⓜ pl de soja bro·tes de so·kha
beans judías khoo·dee·as
beautiful hermoso/a ⓜ/ⓕ er·mo·so/a
beauty salon salón ⓜ de belleza sa·lon de be·lye·tha
because porque por·ke
bed cama ⓕ ka·ma
bedding ropa ⓕ de cama ro·pa de ka·ma
bedroom habitación ⓕ a·bee·ta·thyon

bee abeja ⓕ a·be·kha
beef carne ⓕ de vaca kar·ne de va·ka
beer cerveza ⓕ ther·ve·tha
beetroot remolacha ⓕ re·mo·la·cha
before antes an·tes
beggar mendigo/a ⓜ/ⓕ men·dee·go/a
begin comenzar ko·men·thar
behind detrás de·tras de
Belgium Bélgica ⓕ bel·khee·ka
below abajo a·ba·kho
best lo mejor lo me·khor
bet apuesta ⓕ a·pwes·ta
better mejor me·khor
between entre en·tre
bible biblia ⓕ bee·blya
bicycle bicicleta ⓕ bee·thee·kle·ta
big grande gran·de
bike bici ⓕ bee·thee
bike chain cadena ⓕ de bici ka·de·na de bee·thee
bike path camino ⓜ de bici ka·mee·no de bee·thee
bill cuenta ⓕ kwen·ta
biodegradable biodegradable bee·o·de·gra·da·ble
biography biografía ⓕ bee·o·gra·fee·a
bird pájaro ⓜ pa·kha·ro
birth certificate partida ⓕ de nacimiento par·tee·da de na·thee·myen·to
birthday cumpleaños ⓜ koom·ple·a·nyos
birthday cake pastel ⓜ de cumpleaños pas·tel de koom·ple·a·nyos
biscuit ⓕ galleta ga·lye·ta
bite (dog) mordedura ⓕ mor·de·doo·ra
bite (food) bocado ⓜ bo·ka·do
bite (insect) picadura ⓕ pee·ka·doo·ra
black negro/a ⓜ/ⓕ ne·gro/a
blanket manta ⓕ man·ta
bleed sangrar san·grar
blind ciego/a ⓜ/ⓕ thye·go/a

B

blister ampolla ⓕ am·po·lya

blocked atascado/a ⓜ/ⓕ a·tas·ka·do/a

blood sangre ⓕ san·gre

blood group grupo ⓜ sanguíneo groo·po san·gee·neo

blood pressure presión ⓕ arterial pre·syon ar·te·ryal

blood test análisis ⓜ de sangre a·na·lee·sees de san·gre

blue azul a·thool

board (ship, etc) embarcarse em·bar·kar·se

boarding house pensión ⓕ pen·syon

boarding pass tarjeta ⓕ de embarque tar·khe·ta de em·bar·ke

bone hueso ⓜ we·so

book libro ⓜ lee·bro

book (make a reservation) reservar re·ser·var

booked out lleno/a ⓜ/ⓕ lye·no/a

bookshop librería ⓕ lee·bre·ree·a

boots botas ⓕ pl bo·tas

border frontera ⓕ fron·te·ra

boring aburrido/a ⓜ/ⓕ a·boo·ree·do/a

borrow tomar prestado to·mar pres·ta·do

botanic garden jardín ⓜ botánico khar·deen bo·ta·nee·ko

both ambos/as ⓜ/ⓕ pl am·bos/bas

bottle botella ⓕ bo·te·lya

bottle opener abrebotellas ⓜ a·bre·bo·te·lyas

bowl bol ⓜ bol

box caja ⓕ ka·kha

boxer shorts calzones ⓜ pl kal·tho·nes

boxing boxeo ⓜ bo·se·o

boy chico ⓜ chee·ko

boyfriend novio ⓜ no·vyo

bra sujetador ⓜ soo·khe·ta·dor

brakes frenos ⓜ pl fre·nos

branch (office) sucursal ⓕ soo·koor·sal

brandy coñac ⓜ ko·nyak

brave valiente va·lyen·te

bread pan ⓜ pan

bread (brown) pan moreno pan mo·re·no

bread rolls bollos bo·lyos

bread (rye) pan de centeno pan de then·te·no

bread (sourdough) pan de masa fermentada pan de ma·sa fer·men·ta·da

bread (white) pan blanco pan blan·ko

bread (wholemeal) pan integral pan een·te·gral

break romper rom·per

break down descomponerse des·kom·po·ner·se

breakfast desayuno ⓜ des·a·yoo·no

breasts senos ⓜ pl se·nos

breathe respirar res·pee·rar

brewery fábrica ⓕ de cerveza fab·ree·ka de ther·ve·tha

bribe soborno ⓜ so·bor·no

bribe sobornar so·bor·nar

bridge puente ⓜ pwen·te

briefcase maletín ⓜ ma·le·teen

brilliant cojonudo/a ⓜ/ⓕ ko·kho·noo·do/a

bring traer tra·er

brochure folleto ⓜ fo·lye·to

broken roto/a ⓜ/ⓕ ro·to/a

bronchitis bronquitis ⓕ bron·kee·tees

brother hermano ⓜ er·ma·no

brown marrón ma·ron

bruise cardenal ⓜ kar·de·nal

brussels sprouts coles ⓜ pl de Bruselas ko·les de broo·se·las

bucket cubo ⓜ koo·bo

Buddhist budista ⓜ&ⓕ boo·dees·ta

buffet buffet ⓜ boo·fe

bug bicho ⓜ bee·cho

build construir kons·troo·eer

building edificio ⓜ e·dee·fee·thyo

bull toro ⓜ to·ro

bullfight corrida ⓕ ko·ree·da

bullring plaza ⓕ de toros pla·tha de to·ros

bum (of body) culo ⓜ koo·lo

burn quemadura ① ke·ma·*doo*·ra
bus autobús ⓜ ow·to·*boos*
bus (intercity) autocar ⓜ ow·to·*kar*
bus station estación de auto-
buses/autocares ① es·ta·*thyon* de
ow·to·*boo*·ses/ow·to·*ka*·res
bus stop parada ① de autobús
pa·*ra*·da de ow·to·*boos*
business negocios ⓜ pl ne·*go*·thyos
business class clase ① preferente
kla·se pre·fe·*ren*·te
business person comerciante ⓜ&①
ko·mer·*thyan*·te
busker artista callejero/a ⓜ/①
ar·*tees*·ta ka·lye·*khe*·ro/a
busy ocupado/a ⓜ/① o·koo·*pa*·do/a
but pero *pe*·ro
butcher's shop carnicería ①
kar·nee·the·*ree*·a
butter mantequilla ① man·te·*kee*·lya
butterfly mariposa ① ma·ree·*po*·sa
buttons botónes ⓜ pl bo·*to*·nes
buy comprar kom·*prar*

C

cabbage col kol
cable cable ⓜ *ka*·ble
cable car teleférico ⓜ te·le·fe·*ree*·ko
cafe café ⓜ ka·*fe*
cake pastel ⓜ pas·*tul*
cake shop pastelería ①
pas·te·le·*ree*·a
calculator calculadora ①
kal·koo·la·*do*·ra
calendar calendario ⓜ ka·len·*da*·ryo
calf ternero ⓜ ter·*ne*·ro
camera cámara ① (fotográfica)
ka·ma·ra (fo·to·*gra*·fee·ka)
camera shop tienda ① de fotografía
tyen·da de fo·to·gra·*fee*·a
camp acampar a·kam·*par*
camping store tienda ① de cámping
tyen·da de *kam*·peen
campsite cámping ⓜ *kam*·peen
can lata ① *la*·ta
can (be able) poder po·*der*

can opener abrelatas ⓜ a·bre·*la*·tas
Canada Canadá ① ka·na·*da*
cancel cancelar kan·the·*lar*
cancer cáncer ⓜ *kan*·ther
candle vela ① *ve*·la
cantaloupe cantalupo ⓜ
kan·ta·*loo*·po
capsicum (red/green) pimiento ⓜ
rojo/verde pee·*myen*·to ro·kho/*ver*·de
car coche ⓜ *ko*·che
car hire alquiler ⓜ de coche al·kee·*ler*
de *ko*·che
car owner's title papeles ⓜ pl del
coche pa·*pe*·les del *ko*·che
car registration matrícula ①
ma·tree·koo·la
caravan caravana ① ka·ra·*va*·na
cards cartas ① pl *kar*·tas
care (about something) preocuparse
por pre·o·koo·*par*·se por
care (for someone) cuidar de
kwee·*dar* de
caring bondadoso/a ⓜ/①
bon·da·*do*·so/a
carpark aparcamiento ⓜ
a·par·ka·*myen*·to
carpenter carpintero/a ⓜ/①
kar·peen·*te*·ro/a
carrot zanahoria ① tha·na·o·*rya*
carry llevar lye·*var*
carton cartón ⓜ kar·*ton*
cash dinero ⓜ en efectivo dee·*ne*·ro
en e·fek·*tee*·vo
cash (a cheque) cambiar (un
cheque) kam·*byar* (oon *che*·ke)
cash register caja ① registradora
ka·kha re·khees·tra·*do*·ra
cashew nut anacardo ⓜ a·na·*kar*·do
cashier caja ① *ka*·kha
casino casino ⓜ ka·*see*·no
cassette casete ⓜ ka·*se*·te
castle castillo ⓜ kas·*tee*·lyo
casual work trabajo ⓜ eventual
tra·*ba*·kho e·ven·*twal*
cat gato/a ⓜ/① *ga*·to/a
cathedral catedral ① ka·te·*dral*

C

Catholic católico/a ⓜ/ⓕ ka·to·lee·ko/a

cauliflower coliflor ⓕ ko·lee·*flor*

caves cuevas ⓕ pl *kwe*·vas

CD cómpact ⓜ *kom*·pakt

celebrate (an event) celebrar the·le·*brar*

celebration celebración ⓕ the·le·bra·*thyon*

cemetery cementerio ⓜ the·men·*te*·ryo

cent centavo ⓜ then·*ta*·vo

centimetre centímetro ⓜ then·*tee*·me·tro

central heating calefacción ⓕ central ka·le·fak·*thyon* then·*tral*

centre centro ⓜ *then*·tro

ceramic cerámica ⓕ the·*ra*·mee·ka

cereal cereales ⓜ pl the·re·a·les

certificate certificado ⓜ ther·tee·fee·*ka*·do

chair silla ⓕ *see*·lya

champagne champán ⓜ cham·*pan*

chance oportunidad ⓕ o·por·too·nee·*da*

change (money) cambio ⓜ *kam*·byo

change cambiar kam·*byar*

changing rooms vestuarios ⓜ pl ves·*twa*·ryos

charming encantador/encantadora ⓜ/ⓕ en·kan·ta·*dor*/en·kan·ta·*do*·ra

chat up ligar lee·*gar*

cheap barato/a ⓜ/ⓕ ba·*ra*·to/a

cheat tramposo/a ⓜ/ⓕ tram·*po*·so/a

check revisar re·vee·*sar*

check (bank) cheque ⓜ *che*·ke

check-in facturación ⓕ de equipajes fak·too·ra·*thyon* de e·kee·*pa*·khes

checkpoint control ⓜ kon·*trol*

cheese queso ⓜ *ke*·so

chef cocinero ⓜ ko·thee·*ne*·ro

chemist (person) farmacéutico/a ⓜ/ⓕ far·ma·the·oo·ti·ko/a

chemist (shop) farmacia ⓕ far·*ma*·thya

chess ajedrez ⓜ a·khe·*dreth*

chess board tablero ⓜ de ajedrez ta·*ble*·ro de a·khe·*dreth*

chest pecho ⓜ *pe*·cho

chewing gum chicle ⓜ *chee*·kle

chicken pollo ⓜ *po*·lyo

chicken breast pechuga ⓕ pe·*choo*·ga

chickpeas garbanzos ⓜ pl gar·*ban*·thos

child niño/a ⓜ/ⓕ *nee*·nyo/a

child seat asiento ⓜ de seguridad para bebés a·*syen*·to de se·goo·ree·*da* *pa*·ra be·*bes*

childminding service guardería ⓕ gwar·de·*rec*·a

children hijos ⓜ pl *ee*·khos

chilli guindilla ⓕ geen·*dee*·lya

chilli sauce salsa ⓕ de guindilla *sal*·sa de geen·*dee*·lya

chocolate chocolate ⓜ cho·ko·*la*·te

choose escoger es·ko·*kher*

Christian cristiano/a ⓜ/ⓕ krees·*tya*·no/a

Christian name nombre ⓜ de pila *nom*·bre de *pee*·la

Christmas Navidad ⓕ na·vee·*da*

Christmas Eve Nochebuena ⓕ no·che·*bwe*·na

church iglesia ⓕ ee·*gle*·sya

cider sidra ⓕ *see*·dra

cigar cigarro ⓜ thee·*ga*·ro

cigarette cigarillo ⓜ thee·ga·*ree*·lyo

cigarette lighter mechero ⓜ me·*che*·ro

cigarette machine máquina ⓕ de tabaco *ma*·kee·na de ta·*ba*·ko

cigarette paper papel ⓜ de fumar pa·*pel* de foo·*mar*

cinema cine ⓜ *thee*·ne

circus circo ⓜ *theer*·ko

citizenship ciudadanía ⓕ thyu·da·da·*nee*·a

city ciudad ⓕ thyu·*da*

city centre centro ⓜ de la ciudad *then*·tro de la thyu·*da*

city walls murallas ⓕ pl moo·*ra*·lyas

civil rights derechos civiles ⓜ pl de·*re*·chos thee·*vee*·les

classical clásico/a ⓜ/ⓕ *kla*·see·ko/a

clean limpio/a ⓜ/ⓕ *leem*·pyo/a

cleaning limpieza ⓕ *leem*·pye·tha

client cliente/a ⓜ/ⓕ klee·*en*·te/a

cliff acantilado ⓜ a·kan·tee·*la*·do

climb subir soo·*beer*

cloak capote ⓜ ka·*po*·te

cloakroom guardarropa ⓜ
gwar·da·*ro*·pa

clock reloj ⓜ re·*lokh*

close cerrar the·*rar*

closed cerrado/a ⓜ/ⓕ the·*ra*·do/a

clothes line cuerda ⓕ para tender la
ropa *kwer*·da *pa*·ra ten·*der* la *ro*·pa

clothing ropa ⓕ *ro*·pa

clothing store tienda ⓕ de ropa
tyen·da de *ro*·pa

cloud nube ⓕ *noo*·be

cloudy nublado noo·*bla*·do

clove (garlic) diente ⓜ (de ajo)
dyen·te (de a·kho)

cloves clavos ⓜ pl *kla*·vos

clutch embrague ⓕ em·*bra*·ge

coach entrenador/entrenadora ⓜ/ⓕ
en·tre·na·*dor*/en·tre·na·*do*·ra

coast costa ⓕ *kos*·ta

cocaine cocaína ⓕ ko·ka·*ee*·na

cockroach cucaracha ⓕ koo·ka·*ra*·cha

cocoa cacao ⓜ ka·*kow*

coconut coco ⓜ *ko*·ko

codeine codeína ⓕ ko·de·*ee*·na

coffee café ⓜ ka·*fe*

coins monedas ⓕ pl mo·*ne*·das

cold frío/a ⓜ/ⓕ *free*·o/a

cold (illness) resfriado ⓜ
res·*free*·a·do

colleague colega ⓜ&ⓕ ko·*le*·ga

collect call llamada ⓕ a cobro revertido lya·*ma*·da a *ko*·bro re·ver·*tee*·do

college residencia ⓕ de estudiantes
re·see·*den*·thya de es·too·*dyan*·tes

colour color ⓜ ko·*lor*

colour (film) película ⓕ en color
pe·*lee*·koo·la en ko·*lor*

comb peine ⓜ *pey*·ne

come venir ve·*neer*

come (arrive) llegar lye·*gar*

comedy comedia ⓕ ko·*me*·dya

comfortable cómodo/a ⓜ/ⓕ
ko·mo·do/a

communion comunión ⓕ
ko·moo·*nyon*

communist comunista ⓜ&ⓕ
ko·moo·*nees*·ta

companion compañero/a ⓜ/ⓕ
kom·pa·*nye*·ro/a

company compañía ⓕ kom·pa·*nyee*·a

compass brújula ⓕ *broo*·khoo·la

complain quejarse ke·*khar*·se

computer ordenador ⓜ or·de·na·*dor*

computer game juegos ⓜ pl de
ordenador *khwe*·gos de or·de·na·*dor*

concert concierto ⓜ kon·*thyer*·to

conditioner acondicionador ⓜ
a·kon·dee·thyo·na·*dor*

condoms condones ⓜ pl kon·*do*·nes

confession confesión ⓕ kon·fe·*syon*

confirm confirmar kon·feer·*mar*

connection conexión ⓕ ko·ne·*ksyon*

conservative conservador/
conservadora ⓜ/ⓕ kon·ser·va·*dor*/
kon·ser·va·*do*·ra

constipation estreñimiento ⓜ
es·tre·nyee·*myen*·to

consulate consulado ⓜ kon·soo·*la*·do

contact lenses lentes ⓜ pl de contacto *len*·tes de kon·*tak*·to

contraceptives anticonceptivos ⓜ pl
an·tee·kon·thep·*tee*·vos

contract contrato ⓜ kon·*tra*·to

convenience store negocio ⓜ de
artículos básicos ne·*go*·thyo de
ar·*tee*·koo·los *ba*·see·kos

convent convento ⓜ kon·*ven*·to

cook cocinero ⓜ ko·thee·*ne*·ro

cook cocinar ko·thee·*nar*

cookie galleta ⓕ ga·*lye*·ta

corn maíz ⓜ ma·*eeth*

corn flakes copos ⓜ pl de maíz
ko·pos de ma·*eeth*

corner esquina ⓕ es·*kee*·na

corrupt corrupto/a ⓜ/ⓕ ko·*roop*·to/a

cost costar kos·*tar*

D

cottage cheese requesón ⓜ re·ke·*son*
cotton algodón ⓜ al·go·*don*
cotton balls bolas ⓕ pl de algodón
bo·las de al·go·*don*
cough tos ⓕ tos
cough medicine jarabe ⓜ kha·*ra*·be
count contar kon·*tar*
counter mostrador ⓜ mos·tra·*dor*
country país ⓜ pa·*ees*
countryside campo ⓜ *kam*·po
coupon cupón ⓜ koo·*pon*
courgette calabacín ⓜ ka·la·ba·*theen*
court (tennis) pista ⓕ *pees*·ta
cous cous cus cus ⓜ koos koos
cover charge precio ⓜ del cubierto
pre·thyo del koo·*byer*·to
cow vaca ⓕ *va*·ka
crab cangrejo ⓜ kan·*gre*·kho
crackers galletas ⓕ pl saladas
ga·*lye*·tas sa·*la*·das
crafts artesanía ⓕ ar·te·sa·*nee*·a
crash choque ⓜ *cho*·ke
crazy loco/a ⓜ/ⓕ *lo*·ko/a
cream (food) crema *kre*·ma
cream (moisturising) crema ⓕ
hidratante *kre*·ma ee·dra·*tan*·te
cream cheese queso ⓜ crema *ke*·so
kre·ma
creche guardería ⓕ gwar·de·*ree*·a
credit card tarjeta ⓕ de crédito
tar·*khe*·ta de *kre*·dee·to
cricket críquet ⓜ *kree*·ket
crop cosecha ⓕ ko·*se*·cha
crowded abarrotado/a ⓜ/ⓕ
a·ba·ro·*ta*·do/a
cucumber pepino ⓜ pe·*pee*·no
cuddle abrazo ⓜ a·*bra*·tho
cup taza ⓕ *ta*·tha
cupboard armario ⓜ ar·*ma*·ryo
currency exchange cambio ⓜ (de
dinero) *kam*·byo (de dee·*ne*·ro)
current (electricity) corriente ⓕ
ko·*ryen*·te
current affairs informativo ⓜ
een·for·ma·*tee*·vo
curry curry ⓜ *koo*·ree

curry powder curry ⓜ en polvo
koo·ree en pol·vo
customs aduana ⓕ a·*dwa*·na
cut cortar kor·*tar*
cutlery cubiertos ⓜ pl koo·*byer*·tos
CV historial ⓜ profesional ees·to·*ryal*
pro·fe·syo·*nal*
cycle andar en bicicleta an·*dar* en
bee·thee·*kle*·ta
cycling ciclismo ⓜ thee·*klees*·mo
cyclist ciclista ⓜ&ⓕ thee·*klees*·ta
cystitis cistitis ⓕ thees·*tee*·tees

D

dad papá ⓜ pa·*pa*
daily diariamente dya·rya·*men*·te
dance bailar bai·*lar*
dancing bailar ⓜ bai·*lar*
dangerous peligroso/a ⓜ/ⓕ
pe·lee·*gro*·so/a
dark oscuro/a ⓜ/ⓕ os·*koo*·ro/a
date citarse thee·*tar*·se
date (a person) salir con sa·*leer* kon
date (time) fecha ⓕ *fe*·cha
date of birth fecha ⓕ de nacimiento
fe·cha de na·thee·*myen*·to
daughter hija ⓕ *ee*·kha
dawn alba ⓕ *al*·ba
day día ⓜ *dee*·a
day after tomorrow pasado mañana
pa·*sa*·do ma·*nya*·na
day before yesterday anteayer
an·te·a·*yer*
dead muerto/a ⓜ/ⓕ *mwer*·to/a
deaf sordo/a ⓜ/ⓕ *sor*·do/a
deal (cards) repartir re·par·*teer*
decide decidir de·thee·*deer*
deep profundo/a ⓜ/ⓕ pro·*foon*·do/a
deforestation deforestación ⓕ
de·fo·res·ta·*thyon*
degree título ⓜ *tee*·too·lo
delay demora ⓕ de·*mo*·ra
delirious delirante de·lee·*ran*·te
deliver entregar en·tre·*gar*
democracy democracia ⓕ
de·mo·*kra*·thya

demonstration manifestación ⓕ ma·nee·fes·ta·*thyon*

Denmark Dinamarca ⓕ dee·na·*mar*·ka

dental floss hilo ⓜ dental ee·lo den·*tal*

dentist dentista ⓜ&ⓕ den·*tees*·ta

deny negar ne·*gar*

deodorant desodorante ⓜ de·so·do·*ran*·te

depart salir de sa·*leer* de

department store grande almacen ⓜ *gran*·de al·ma·*then*

departure salida ⓕ sa·*lee*·da

deposit depósito ⓜ de·*po*·see·to

descendant descendiente ⓜ des·then·*dyen*·te

desert desierto ⓜ de·*syer*·to

design diseño ⓜ dee·*se*·nyo

destination destino ⓜ des·*tee*·no

destroy destruir des·troo·*eer*

detail detalle ⓜ de·*ta*·lye

diabetes diabetes ⓕ dee·a·*be*·tes

diaper pañal ⓜ pa·*nyal*

diaphragm diafragma ⓜ dee·a·*frag*·ma

diarrhoea diarrea ⓕ dee·a·*re*·a

diary agenda ⓕ a·*khen*·da

dice (die) dados ⓜ pl da·dos

dictionary diccionario ⓜ deek·thyo·*na*·ryo

die morir mo·*reer*

diet régimen ⓜ *re*·khee·men

different diferente ⓜ/ⓕ dee·fe·*ren*·te

difficult difícil ⓜ/ⓕ dee·*fee*·theel

dining car vagón ⓜ restaurante va·*gon* res·tow·*ran*·te

dinner cena ⓕ *the*·na

direct directo/a ⓜ/ⓕ dee·*rek*·to/a

direct-dial marcar directo mar·*kar* dee·*rek*·to

director director/directora ⓜ/ⓕ dee·rek·*tor*/dee·rek·*to*·ra

dirty sucio/a ⓜ/ⓕ *soo*·thyo/a

disabled minusválido/a ⓜ/ⓕ mee·noos·*va*·lee·do/a

disco discoteca ⓕ dees·ko·*te*·ka

discount descuento ⓜ des·*kwen*·to

discover descubrir des·koo·*breer*

discrimination discriminación ⓕ dees·kree·mee·na·*thyon*

disease enfermedad ⓕ en·fer·me·*da*

disk disco ⓜ *dees*·ko

dive bucear boo·the·*ar*

diving submarinismo ⓜ soob·ma·ree·*nees*·mo

diving equipment equipo ⓜ de inmersión ⓜ e·*kee*·po de een·mer·*syon*

dizzy mareado/a ⓜ/ⓕ ma·re·a·do/a

do hacer a·*ther*

doctor doctor/doctora ⓜ/ⓕ dok·*tor*/dok·*to*·ra

documentary documental ⓜ do·koo·men·*tal*

dog perro/a ⓜ/ⓕ *pe*·ro/a

dole paro ⓜ *pa*·ro

doll muñeca ⓕ moo·*nye*·ka

domestic flight vuelo ⓜ doméstico *vwe*·lo do·*mes*·tee·ko

donkey burro ⓜ *boo*·ro

door puerta ⓕ *pwer*·ta

dope droga ⓕ *dro*·ga

double doble ⓜ/ⓕ *do*·ble

double bed cama ⓕ de matrimonio *ka*·ma de ma·tree·*mo*·nyo

double room habitación ⓕ doble a·bee·ta·*thyon* *do*·ble

down abajo a·*ba*·kho

downhill cuesta abajo *kwes*·ta a·*ba*·kho

dozen docena ⓕ do·*the*·na

draw dibujar dee·boo·*khar*

dream soñar so·*nyar*

dress vestido ⓜ ves·*tee*·do

dried fruit fruto ⓜ seco *froo*·to *se*·ko

drink bebida ⓕ be·*bee*·da

drink beber be·*ber*

drive conducir kon·doo·*theer*

drivers licence carnet ⓜ de conducir kar·*ne* de kon·doo·*theer*

drug droga ⓕ *dro*·ga

drug addiction drogadicción ⓕ dro·ga·deek·*thyon*

drug dealer traficante ⓜ de drogas tra·fee·*kan*·te de *dro*·gas
drums batería ① ba·te·*ree*·a
drumstick (chicken) muslo *moos*·lo
drunk borracho/a ⓜ/① bo·*ra*·cho/a
dry secar se·*kar*
duck pato ⓜ *pa*·to
dummy (pacifier) chupete ⓜ choo·*pe*·te

E

each cada *ka*·da
ear oreja ① o·*re*·kha
early temprano tem·*pra*·no
earn ganar ga·*nar*
earplugs tapones ⓜ pl para los oídos ta·*po*·nes *pa*·ra los o·*ee*·dos
earrings pendientes ⓜ pl pen·*dyen*·tes
Earth Tierra ① *tye*·ra
earthquake terremoto ⓜ te·re·*mo*·to
east este *es*·te
Easter Pascua ① *pas*·kwa
Easter Week Semana ① Santa se·*ma*·na *san*·ta
easy fácil *fa*·theel
eat comer ko·*mer*
economy class clase ① turística *kla*·se too·*rees*·tee·ka
eczema eczema ① ek·*the*·ma
editor editor/editora ⓜ/① e·dee·*tor*/e·dee·*to*·ra
education educación ① e·doo·ka·*thyon*
eggplant berenjenas ① pl be·ren·*khe*·nas
egg huevo ⓜ *we*·vo
elections elecciones ① pl e·lek·*thyo*·nes
electrical store tienda ① de productos eléctricos *tyen*·da de pro·*dook*·tos e·*lek*·tree·kos
electricity electricidad ① e·lek·tree·thee·*da*
elevator ascensor ⓜ as·then·*sor*
embarrassed avergonzado/a ⓜ/① a·ver·gon·*tha*·do/a

embassy embajada ① em·ba·*kha*·da
emergency emergencia ① e·mer·*khen*·thya
emotional emocional e·mo·thyo·*nal*
employee empleado/a ⓜ/① em ple·a·do/a
employer jefe/a ⓜ/① *khe*·fe/a
empty vacío/a ⓜ/① va·*thee*·o/a
end fin ⓜ feen
end acabar a·ka·*bar*
endangered species especies ① pl en peligro de extinción es·*pe*·thyes en pe·*lee*·gro de eks·teen·*thyon*
engagement compromiso ⓜ kom·pro·*mee*·so
engine motor ⓜ mo·*tor*
engineer ingeniero/a ⓜ/① een·khe·*nye*·ro/a
engineering ingeniería ① een·khe·nye·*ree*·a
England Inglaterra ① een·gla·*te*·ra
English inglés ⓜ een·*gles*
enjoy (oneself) divertirse dee·ver·*teer*·se
enough suficiente ⓜ/① soo·fee·*thyen*·te
enter entrar en·*trar*
entertainment guide guía ① del ocio *gee*·a del o·*thyo*
envelope sobre ⓜ *so*·bre
environment medio ⓜ ambiente *me*·dyo am·*byen*·te
epilepsy epilepsia ① e·pee·*lep*·sya
equal opportunity igualdad ① de oportunidades ee·gwal·*da* de o·por·too·nee·*da*·des
equality igualdad ① ee·gwal·*da*
equipment equipo ⓜ e·*kee*·po
escalator escaleras ① pl mecánicas es·ka·*le*·ras me·*ka*·nee·kas
euro euro ⓜ e·oo·ro
Europe Europa ① e·oo·*ro*·pa
euthanasia eutanasia ① e·oo·ta·*na*·sya
evening noche ① *no*·che
everything todo *to*·do

example ejemplo ⓜ e·*khem*·plo
excellent excelente ⓜ/ⓕ
eks·the·*len*·te
exchange cambio ⓜ *kam*·byo
exchange (money) cambiar kam·*byar*
exchange rate tipo ⓜ de cambio
tee·po de *kam*·byo
exchange (give gifts) regalar
re·ga·*lar*
excluded no incluido no
een·kloo·*ee*·do
exhaust tubo ⓜ de escape *too*·bo de
es·*ka*·pe
exhibit exponer eks·po·*ner*
exhibition exposición ⓕ
eks·po·see·*thyon*
exit salida ⓕ sa·*lee*·da
expensive caro/a ⓜ/ⓕ *ka*·ro/a
experience experiencia ⓕ
eks·pe·*ryen*·thya
express expreso/a ⓜ/ⓕ eks·*pre*·so/a
express mail correo ⓜ urgente
ko·re·o oor·*khen*·te
extension (visa) prolongación ⓕ
pro·lon·ga·*thyon*
eye ojo ⓜ o·kho
eye drops gotas ⓕ pl para los ojos
go·tas *pa*·ra los o·khos

F

fabric tela ⓕ *te*·la
face cara ⓕ *ka*·ra
face cloth toallita ⓕ to·a·*lyee*·ta
factory fábrica ⓕ *fa*·bree·ka
factory worker obrero/a ⓜ/ⓕ
o·*bre*·ro/a
fall caída ⓕ ka·*ee*·da
family familia ⓕ fa·*mee*·lya
family name apellido ⓜ a·pe·*lyee*·do
famous famoso/a ⓜ/ⓕ fa·*mo*·so/a
fan (hand held) abanico ⓜ
a·ba·*nee*·ko
fan (electric) ventilador ⓜ
ven·tee·la·*dor*
fanbelt correa ⓕ del ventilador
ko·re·a del ven·tee·la·*dor*

far lejos *le*·khos
farm granja ⓕ *gran*·kha
farmer agricultor/agricultora ⓜ/ⓕ
a·gree·kool·*tor*/a·gree·kool·*to*·ra
fast rápido/a ⓜ/ⓕ *ra*·pee·do/a
fat gordo/a ⓜ/ⓕ *gor*·do/a
father padre ⓜ *pa*·dre
father-in-law suegro ⓜ *swe*·gro
fault falta ⓕ *fal*·ta
faulty defectuoso/a ⓜ/ⓕ
de·fek·*two*·so/a
feed dar de comer dar de ko·*mer*
feel sentir sen·*teer*
feelings sentimientos ⓜ pl
sen·tee·*myen*·tos
fence cerca ⓕ *ther*·ka
fencing esgrima ⓕ es·*gree*·ma
festival festival ⓜ fes·tee·*val*
fever fiebre ⓕ *fye*·bre
few pocos/as ⓜ/ⓕ *po*·kos/as
fiance prometido ⓜ pro·me·*tee*·do
fiancee prometida ⓕ pro·me·*tee*·da
fiction ficción ⓕ feek·*thyon*
field campo ⓜ *kam*·po
fig higo ⓜ *ee*·go
fight pelea ⓕ pe·*le*·a
fight luchar loo·*char*
fill llenar lye·*nar*
fillet filete ⓜ fee·*le*·te
film película ⓕ pe·*lee*·koo·la
film speed sensibilidad ⓕ
sen·see·bee·lee·*da*
filtered con filtro kon *feel*·tro
find encontrar en·kon·*trar*
fine multa ⓕ *mool*·ta
finger dedo ⓜ *de*·do
finish terminar ter·mee·*nar*
fire fuego ⓜ *fwe*·go
firewood leña ⓕ *le*·nya
first primero/a ⓜ/ⓕ pree·*me*·ro/a
first class primera clase pree·*me*·ra
kla·se
first-aid kit maletín ⓜ de primeros
auxilios ma·le·*teen* de pree·*me*·ros
ow·*ksee*·lyos
fish pez ⓜ peth

G

fish (as food) pescado ⓜ pes·*ka*·do
fish shop pescadería ⓕ
pes·ka·de·*ree*·a
fishing pesca ⓕ *pes*·ka
flag bandera ⓕ ban·*de*·ra
flannel franela ⓕ fra·*ne*·la
flashlight linterna ⓕ leen·*ter*·na
flat llano/a ⓜ/ⓕ *lya*·no/a
flea pulga ⓕ *pool*·ga
flooding inundación ⓕ
ee·noon·da·*thyon*
floor suelo ⓜ *swe*·lo
florist florista ⓜ&ⓕ flo·*rees*·ta
flour harina ⓕ a·*ree*·na
flower flor ⓕ flor
flower seller vendedor/vend-
edora ⓜ/ⓕ de flores ven·de·*dor*/
ven·de·*do*·ra de *flo*·res
fly volar vo·*lar*
foggy brumoso/a ⓜ/ⓕ broo·*mo*·so
follow seguir se·*geer*
food comida ⓕ ko·*mee*·da
food supplies víveres ⓜ pl *vee*·ve·res
foot pie ⓜ pye
football fútbol ⓜ *foot*·bol
footpath acera ⓕ a·*the*·ra
foreign extranjero/a ⓜ/ⓕ
eks·tran·*khe*·ro/a
forest bosque ⓜ *bos*·ke
forever para siempre *pa*·ra syem·pre
forget olvidar ol·vee·*dar*
forgive perdonar per·do·*nar*
fork tenedor ⓜ te·ne·*dor*
fortnight quincena ⓕ keen·*the*·na
foul sucio/a ⓜ/ⓕ *soo*·thyo/a
foyer vestíbulo ⓜ ves·*tee*·boo·lo
fragile frágil *fra*·kheel
France Francia ⓕ *fran*·thya
free (not bound) libre *lee*·bre
free (of charge) gratis *gra*·tees
freeze helarse e·*lar*·se
friend amigo/a ⓜ/ⓕ a·*mee*·go/a
frost escarcha ⓕ es·*kar*·cha
frozen foods productos congelados
ⓜ pl pro·*dook*·tos kon·khe·*la*·dos
fruit fruta ⓕ *froo*·ta

fruit picking recolección ⓕ de fruta
re·ko·lek·*thyon* de *froo*·ta
fry freír fre·*eer*
frying pan sartén ⓕ sar·*ten*
full lleno/a ⓜ/ⓕ *lye*·no/a
full-time a tiempo completo a
tyem·po kom·*ple*·to
fun diversión ⓕ dee·ver·*syon*
funeral funeral ⓜ foo·ne·*ral*
funny gracioso/a ⓜ/ⓕ gra·*thyo*·so/a
furniture muebles ⓜ pl *mwe*·bles
future futuro ⓜ foo·*too*·ro

G

gay gay gai
general general khe·ne·*ral*
Germany Alemania ⓕ a·le·*ma*·nya
gift regalo ⓜ re·*ga*·lo
gig bolo ⓜ *bo*·lo
gin ginebra ⓕ khee·*ne*·bra
ginger jengibre ⓜ khen·*khee*·bre
girl chica ⓕ *chee*·ka
girlfriend novia ⓕ *no*·vya
give dar dar
glandular fever fiebre ⓕ glandular
fye·bre glan·doo·*lar*
glass (material) vidrio ⓜ *vee*·dryo
glass (drinking) vaso ⓜ *va*·so
glasses gafas ⓕ pl *ga*·fas
gloves guantes ⓜ pl *gwan*·tes
go ir eer
go out with salir con sa·*leer* kon
go shopping ir de compras eer de
kom·pras
goal gol ⓜ gol
goalkeeper portero/a ⓜ/ⓕ por·*te*·ro/a
goat cabra ⓕ *ka*·bra
goat's cheese queso ⓜ de cabra
ke·so de *ka*·bra
god Dios ⓜ dyos
goggles gafas ⓕ pl de submarinismo
ga·fas de soob·ma·ree·*nees*·mo
golf ball pelota ⓕ de golf pe·*lo*·ta
de golf
golf course campo ⓜ de golf *kam*·po
de golf

H

good bueno/a ⓜ/ⓕ *bwe·no·a*

government gobierno ⓜ *go·byer·no*

gram gramo ⓜ *gra·mo*

grandchild nieto/a ⓜ/ⓕ *nye·to/a*

grandfather abuelo ⓜ *a·bwe·lo*

grandmother abuela ⓕ *a·bwe·la*

grapefruit pomelo ⓜ *po·me·lo*

grapes uvas ⓕ pl *oo·vas*

graphic art arte ⓜ gráfico *ar·te gra·fee·ko*

grass hierba ⓕ *yer·ba*

grave tumba ⓕ *toom·ba*

gray gris *grees*

great fantástico/a ⓜ/ⓕ *fan·tas·tee·ko/a*

green verde *ver·de*

greengrocery (shop) verdulería ⓕ *ver·doo·le·ree·a*

grocer (shopkeeper) verdulero/a ⓜ/ⓕ *ver·doo·le·ro/a*

grey gris *grees*

grocery tienda ⓕ de comestibles *tyen·da de ko·mes·tee·bles*

grow crecer *kre·ther*

g-string tanga ⓕ *tan·ga*

guess adivinar *a·dee·vee·nar*

guide (audio) guía ⓕ audio *gee·a ow·dyo*

guide (person) guía ⓜ&ⓕ *gee·a*

guide dog perro lazarillo ⓜ *pe·ro la·tha·ree·lyo*

guidebook guía ⓕ *gee·a*

guided tour recorrido ⓜ guiado *re·ko·ree·do gee·a·do*

guilty culpable *kool·pa·ble*

guitar guitarra ⓕ *gee·ta·ra*

gum chicle ⓜ *chee·kle*

gymnastics gimnasia ⓕ rítmica *kheem·na·sya reet·mee·ka*

gynaecologist ginecólogo ⓜ *khee·ne·ko·lo·go*

H

hair pelo ⓜ *pe·lo*

hairbrush cepillo ⓜ *the·pee·lyo*

hairdresser peluquero/a ⓜ/ⓕ *pe·loo·ke·ro/a*

halal halal *a·lal*

half medio/a ⓜ/ⓕ *me·dyo/a*

half a litre medio litro ⓜ *me·dyo lee·tro*

hallucinate alucinar *a·loo·thee·nar*

ham jamón ⓜ *kha·mon*

hammer martillo ⓜ *mar·tee·lyo*

hammock hamaca ⓕ *a·ma·ka*

hand mano ⓕ *ma·no*

handbag bolso ⓜ *bol·so*

handicrafts artesanía ⓕ *ar·te·sa·nee·a*

handlebar manillar ⓜ *ma·nee·lyar*

handmade hecho a mano *e·cho a ma·no*

handsome hermoso ⓜ *er·mo·so*

happy feliz *fe·leeth*

harassment acoso ⓜ *a·ko·so*

harbour puerto ⓜ *pwer·to*

hard duro/a ⓜ/ⓕ *doo·ro/a*

hardware store ferretería ⓕ *fe·re·te·ree·a*

hash hachís ⓜ *a·chees*

hat sombrero ⓜ *som·bre·ro*

have tener *te·ner*

have a cold estar constipado/a ⓜ/ⓕ *es·tar kons·tee·pa·do/a*

have fun divertirse *dee·ver·teer·se*

hay fever alergia ⓕ al polen *a·ler·khya al po·len*

he él *el*

head cabeza ⓕ *ka·be·tha*

headache dolor ⓜ de cabeza *do·lor de ka·be·tha*

headlights faros ⓜ pl *fa·ros*

health salud ⓕ *sa·loo*

hear oír *o·eer*

hearing aid audífono ⓜ *ow·dee·fo·no*

heart corazón ⓜ *ko·ra·thon*

heart condition condición ⓕ cardíaca *kon·dee·thyon kar·dee·a·ka*

heat calor ⓜ *ka·lor*

heater estufa ⓕ *es·too·fa*

heavy pesado/a ⓜ/ⓕ *pe·sa·do/a*

I

helmet casco ⓜ *kas*·ko
help ayudar a·yoo·*dar*
hepatitis hepatitis ① e·pa·*tee*·tees
her su soo
herbalist herbolario/a ⓜ/①
er·bo·*la*·ree·o/a
herbs hierbas ① pl *yer*·bas
here aquí a·*kee*
heroin heroína ① e·ro·*ee*·na
herring arenque ⓜ a·*ren*·ke
high alto/a ⓜ/① *al*·to/a
high school instituto ⓜ
eens·tee·*too*·to
hike ir de excursión eer de
eks·koor·*syon*
hiking excursionismo ⓜ
eks·koor·syo·*nees*·mo
hiking boots botas ① pl de montaña
bo·tas de mon·*ta*·nya
hiking routes caminos ⓜ pl rurales
ka·*mee*·nos roo·*ra*·les
hill colina ① ko·*lee*·na
Hindu hindú ⓜ&① een·*doo*
hire alquilar al·kee·*lar*
his su soo
historical histórico/a ⓜ/①
ees·to·*ree*·ko/a
hitchhike hacer dedo a·*ther* de·do
HIV positive seropositivo/a ⓜ/①
se·ro po·see·*tee*·vo/a
hockey hockey ⓜ *kho*·kee
holiday día festivo ⓜ *dee*·a fes·*tee*·vo
holidays vacaciones ① pl
va·ka·*thyo*·nes
homeless sin hogar seen o·*gar*
homemaker ama ① de casa *a*·ma
de *ka*·sa
homosexual homosexual ⓜ&①
o·mo·sek·*swal*
honey miel ① myel
honeymoon luna ① de miel *loo*·na
de myel
horoscope horóscopo ⓜ
o·*ros*·ko·po
horse caballo ⓜ ka·*ba*·lyo
horse riding equitación ①
e·kee·ta·*thyon*

horseradish rábano ⓜ picante
ra·ba·no pee·*kan*·te
hospital hospital ⓜ os·pee·*tal*
hospitality hosteleria ① os·te·le·*ree*·a
hot caliente ka·*lyen*·te
hot water agua caliente ① *a*·gwa
ka·*lyen*·te
hotel hotel ⓜ o·*tel*
house casa ① *ka*·sa
housework trabajo ⓜ de casa
tra·*ba*·kho de *ka*·sa
how cómo *ko*·mo
how much cuánto *kwan*·to
hug abrazo ⓜ a·*bra*·tho
huge enorme e·*nor*·me
human rights derechos ⓜ pl hu·
manos de·*re*·chos oo·*ma*·nos
humanities humanidades ① pl
oo·ma·nee·*da*·des
hungry hambriento/a ⓜ/①
am·*bryen*·to/a
hungry tener hambre te·*ner* am·bre
hunting caza ① *ka*·tha
hurt dañar da·*nyar*
husband marido ⓜ ma·*ree*·do

I

I yo yo
ice hielo ⓜ *ye*·lo
ice axe piolet ⓜ pyo·*le*
ice cream helado ⓜ e·*la*·do
ice cream parlour heladería ①
e·la·de·*ree*·a
ice hockey hockey ⓜ sobre hielo
kho·kee so·bre *ye*·lo
identification identificación ①
ee·den·tee·fee·ka·*thyon*
identification card carnet ⓜ de
identidad kar·*net* de ee·den·tee·*da*
idiot idiota ⓜ&① ee·*dyo*·ta
if si see
ill enfermo/a ⓜ/① en·*fer*·mo/a
immigration inmigración ①
een·mee·gra·*thyon*
important importante eem·por·*tan*·te
in a hurry de prisa de *pree*·sa

in front of enfrente de en·*fren*·te de
included incluido een·kloo·ee·do
income tax impuesto ⓜ sobre la renta eem·*pwes*·to so·bre la *ren*·ta
India India ⓕ een·dya
indicator indicador ⓜ een·dee·ka·*dor*
indigestion indigestión ⓕ een·dee·khes·*tyon*
industry industria ⓕ een·*doos*·trya
infection infección ⓕ een·fek·*thyon*
inflammation inflamación ⓕ een·fla·ma·*thyon*
influenza gripe ⓕ *gree*·pe
ingredient ingrediente ⓜ een·gre·*dyen*·te
inject inyectarse een·yek·*tar*·se
injection inyección ⓕ een·yek·*thyon*
injury herida ⓕ e·*ree*·da
innocent inocente ee·no·*then*·te
inside adentro a·*den*·tro
instructor profesor/profesora ⓜ/ⓕ pro·fe·*sor*/pro·fe·*sor*·ra
insurance seguro ⓜ se·*goo*·ro
interesting interesante een·te·re·*san*·te
intermission descanso ⓜ des·*kan*·so
international internacional een·ter·na·thyo·*nal*
internet internet een·ter·net
internet cafe cibercafé thee·ber·ka·*fe*
interpreter intérprete ⓜ&ⓕ een·*ter*·pre·te
intersection cruce ⓜ *croo*·the
interview entrevista ⓕ en·tre·*vees*·ta
invite invitar een·vee·*tar*
Ireland Irlanda ⓕ eer·*lan*·da
iron plancha ⓕ *plan*·cha
island isla ⓕ *ees*·la
IT informática ⓕ een·for·*ma*·tee·ka
Italy Italia ⓕ ee·*ta*·lya
itch picazón ⓕ pee·ka·*thon*
itemised detallado/a ⓜ/ⓕ de·ta·*lya*·do/a
itinerary itinerario ⓜ ee·tee·ne·*ra*·ryo
IUD DIU ⓜ de·ee·oo

J

jacket chaqueta ⓕ cha·*ke*·ta
jail cárcel ⓕ *kar*·thel
jam mermelada ⓕ mer·me·*la*·da
Japan Japón ⓜ kha·*pon*
jar jarra ⓕ *kha*·ra
jaw mandíbula ⓕ man·*dee*·boo·la
jealous celoso/a ⓜ/ⓕ the·*lo*·so/a
jeans vaqueros ⓜ pl va·*ke*·ros
jeep yip ⓜ yeep
jet lag jet lag ⓜ dyet lag
jewellery shop joyería ⓕ kho·ye·*ree*·a
Jewish judío/a ⓜ/ⓕ khoo·*dee*·o/a
job trabajo ⓜ tra·*ba*·kho
jockey jockey ⓜ *dyo*·kee
juggling footing ⓜ *foo*·teen
joke broma ⓕ *bro*·ma
joke bromear bro·me·*ar*
journalist periodista ⓜ&ⓕ pe·ryo·*dees*·ta
judge juez ⓜ&ⓕ khweth
juice jugo ⓜ *khoo*·go • zumo ⓜ *thoo*·mo
jump saltar sal·*tar*
jumper (sweater) jersey ⓜ kher·*say*
jumper leads cables ⓜ pl de arranque *ka*·bles de a·*ran*·ke

K

ketchup salsa ⓕ de tomate *sal*·sa de to·*ma*·te
key llave ⓕ *lya*·ve
keyboard teclado ⓜ te·*kla*·do
kick dar una patada dar oo·na pa·*ta*·da
kick (a goal) meter (un gol) me·*ter* (oon gol)
kill matar ma·*tar*
kilogram kilogramo ⓜ kee·lo·*gra*·mo
kilometre kilómetro ⓜ kee·*lo*·me·tro
kind amable a·*ma*·ble
kindergarten escuela ⓕ de párvulos es·*kwe*·la de *par*·voo·los
king rey ⓜ rey
kiss beso ⓜ *be*·so
kiss besar be·*sar*

kitchen cocina ① ko·*thee*·na
kitten gatito/a ⓜ/① ga·*tee*·to/a
kiwifruit kiwi ⓜ *kee*·wee
knapsack mochila ① mo·*chee*·la
knee rodilla ① ro·*dee*·lya
knife cuchillo ⓜ koo·*chee*·lyo
know (someone) conocer ko·no·*ther*
know (something) saber sa·*ber*
kosher kosher *ko*·sher

L

labourer obrero/a ⓜ/① o·*bre*·ro/a
lace encaje ⓜ en·*ka*·khe
lager cerveza ① rubia ther·*ve*·tha *roo*·bya
lake lago ⓜ *la*·go
lamb cordero ⓜ kor·*de*·ro
land tierra ① *tye*·ra
landlady propietaria ① pro·pye·*ta*·rya
landlord propietario ⓜ pro·pye·*ta*·ryo
languages idiomas ⓜ pl ee·*dyo*·mas
laptop ordenador ⓜ portátil or·de·na·*dor* por·*ta*·teel
lard manteca ① man·*te*·ka
large grande *gran*·de
late tarde *tar*·de
laugh reírse re·*eer*·se
laundrette lavandería ① la·van·de·*ree*·a
laundry lavadero ⓜ la·va·*de*·ro
law ley ① ley
lawyer abogado/a ⓜ/① a·bo·*ga*·do/a
leader líder ⓜ&① *lee*·der
leaf hoja ① *o*·kha
learn aprender a·pren·*der*
leather cuero ⓜ *kwe*·ro
leave dejar de·*khar*
leave (behind/over) quedar ke·*dar*
lecturer profesor/profesora ⓜ/① pro·fe·*sor*/pro·fe·*so*·ra
ledge saliente ⓜ sa·*lyen*·te
leek puerro ⓜ *pwe*·ro
left izquierda ① eeth·*kyer*·da
left luggage consigna ① kon·*seeg*·na
left-wing de izquierdas de eeth·*kyer*·das

leg pierna ① *pyer*·na
legal legal le·*gal*
legislation legislación ① le·khees·la·*thyon*
lemon limón ⓜ lee·*mon*
lemonade limonada ① lee·mo·*na*·da
lens objetivo ⓜ ob·khe·*tee*·vo
Lent Cuaresma ① kwa·*res*·ma
lentils lentejas ① pl len·*te*·khas
lesbian lesbiana ① les·bee·*a*·na
less menos *me*·nos
letter carta ① *kar*·ta
lettuce lechuga ① le·*choo*·ga
liar mentiroso/a ⓜ/① men·tee·ro·so/a
library biblioteca ① bee·blyo·*te*·ka
lice piojos ⓜ pl *pyo*·khos
license plate number matrícula ① ma·*tree*·koo·la
lie (not stand) tumbarse toom·*bar*·se
life vida ① *vee*·da
lifejacket chaleco ⓜ salvavidas cha·*le*·ko sal·va·*vee*·das
lift ascensor ⓜ as·then·*sor*
light (weight) leve *le*·ve
light luz ① looth
light bulb bombilla ① bom·*bee*·lya
light meter fotómetro ⓜ fo·*to*·me·tro
lighter encendedor ⓜ en·then·de·*dor*
like gustar(le) goos·*tar*(le)
lime lima ① *lee*·ma
line línea ① *lee*·ne·a
lip balm bálsamo ⓜ de labios *bal*·sa·mo de *la*·byos
lips labios ⓜ pl *la*·byos
lipstick pintalabios ⓜ peen·ta·*la*·byos
liquor store bodega ① bo·*de*·ga
listen escuchar es·koo·*char*
live (life) vivir vee·*veer*
live (somewhere) ocupar o·koo·*par*
liver hígado ⓜ *ee*·ga·do
lizard lagartija ① la·gar·*tee*·kha
local de cercanías de ther·ka·*nee*·as
lock cerradura ① the·ra·*doo*·ra
lock cerrar the·*rar*
locked cerrado/a ⓜ/① con llave the·*ra*·do/a kon *lya*·ve

lollies caramelos ⓜ pl ka·ra·me·los
long largo/a ⓜ/ⓕ lar·go/a
long-distance a larga distancia a lar·ga dees·tan·thya
look mirar mee·rar
look after cuidar kwee·dar
look for buscar boos·kar
lookout mirador ⓜ mee·ra·dor
lose perder per·der
lost perdido/a ⓜ/ⓕ per·dee·do/a
lost property office oficina ⓕ de objetos perdidos o·fee·thee·na de ob·khe·tos per·dee·dos
loud ruidoso/a ⓜ/ⓕ rwee·do·so/a
love querer ke·rer
lover amante ⓜ&ⓕ a·man·te
low bajo/a ⓜ/ⓕ ba·kho/a
lubricant lubricante ⓜ loo·bree·kan·te
luck suerte ⓕ swer·te
lucky afortunado/a ⓜ/ⓕ a·for·too·na·do/a
luggage equipaje ⓜ e·kee·pa·khe
luggage lockers consigna ⓕ automática kon·seeg·na ow·to·ma·tee·ka
luggage tag etiqueta ⓕ de equipaje e·tee·ke·ta de e·kee·pa·khe
lump bulto ⓜ bool·to
lunch almuerzo ⓜ al·mwer·tho
lungs pulmones ⓜ pl pool·mo·nes
luxury lujo ⓜ loo·kho

M

machine máquina ⓕ ma·kee·na
made of (cotton) hecho a de (algodón) e·cho a de (al·go·don)
magazine revista ⓕ re·vees·ta
magician mago/a ⓜ/ⓕ ma·go/a
mail correo ⓜ ko·ro·o
mailbox buzón ⓜ boo·thon
main principal preen·thee·pal
make hacer a·ther
make fun of burlarse de boor·lar·se de
make-up maquillaje ⓜ ma·kee·lya·khe
mammogram mamograma ⓜ ma·mo·gra·ma

man hombre ⓜ om·bre
manager gerente ⓜ&ⓕ khe·ren·te
mandarin mandarina ⓕ man·da·ree·na
mango mango ⓜ man·go
manual worker obrero/a ⓜ/ⓕ o·bre·ro/a
many muchos/as ⓜ/ⓕ pl moo·chos/as
map mapa ⓜ ma·pa
margarine margarina ⓕ mar·ga·ree·na
marijuana marihuana ⓕ ma·ree·wa·na
marital status estado ⓜ civil es·ta·do thee·veel
market mercado ⓜ mer·ka·do
marmalade mermelada ⓕ mer·me·la·da
marriage matrimonio ⓜ ma·tree·mo·nyo
marry casarse ka·sar·se
martial arts marciales ⓜ pl ar·tes mar·thya·les
mass misa ⓕ mee·sa
massage masaje ⓜ ma·sa·khe
masseur/masseuse masajista ⓜ&ⓕ ma·sa·khees·ta
mat esterilla ⓕ es·te·ree·lya
match partido ⓜ par·tee·do
matches cerillas ⓕ pl the·ree·lyas
mattress colchón ⓜ kol·chon
maybe quizás kee·thas
mayonnaise mayonesa ⓕ ma·yo·ne·sa
mayor alcalde ⓜ&ⓕ al·kal·de
measles sarampión ⓜ sa·ram·pyon
meat carne ⓕ kar·ne
mechanic mecánico/a ⓜ/ⓕ me·ka·nee·ko
media medios ⓜ pl de comunicación me·dyos de ko·moo·nee·ka·thyon
medicine medicina ⓕ me·dee·thee·na
meditation meditación ⓕ me·dee·ta·thyon
meet encontrar en·kon·trar

melon melón ⓜ me·*lon*

member miembro ⓜ *myem*·bro

menstruation menstruación ⓕ mens·trwa·*thyon*

menu menú ⓜ me·*noo*

message mensaje ⓜ men·*sa*·khe

metal metal ⓜ me·*tal*

metre metro ⓜ *me*·tro

metro station estación ⓕ de metro es·ta·*thyon* de *me*·tro

microwave microondas ⓜ mee·kro·*on*·das

midnight medianoche ⓕ me·dya·*no*·che

migraine migraña ⓕ mee·*gra*·nya

military service servicio ⓜ militar ser·*vee*·thyo mee·lee·*tar*

milk leche ⓕ *le*·che

millimetre milímetro ⓜ mee·*lee*·me·tro

million millón ⓜ mee·*lyon*

mince (meat) carne ⓜ molida *kar*·ne mo·*lee*·da

mind (object) cuidar kwee·*dar*

mineral water agua ⓜ mineral *a*·gwa mee·ne·*ral*

mints pastillas ⓕ pl de menta pas·*tee*·lyas de *men*·ta

minute minuto ⓜ mee·*noo*·to

mirror espejo ⓜ es·*pe*·kho

miscarriage aborto ⓜ natural a·*bor*·to na·too·*ral*

miss (feel sad) echar de menos e·*char* de *me*·nos

mistake error ⓜ e·*ror*

mix mezclar meth·*klar*

mobile phone teléfono ⓜ móvil te·*le*·fo·no *mo*·veel

modem módem ⓜ *mo*·dem

moisturiser crema ⓕ hidratante *kre*·ma ee·dra·*tan*·te

monastery monasterio ⓜ mo·nas·*te*·ryo

money dinero ⓜ dee·*ne*·ro

month mes ⓜ mes

monument monumento ⓜ mo·noo·*men*·to

(full) moon luna ⓕ (llena) *loo*·na (*lye*·na)

morning (6am–1pm) mañana ⓕ ma·*nya*·na

morning sickness náuseas ⓕ pl del embarazo *now*·se·as del em·ba·*ra*·tho

mosque mezquita ⓕ meth·*kee*·ta

mosquito mosquito ⓜ mos·*kee*·to

mosquito coil rollo ⓜ repelente contra mosquitos *ro*·lyo re·pe·*len*·te *kon*·tra mos·*kee*·tos

mosquito net mosquitera ⓕ mos·kee·*te*·ra

mother madre ⓕ *ma*·dre

mother-in-law suegra ⓕ *swe*·gra

motorboat motora ⓕ mo·*to*·ra

motorcycle motocicleta ⓕ mo·to·thee·*kle*·ta

motorway autovía ⓕ ow·to·*vee*·a

mountain montaña ⓕ mon·*ta*·nya

mountain bike bicicleta ⓕ de montaña bee·thee·*kle*·ta de mon·*ta*·nya

mountain path sendero ⓜ sen·*de*·ro

mountain range cordillera ⓕ kor·dee·*lye*·ra

mountaineering alpinismo ⓜ al·pee·*nees*·mo

mouse ratón ⓜ ra·*ton*

mouth boca ⓕ *bo*·ka

movie película ⓕ pe·*lee*·koo·la

mud lodo ⓜ *lo*·do

muesli muesli ⓜ *mwes*·lee

mum mamá ⓕ ma·*ma*

muscle músculo ⓜ *moos*·koo·lo

museum museo ⓜ moo·*se*·o

mushroom champiñón ⓜ cham·pee·*nyon*

music música ⓕ *moo*·see·ka

musician músico/a ⓜ/ⓕ *moo*·see·ko/a

Muslim musulmán/musulmana ⓜ/ⓕ moo·sool·*man*/moo·sool·*ma*·na

mussels mejillones ⓜ pl me·khee·*lyo*·nes

mustard mostaza ⓕ mos·*ta*·tha

mute mudo/a ⓜ/ⓕ *moo·do/a*
my mi *mee*

N

nail clippers cortauñas ⓜ pl
kor·ta·oo·nyas
name nombre ⓜ *nom·bre*
napkin servilleta ⓕ *ser·vee·lye·ta*
nappy pañal ⓜ *pa·nyal*
nappy rash irritación ⓕ de pañal
ee·ree·ta·thyon de pa·nyal
national park parque ⓜ nacional
par·ke na·thyo·nal
nationality nacionalidad ⓕ
na·thyo·na·lee·da
nature naturaleza ⓕ *na·too·ra·le·tha*
naturopathy naturopatia ⓕ
na·too·ro·pa·tya
nausea náusea ⓕ *now·se·a*
near cerca *ther·ka*
nearby cerca *ther·ka*
nearest más cercano/a ⓜ/ⓕ *mas
ther·ka·no/a*
necessary necesario/a ⓜ/ⓕ
ne·the·sa·ryo/a
neck cuello ⓜ *kwe·lyo*
necklace collar ⓜ *ko·lyar*
need necesitar *ne·the·see·tar*
needle (sewing) aguja ⓕ *a·goo·kha*
needle (syringe) jeringa ⓕ
khe·reen·ga
neither tampoco *tam·po·ko*
net red ⓕ *red*
Netherlands Holanda ⓕ *o·lan·da*
never nunca *noon·ka*
new nuevo/a ⓜ/ⓕ *nwe·vo/a*
New Year Año Nuevo ⓜ *a·nyo nwe·vo*
New Year's Eve Nochevieja ⓕ
no·che·vye·kha
New Zealand Nueva Zelanda ⓕ
nwe·va·the·lan·da
news noticias ⓕ pl *no·tee·thyas*
news stand quiosco ⓜ *kyos·ko*
newsagency quiosco ⓜ *kyos·ko*
newspaper periódico ⓜ
pe·ryo·dee·ko

next (month) el próximo (mes) el
prok·see·mo (mes)
next to al lado de al *la·do de*
nice simpático/a ⓜ/ⓕ
seem·pa·tee·ko/a
nickname apodo ⓜ *a·po·do*
night noche ⓕ *no·che*
no no *no*
noisy ruidoso/a ⓜ/ⓕ *rwee·do·so/a*
none nada *na·da*
nonsmoking no fumadores no
foo·ma·do·res
noodles fideos ⓜ pl *fee·de·os*
noon mediodía ⓜ *me·dyo·dee·a*
north norte ⓜ *nor·te*
nose nariz ⓕ *na·reeth*
notebook cuaderno ⓜ *kwa·der·no*
nothing nada *na·da*
now ahora *a·o·ra*
nuclear energy energía ⓕ nuclear
e·ner·khee·a noo·kle·ar
nuclear testing pruebas ⓕ pl
nucleares *prwe·bas noo·kle·a·res*
nuclear waste desperdicios ⓜ
pl nucleares *des·per·dee·thyos
noo·kle·a·res*
number número ⓜ *noo·me·ro*
nun monja ⓕ *mon·kha*
nurse enfermero/a ⓜ/ⓕ
en·fer·me·ro/a
nuts nueces ⓕ pl *nwe·thes*
nuts (raw) nueces ⓕ pl (crudas)
nwe·thes (kroo·das)
nuts (roasted) nueces ⓕ pl
(tostadas) *nwe·thes (tos·ta·das)*

O

oats avena ⓕ *a·ve·na*
ocean océano ⓜ *o·the·a·no*
off (food) pasado/a ⓜ/ⓕ *pa·sa·do/a*
office oficina ⓕ *o·fee·thee·na*
office worker oficinista ⓜ&ⓕ
o·fee·thee·nees·ta
offside fuera de juego *fwe·ra de khwe·go*
often a menudo a *me·noo·do*
oil aceite ⓜ *a·they·te*

P

old viejo/a ⓜ/ⓕ *vye·*kho/a
olive oil aceite ⓜ de oliva a·*they·*te de o·*lee·*va
Olympic Games Juegos ⓜ pl Olímpicos *khwe·*gos o·*leem·*pee·kos
on en en
once vez ⓕ veth
one-way ticket billete ⓜ sencillo bee·*lye·*te sen·*thee·*lyo
onion ⓕ cebolla the·*bo·*lya
only sólo *so·*lo
open abierto/a ⓜ/ⓕ a·*byer·*to/a
open abrir a·*breer*
opening hours horas ⓕ pl de abrir *o·*ras de a·*breer*
opera ópera ⓕ *o·*pe·ra
opera house teatro ⓜ de la ópera te·*a·*tro de la *o·*pe·ra
operation operación ⓕ o·pe·ra·*thyon*
operator operador/operadora ⓜ/ⓕ o·pe·ra·*dor/*o·pe·ra·*do·*ra
opinion opinión ⓕ o·pee·*nyon*
opposite frente a *fren·*te a
or o o
orange (fruit) naranja ⓕ na·*ran·*kha
orange (colour) naranja na·*ran·*kha
orange juice zumo ⓜ de naranja *thoo·*mo de na·*ran·*kha
orchestra orquesta ⓕ or·*kes·*ta
order orden ⓜ *or·*den
order ordenar or·de·*nar*
ordinary corriente ko·*ryen·*te
orgasm orgasmo ⓜ or·*gas·*mo
original original o·ree·khee·*nal*
other otro/a ⓜ/ⓕ *o·*tro/a
our nuestro/a ⓜ/ⓕ *nwes·*tro/a
outside exterior ⓜ eks·te·*ryor*
ovarian cyst quiste ⓜ ovárico *kees·*te o·*va·*ree·ko
oven horno ⓜ *or·*no
overcoat abrigo ⓜ a·*bree·*go
overdose sobredosis ⓕ so·bre·*do·*sees
owe deber de·*ber*
owner dueño/a ⓜ/ⓕ *dwe·*nyo/a
oxygen oxígeno ⓜ ok·*see·*khe·no
oyster ⓕ ostra *os·*tra

ozone layer capa ⓕ de ozono *ka·*pa de o·*tho·*no

P

pacemaker marcapasos ⓜ mar·ka·*pa·*sos
pacifier chupete ⓜ choo·*pe·*te
package paquete ⓜ pa·*ke·*te
packet paquete ⓜ pa·*ke·*te
padlock candado ⓜ kan·*da·*do
page página ⓕ *pa·*khee·na
pain dolor ⓜ do·*lor*
painful doloroso/a ⓜ/ⓕ do·lo·*ro·*so/a
painkillers analgésicos ⓜ pl a·nal·*khe·*see·kos
paint pintar peen·*tar*
painter pintor/pintora ⓜ/ⓕ peen·*tor/*peen·*to·*ra
painting pintura ⓕ peen·*too·*ra
pair (couple) pareja ⓕ pa·*re·*kha
palace palacio ⓜ pa·*la·*thyo
pan cazuela ⓕ ka·*thwe·*la
pants pantalones ⓜ pl pan·ta·*lo·*nes
panty liners salvaeslips ⓜ pl sal·va·e·*sleeps*
pantyhose medias ⓕ pl *me·*dyas
pap smear citología ⓕ thee·to·lo·*khee·*a
paper papel ⓜ pa·*pel*
paperwork trabajo ⓜ administrativo tra·*ba·*kho ad·mee·nees·tra·*tee·*vo
paraplegic parapléjico/a ⓜ/ⓕ pa·ra·ple·*khee·*ko/a
parasailing esqui ⓜ acuático con paracaídas es·*kee* a·*kwa·*tee·ko kon pa·ra·ka·*ee·*das
parcel paquete ⓜ pa·*ke·*te
parents padres ⓜ pl *pa·*dres
park parque ⓜ *par·*ke
park (car) estacionar es·ta·thyo·*nar*
parliament parlamento ⓜ par·la·*men·*to
parsley perejil ⓜ pe·re·*kheel*
part parte ⓕ *par·*te
part-time a tiempo parcial a *tyem·*po par·*thyal*

P

party fiesta ① *fyes*·ta
party (political) partido ⓜ par·*tee*·do
pass pase ⓜ *pa*·se
passenger pasajero/a ⓜ/①
pa·sa·*khe*·ro
passport pasaporte ⓜ pa·sa·*por*·te
passport number número ⓜ de
pasaporte *noo*·me·ro de pa·sa·*por*·te
past pasado ⓜ pa·*sa*·do
pasta pasta ① *pas*·ta
pate (food) paté ⓜ pa·*te*
path sendero ⓜ sen·*de*·ro
pay pagar pa·*gar*
payment pago ⓜ *pa*·go
peace paz ① path
peach melocotón ⓜ me·lo·ko·*ton*
peak cumbre ① *koom*·bre
peanuts cacahuetes ⓜ pl
ka·ka·*we*·tes
pear pera ① *pe*·ra
peas guisantes ⓜ pl gee·*san*·tes
pedal pedal ⓜ pe·*dal*
pedestrian peatón ⓜ&① pe·a·*ton*
pedestrian crossing paso ⓜ de
cebra pa·so de *the*·bra
pen bolígrafo ⓜ bo·*lee*·gra·fo
pencil lápiz ⓜ *la*·peeth
penis pene ⓜ *pe*·ne
penknife navaja ① na·*va*·kha
pensioner pensionista ⓜ&①
pen·syo·*nees*·ta
people gente ① *khen*·te
pepper (vegetable) pimiento ⓜ
pee·*myen*·to
pepper (spice) pimienta ①
pee·*myen*·ta
per (day) por (dia) por (*dee*·a)
percent por ciento por *thyen*·to
performance actuación ①
ak·twa·*thyon*
perfume perfume ⓜ per·*foo*·me
period pain dolor ⓜ menstrual do·*lor*
mens·*trwal*
permission permiso ⓜ per·*mee*·so
permit permiso ⓜ per·*mee*·so
permit permitir per·mee·*teer*

person persona ① per·*so*·na
perspire sudar soo·*dar*
petition petición ① pe·tee·*thyon*
petrol gasolina ① ga·so·*lee*·na
pharmacy farmacia ① far·*ma*·thya
phone book guía ① telefónica gee·a
te·le·*fo*·nee·ka
phone box cabina ① telefónica
ka·*bee*·ka te·le·*fo*·nee·ka
phone card tarjeta ① de teléfono
tar·*khe*·ta de te·le·*fo*·no
photo foto ① *fo*·to
photographer fotógrafo/a ⓜ/①
to·*to*·gra·fo/a
photography fotografía ①
fo·to·gra·*fee*·a
phrasebook libro ⓜ de frases *lee*·bro
de *fra*·ses
pick up ligar lee·*gar*
pickaxe piqueta ① pee·*ke*·ta
pickles encurtidos ⓜ pl
en·koor·*tee*·dos
picnic comida ① en el campo
ko·*mee*·da en el *kam*·po
ple pastel ⓜ pas·*tel*
piece pedazo ⓜ pe·*da*·tho
pig cerdo ⓜ *ther*·do
pill pastilla ① pas·*tee*·lya
pill, the (contraceptive) píldora ①
peel·do·ra
pillow almohada ① al·*mwa*·da
pillowcase funda ① de almohada
foon·da de al·*mwa*·da
pineapple piña ① *pee*·nya
pink rosa *ro*·sa
pistachio pistacho ⓜ pees·*ta*·cho
place lugar ⓜ loo·*gar*
place of birth lugar ⓜ de nacimiento
loo·*gar* de na·thee·*myen*·to
plane avión ⓜ a·*vyon*
planet planeta ⓜ pla·*ne*·ta
plant planta ① *plan*·ta
plant sembrar sem·*brar*
plastic plástico ⓜ *plas*·tee·ko
plate plato ⓜ *pla*·to
plateau meseta ① me·*se*·ta

P

platform plataforma ① pla·ta·for·ma
play obra ① o·bra
play (musical instrument) tocar to·kar
play (sport/games) jugar khoo·gar
plug tapar ta·par
plum ciruela thee·rwe·la
pocket bolsillo ⑩ bol·see·lyo
poetry poesía ① po·e·se·a
point apuntar a·poon·tar
point (tip) punto ⑩ poon·to
poisonous venenoso/a ⑩/① ve·ne·no·so/a
poker póquer ⑩ po·ker
police policía ① po·lee·thee·a
police station comisaría ① ko·mee·sa·ree·a
policy política ① po·lee·tee·ka
policy (insurance) póliza ① po·lee·tha
politician político ⑩ po·lee·tee·ko
politics política ① po·lee·tee·ka
pollen polen ⑩ po·len
polls sondeos ⑩ pl son·de·os
pollution contaminación ① kon·ta·mee·na·thyon
pool (swimming) piscina ① pees·thee·na
poor pobre po·bre
popular popular po·poo·lar
pork cerdo ⑩ ther·do
pork sausage chorizo ⑩ cho·ree·tho
port puerto ⑩ pwer·to
port (wine) oporto ⑩ o·por·to
possible posible po·see·ble
post code código postal ⑩ ko·dee·go pos·tal
post office correos ⑩ ko·re·os
postage franqueo ⑩ fran·ke·o
postcard postal ① pos·tal
poster póster ⑩ pos·ter
pot (kitchen) cazuela ① ka·thwe·la
pot (plant) tiesto ⑩ tyes·to
potato patata ① pa·ta·ta
pottery alfarería ① al·fa·re·ree·a
pound (money) libra ① lee·bra

poverty pobreza ① po·bre·tha
power poder ⑩ po·der
prawns gambas ① pl gam·bas
prayer oración ① o·ra·thyon
prayer book devocionario ⑩ de·vo·thyo·na·ryo
prefer preferir pre·fe·reer
pregnancy test prueba ① del embarazo prwe·ba del em·ba·ra·tho
pregnant embarazada ① em·ba·ra·tha·da
premenstrual tension tensión ① premenstrual ten·syon pre·mens·trwal
prepare preparar pre·pa·rar
president presidente/a ⑩/① pre·see·den·te/a
pressure presión ① pre·syon
pretty bonito/a ⑩/① bo·nee·to/a
prevent prevenir pre·ve·neer
price precio ⑩ pre·thyo
priest sacerdote ⑩ sa·ther·do·te
prime minister primer ministro/ primera ministra ⑩/① pree·mer mee·nees·tro/pree·me·ra mee·nees·tra
prison cárcel ① kar·thel
prisoner prisionero/a ⑩/① pree·syon·ne·ro/a
private privado/a ⑩/① pree·va·do/a
private hospital clínica ① klee·nee·ka
produce producir pro·doo·theer
profit beneficio ⑩ be·ne·fee·thyo
programme programa ⑩ pro·gra·ma
projector proyector ⑩ pro·yek·tor
promise promesa ① pro·me·sa
protect proteger pro·te·kher
protected (species) protegido/a ⑩/① pro·te·khee·do/a
protest protesta ① pro·tes·ta
protest protestar pro·tes·tar
provisions provisiones ① pl pro·vee·syo·nes
prune ciruela ① pasa thee·rwe·la pa·sa
pub pub ⑩ poob
public telephone teléfono ⑩ público te·le·fo·no poo·blee·ko

public toilet servicios ⓜ pl
ser·vee·thyos
pull tirar tee·rar
pump bomba ⓕ bom·ba
pumpkin calabaza ⓕ ka·la·ba·tha
puncture pinchar peen·char
punish castigar kas·tee·gar
puppy cachorro ⓜ ka·cho·ro
pure puro/a ⓜ/ⓕ poo·ro/a
purple lila lee·la
push empujar em·poo·khar
put poner po·ner

Q

qualifications cualificaciones ⓕ pl
kwa·lee·fee·ka·thyo·nes
quality calidad ⓕ ka·lee·da
quarantine cuarentena ⓕ
kwa·ren·te·na
quarrel pelea ⓕ pe·le·a
quarter cuarto ⓜ kwar·to
queen reina ⓕ rey·na
question pregunta ⓕ pre·goon·ta
question cuestionar kwes·tyo·nar
queue cola ⓕ ko·la
quick rápido/a ⓜ/ⓕ ra·pee·do/a
quiet tranquilo/a ⓜ/ⓕ tran·kee·lo/a
quiet tranquilidad ⓕ tran·kee·lee·da
quit dejar de·khar

R

rabbit conejo ⓜ ko·ne·kho
race (people) raza ⓕ ra·tha
race (sport) carrera ⓕ ka·re·ra
racetrack (bicycles) velódromo ⓜ
ve·lo·dro·mo
racetrack (cars) circuito ⓜ de
carreras theer·kwee·to de ka·re·ras
racetrack (horses) hipódromo ⓜ
ee·po·dro·mo
racetrack (runners) pista ⓕ pees·ta
racing bike bicicleta ⓕ de carreras
bee·thee·kle·ta de ka·re·ras
racquet raqueta ⓕ ra·ke·ta
radiator radiador ⓜ ra·dya·dor
radish rábano ⓜ ra·ba·no

railway station estación ⓕ de tren
es·ta·thyon de tren
rain lluvia ⓕ lyoo·vya
raincoat impermeable ⓜ
eem·per·me·a·ble
raisin uva ⓕ pasa oo·va pa·sa
rally concentración ⓕ
kon·then·tra·thyon
rape violar vyo·lar
rare raro/a ⓜ/ⓕ ra·ro/a
rash irritación ⓕ ee·ree·ta·thyon
raspberry frambuesa ⓕ fram·bwe·sa
rat rata ⓕ ra·ta
rate of pay salario ⓜ sa·la·ryo
raw crudo/a ⓜ/ⓕ kroo·do/a
razor afeitadora ⓕ a·fey·ta·do·ra
razor blades cuchillas ⓕ pl de afeitar
koo·chee·lyas de a·fey·tar
read leer le·er
ready listo/a ⓜ/ⓕ lees·to/a
real estate agent agente inmobiliario
ⓜ a·khen·te een·mo·bee·lya·ryo
realise darse cuenta de dar·se
kwen·ta de
realistic realista re·a·lees·ta
reason razón ⓕ ra·thon
receipt recibo ⓜ re·thee·bo
receive recibir re·thee·beer
recently recientemente
re·thyen·te·men·te
recognise reconocer re·ko·no·ther
recommend recomendar
re·ko·men·dar
recording grabación ⓕ gra·ba·thyon
recyclable reciclable re·thee·kla·ble
recycle reciclar re·thee·klar
red rojo/a ⓜ/ⓕ ro·kho/a
referee árbitro ⓜ ar·bee·tro
reference referencias ⓕ pl
re·fe·ren·thyas
refrigerator nevera ⓕ ne·ve·ra •
frigerífico ⓜ free·ge·ree·fee·ko
refugee refugiado/a ⓜ/ⓕ
re·foo·khya·do/a
refund reembolso ⓜ re·em·bol·so
refund reembolsar re·em·bol·sar
refuse negar ne·gar

registered mail correo Ⓜ certificado ko·*re*·o ther·*tee*·fee·*ka*·do
regret lamentar la·men·*tar*
relationship relación Ⓕ re·la·*thyon*
relax relajarse re·la·*khar*·se
relic reliquia Ⓕ re·*lee*·kya
religion religión Ⓕ re·lee·*khyon*
religious religioso/a Ⓜ/Ⓕ re·lee·*khyo*·so/a
remember recordar re·kor·*dar*
remote remoto/a Ⓜ/Ⓕ re·*mo*·to/a
remote control mando Ⓜ a distancia *man*·do a dees·*tan*·thya
rent alquiler Ⓜ al·kee·*ler*
rent alquilar al·kee·*lar*
repair reparar re·pa·*rar*
repeat repetir re·pe·*teer*
republic república Ⓕ re·*poo*·blee·ka
reservation reserva Ⓕ re·*ser*·va
reserve reservar re·ser·*var*
rest descansar des·kan·*sar*
restaurant restaurante Ⓜ res·tow·*ran*·te
retired jubilado/a Ⓜ/Ⓕ khoo·bee·*la*·do/a
return volver vol·*ver*
return ticket billete Ⓜ de ida y vuelta bee·*lye*·te de *ee*·da ee *vwel*·ta
review crítica Ⓕ *kree*·tee·ka
rhythm ritmo Ⓜ *reet*·mo
rice arroz Ⓜ a·*roth*
rich rico/a Ⓜ/Ⓕ *ree*·ko/a
ride paseo Ⓜ pa·*se*·o
ride montar mon·*tar*
right (correct) correcto/a Ⓜ/Ⓕ ko·*rek*·to/a
right (not left) derecha de·*re*·cha
right-wing derechista de·re·*chees*·ta
ring (phone) llamada Ⓕ lya·*ma*·da
ring llamar por telefono lya·*mar* por te·*le*·fo·no
rip-off estafa Ⓕ es·*ta*·fa
risk riesgo Ⓜ *ryes*·go
river río Ⓜ *ree*·o
road carretera Ⓕ ka·re·*te*·ra
rob robar ro·*bar*
rock (stone) roca Ⓕ *ro*·ka

rock (music) rock Ⓜ rok
rock climbing escalada Ⓕ es·ka·*la*·da
rock group grupo Ⓜ de rock *groo*·po de rok
rollerblading patinar pa·*tee*·nar
romantic romántico/a Ⓜ/Ⓕ ro·*man*·tee·ko/a
room habitación Ⓕ a·bee·ta·*thyon*
room number número Ⓜ de la habitación *noo*·me·ro de la a·bee·ta·*thyon*
rope cuerda Ⓕ *kwer*·da
round redondo/a Ⓜ/Ⓕ re·*don*·do/a
roundabout glorieta Ⓕ glo·*rye*·ta
route ruta Ⓕ *roo*·ta
rowing remo Ⓜ *re*·mo
rubbish basura Ⓕ ba·*soo*·ra
rug alfombra Ⓕ al·*fom*·bra
rugby rugby Ⓜ *roog*·bee
ruins ruinas Ⓕ pl *rwee*·nas
rules reglas Ⓕ pl *re*·glas
rum ron ron
run correr ko·*rer*
run out of quedarse sin ke·*dar*·se seen

sad triste *trees*·te
saddle sillín Ⓜ see·*lyeen*
safe seguro/a Ⓜ/Ⓕ se·*goo*·ro/a
safe caja Ⓕ fuerte *ka*·kha *fwer*·te
safe sex sexo Ⓜ seguro *sek*·so se·*goo*·ro
saint santo/a Ⓜ/Ⓕ *san*·to/a
salad ensalada Ⓕ en·sa·*la*·da
salami (Spanish sausage) chorizo cho·*ree*·tho
salary salario Ⓜ sa·*la*·ryo
sales tax IVA Ⓜ *ee*·va
salmon salmón Ⓜ sal·*mon*
salt sal Ⓕ sal
same igual ee·*gwal*
sand arena Ⓕ a·*re*·na
sandals sandalias Ⓕ pl san·*da*·lyas
sanitary napkins compresas Ⓕ pl kom·*pre*·sas

sauna sauna ⓕ *sow*·na
sausage salchicha ⓕ sal·*chee*·cha
save salvar sal·*var*
save (money) ahorrar a·o·*rar*
say decir de·*theer*
scale/climb trepar tre·*par*
scarf bufanda ⓕ boo·*fan*·da
school escuela ⓕ es·*kwe*·la
science ciencias ⓕ pl *thyen*·thyas
scientist científico/a ⓜ/ⓕ *thyen·tee·fee·ko/a*
scissors tijeras ⓕ pl tee·*khe*·ras
score marcar mar·*kar*
scoreboard marcador ⓜ mar·ka·*dor*
Scotland Escocia ⓕ es·*ko*·thya
screen pantalla ⓕ pan·*ta*·lva
script guión ⓜ *gee*·on
sculpture escultura ⓕ es·kool·*too*·ra
sea mar ⓜ mar
seasick mareado/a ⓜ/ⓕ ma·re·*a*·do/a
seaside costa ⓕ *kos*·ta
season estación ⓕ es·ta·*thyon*
season (in sport) temporada ⓕ tem·po·*ra*·da
seat asiento ⓜ a·*syen*·to
seatbelt cinturón ⓜ de seguridad theen·too·ron de se·goo·ree·*da*
second (place) segundo/a ⓜ/ⓕ se·*goon*·do/a
second (time) segundo ⓜ se·*goon*·do
secondhand de segunda mano de se·*goon*·da *ma*·no
secretary secretario/a ⓜ/ⓕ se·kre·*ta*·ryo/a
see ver ver
selfish egoísta e·go·*ees*·ta
self-service autoservicio ⓜ ow·to·ser·*vee*·thyo
sell vender ven·*der*
send enviar en·vee·*ar*
sensible prudente proo·*den*·te
sensual sensual sen·*swal*
separate separado/a ⓜ/ⓕ se·pa·*ra*·do/a
separate separar se·pa·*rar*
series serie ⓕ *se*·rye

serious serio/a ⓜ/ⓕ *se*·ryo/a
service station gasolinera ⓕ ga·so·lee·*ne*·ra
service charge carga ⓕ *kar*·ga
several varias/os ⓜ/ⓕ *va*·ryas/os
sew coser ko·*ser*
sex sexo ⓜ *sek*·so
sexism machismo ⓜ ma·*chees*·mo
sexy sexy *sek*·see
shadow sombra ⓕ *som*·bra
shampoo champú ⓜ cham·*poo*
shape forma ⓕ *for*·ma
share (a dorm) compartir (un dormitorio) kom·par·*teer* (oon dor·mee·to·ryo)
share (with) compartir kom·par·*teer*
shave afeitarse a·fey·*tar*·se
shaving cream espuma ⓕ de afeitar es·*poo*·ma de a·fey·*tar*
she ella ⓕ *e*·lya
sheep oveja ⓕ o·*ve*·kha
sheet (bed) sábana ⓕ *sa*·ba·na
sheet (of paper) hoja ⓕ *o*·kha
shelf estante ⓜ es·*tan*·te
ship barco ⓜ *bar*·ko
ship enviar en·vee·*ar*
shirt camisa ⓕ ka·*mee*·sa
shoe shop zapatería ⓕ tha·pa·te·*ree*·a
shoes zapatos ⓜ pl tha·*pa*·tos
shoot disparar dees·pa·*rar*
shop tienda ⓕ *tyen*·da
shoplifting ratería ⓕ ra·te·*ree*·a
shopping centre centro ⓜ comercial *then*·tro ko·mer·*thyal*
short (height) bajo/a ⓜ/ⓕ *ba*·kho/a
short (length) corto/a ⓜ/ⓕ *kor*·to/a
shortage escasez ⓕ es·ka·*seth*
shorts pantalones ⓜ pl cortos *kor*·tos pan·ta·*lo*·nes
shoulders hombros ⓜ pl *om*·bros
shout gritar gree·*tar*
show espectáculo ⓜ es·pek·*ta*·koo·lo
show mostrar mos·*trar*
show enseñar en·se·*nyar*
shower ducha ⓕ *doo*·cha

S

shrine capilla ① ka·*pee*·lya
shut cerrado/a ⑩/① the·*ra*·do/a
shut cerrar the·*rar*
shy tímido/a ⑩/① *tee*·mee·do/a
sick enfermo/a ⑩/① en·*fer*·mo/a
side lado ⑩ *la*·do
sign señal ① se·*nyal*
sign firmar feer·*mar*
signature firma ① *feer*·ma
silk seda ① *se*·da
silver plateado/a ⑩/① pla·te·a·do/a
silver plata ① *pla*·ta
similar similar see·mee·*lar*
simple sencillo/a ⑩/① sen·*thee*·lyo/a
since desde (mayo) *des*·de (*ma*·yo)
sing cantar kan·*tar*
Singapore Singapur ⑩ seen·ga·*poor*
singer cantante ⑩&① kan·*tan*·te
single soltero/a ⑩/① sol·*te*·ro/a
single room habitación ① individual
a·bee·ta·*thyon* een·dee·vee·*dwal*
singlet camiseta ① ka·mee·*se*·ta
sister hermana ① er·*ma*·na
sit sentarse sen·*tar*·se
size (clothes) talla ① *ta*·lya
skateboarding monopatinaje ⑩
mo·no·pa·tee·*na*·khe
ski esquiar es·kee·*ar*
skiing esquí ⑩ es·*kee*
skimmed milk leche ① desnatada
le·che des·na·*ta*·da
skin piel ① pyel
skirt falda ① *fal*·da
sky cielo ⑩ *thye*·lo
skydiving paracaidismo ⑩
pa·ra·kai·*dees*·mo
sleep dormir dor·*meer*
sleeping bag saco ⑩ de dormir *sa*·ko
de dor·*meer*
sleeping car coche cama ⑩ *ko*·che
ka·ma
sleeping pills pastillas ① pl para
dormir pas·*tee*·lyas *pa*·ra dor·*meer*
(to be) sleepy tener sueño te·*ner*
swe·nyo
slide diapositiva ① dya·po·see·*tee*·va

slow lento/a ⑩/① *len*·to/a
slowly despacio des·*pa*·thyo
small pequeño/a ⑩/① pe·*ke*·nyo/a
smell olor ⑩ o·*lor*
smell oler o·*ler*
smile sonreír son·re·*eer*
smoke fumar foo·*mar*
snack tentempié ⑩ ten·tem·*pye*
snail caracol ⑩ ka·ra·*kol*
snake serpiente ① ser·*pyen*·te
snorkel tubos ⑩ pl respiratorios
too·bos res·pee·ra·*to*·ryos
snorkel buceo ⑩ boo·*the*·o
snow nieve ① *nye*·ve
snowboarding surf ⑩ sobre la nieve
soorf *so*·bre la *nye*·ve
soap jabón ⑩ kha·*bon*
soap opera telenovela ①
te·le·no·*ve*·la
soccer fútbol ⑩ *foot*·bol
social welfare estado ⑩ del
bienestar es·*ta*·do del byen·es·*tar*
socialist socialista ⑩&①
so·thya·*lees*·ta
socks calcetines ⑩ pl kal·the·*tee*·nes
soft drink refresco ⑩ re·*fres*·ko
soldier soldado ⑩ sol·*da*·do
some alguno/a ⑩/① al·*goon*/al·*goo*·na
someone alguien al·*gyen*
something algo *al*·go
sometimes de vez en cuando de veth
en *kwan*·do
son hijo ⑩ *ee*·kho
song canción ① kan·*thyon*
soon pronto *pron*·to
sore dolorido/a ⑩/① do·lo·*ree*·do/a
soup sopa ① *so*·pa
sour cream nata ① agria *na*·ta *a*·grya
south sur ⑩ soor
souvenir recuerdo ⑩ re·*kwer*·do
souvenir shop tienda ① de recuerdos
tyen·da de re·*kwer*·dos
soy milk leche ① de soja *le*·che de
so·kha
soy sauce salsa ① de soja *sal*·sa de
so·kha

space espacio ⓜ es·pa·thyo

Spain España ⓕ es·pa·nya

sparkling espumoso/a ⓜ/ⓕ es·poo·mo·so

speak hablar a·blar

special especial es·pe·thyal

specialist especialista ⓜ&ⓕ es·pe·thya·lees·ta

speed velocidad ⓕ ve·lo·thee·da

speeding exceso ⓜ de velocidad eks·the·so de ve·lo·thee·da

speedometer velocímetro ⓜ ve·lo·thee·me·tro

spider araña ⓕ a·ra·nya

spinach espinacas ⓕ pl es·pee·na·kas

spoon cuchara ⓕ koo·cha·ra

sport deportes ⓜ pl de·por·tes

sports store tienda ⓕ deportiva tyen·da de·por·tee·va

sportsperson deportista ⓜ&ⓕ de·por·lees·ta

sprain torcedura ⓕ tor·the·doo·ra

spring (wire) muelle ⓜ mwe·lye

spring (season) primavera ⓕ pree·ma·ve·ra

square (shape) cuadrado ⓜ kwa·dra·do

(main) square plaza ⓕ (mayor) pla·tha (ma·yor)

stadium estadio ⓜ es·ta·dyo

stage escenario ⓜ es·the·na·ryo

stairway escalera ⓕ es·ka·le·ra

stamp sello ⓜ se·lyo

standby ticket billete ⓜ de lista de espera bee·lye·te de lees·ta de es·pe·ra

stars estrellas ⓕ pl es·tre·lyas

start comenzar ko·men·thar

station estación ⓕ es·ta·thyon

statue estatua ⓕ es·ta·twa

stay (remain) quedarse ke·dar·se

stay (somewhere) alojarse a·lo·khar·se

steak (beef) bistec ⓜ bees·tek

steal robar ro·bar

steep escarpado/a ⓜ/ⓕ es·kar·pa·do/a

step paso ⓜ pa·so

stereo equipo ⓜ de música e·kee·po de moo·see·ka

stingy tacaño/a ⓜ/ⓕ ta·ka·nyo/a

stock caldo ⓜ kal·do

stockings medias ⓕ pl me·dyas

stomach estómago ⓜ es·to·ma·go

stomachache dolor ⓜ de estómago do·lor de es·to·ma·go

stone piedra ⓕ pye·dra

stoned colocado/a ⓜ/ⓕ ko·lo·ka·do/a

stop parada ⓕ pa·ra·da

stop parar pa·rar

storm tormenta ⓕ tor·men·ta

story cuento ⓜ kwen·to

stove cocina ⓕ ko·thee·na

straight recto/a ⓜ/ⓕ rek·to/a

strange extraño/a ⓜ/ⓕ ek·stra·nyo/a

stranger desconocido/a ⓜ/ⓕ des·ko·no·thee·do/a

strawberry fresa ⓕ fre·sa

stream arroyo ⓜ a·ro·yo

street calle ⓕ ka·lye

string cuerda ⓕ kwer·da

strong fuerte fwer·te

stubborn testarudo/a ⓜ/ⓕ tes·ta·roo·do/a

student estudiante ⓜ&ⓕ es·too·dyan·te

studio estudio ⓜ es·too·dyo

stupid estúpido/a ⓜ/ⓕ es·too·pee·do/a

style estilo ⓜ es·tee·lo

subtitles subtítulos ⓜ pl soob·tee·too·los

suburb barrio ⓜ ba·ryo

subway parada ⓕ de metro pa·ra·da de me·tro

suffer sufrir soo·freer

sugar azúcar ⓜ a·thoo·kar

suitcase maleta ⓕ ma·le·ta

summer verano ⓜ ve·ra·no

sun sol ⓜ sol

sunblock crema ⓕ solar kre·ma so·lar

sunburn quemadura ⓕ de sol ke·ma·doo·ra de sol

T

sun-dried tomato tomate ⓜ secado al sol to·*ma*·te se·*ka*·do al sol

sunflower oil aceite ⓜ de girasol a·*they*·te de khee·ra·*sol*

sunglasses gafas ⓕ pl de sol *ga*·fas de sol

(to be) sunny hace sol a·the sol

sunrise amanecer ⓜ a·ma·ne·*ther*

sunset puesta ⓕ del sol *pwes*·ta del sol

supermarket supermercado ⓜ soo·per·mer·*ka*·do

superstition superstición ⓕ soo·pers·tee·*thyon*

supporters hinchas ⓜ&ⓕ pl *een*·chas

surf hacer surf a·*ther* soorf

surface mail por vía terrestre por *vee*·a te·*res*·tre

surfboard tabla de surf ⓕ *ta*·bla de soorf

surname apellido ⓜ a·pe·*lyee*·do

surprise sorpresa ⓕ sor·*pre*·sa

survive sobrevivir so·bre·vee·*veer*

sweater jersey ⓜ kher·*sey*

Sweden Suecia ⓕ *swe*·thya

sweet dulce *dool*·the

sweets (candy) dulces ⓜ pl *dool*·thes

swim nadar na·*dar*

swimming pool piscina ⓕ pees·*thee*·na

swimsuit bañador ⓜ ba·nya·*dor*

Switzerland Suiza ⓕ *swee*·tha

synagogue sinagoga ⓕ see·na·go·ga

synthetic sintético/a ⓜ/ⓕ seen·*te*·tee·ko/a

syringe jeringa ⓕ khe·*reen*·ga

T

table mesa ⓕ *me*·sa

table tennis ping pong ⓜ peeng pong

tablecloth mantel ⓜ man·*tel*

tail rabo ⓜ *ra*·bo

tailor sastre ⓜ *sas*·tre

take (away) llevar lye·*var*

take (the train) tomar to·*mar*

take (photo) sacar sa·*kar*

take photographs sacar fotos sa·*kar* *fo*·tos

talk hablar a·*blar*

tall alto/a ⓜ/ⓕ *al*·to/a

tampons tampones ⓜ pl tam·*po*·nes

tanning lotion bronceador ⓜ bron·the·a·*dor*

tap grifo ⓜ *gree*·fo

tasty sabroso/a ⓜ/ⓕ sa·*bro*·so/a

taxes impuestos ⓜ pl eem·*pwes*·tos

taxi taxi ⓜ *tak*·see

taxi stand parada ⓕ de taxis pa·*ra*·da de *tak*·sees

tea té ⓜ te

teacher profesor/profesora ⓜ/ⓕ pro·fe·*sor*/pro·fe·*so*·ra

team equipo ⓜ e·*kee*·po

teaspoon cucharita ⓕ koo·cha·*ree*·ta

technique técnica ⓕ *tek*·nee·ka

teeth dientes ⓜ pl *dyen*·tes

telegram telegrama ⓜ te·le·*gra*·ma

telephone teléfono ⓜ te·*le*·fo·no

telephone llamar (por teléfono) lya·*mar* (por te·*le*·fo·no)

telephone centre central ⓕ telefónica then·*tral* te·le·*fo*·nee·ka

telescope telescopio ⓜ te·les·ko·pyo

television televisión ⓕ te·le·vee·*syon*

tell decir de·*theer*

temperature (fever) fiebre ⓕ *fye*·bre

temperature (weather) temperatura ⓕ tem·pe·ra·*too*·ra

temple templo ⓜ *tem*·plo

tennis tenis ⓜ *te*·nees

tennis court pista ⓕ de tenis *pees*·ta de *te*·nees

tent tienda ⓕ (de campaña) *tyen*·da (de kam·*pa*·nya)

tent pegs piquetas ⓕ pl pee·*ke*·tas

terrible terrible te·*ree*·ble

test prueba ⓕ *prwe*·ba

thank dar gracias dar *gra*·thyas

theatre teatro ⓜ te·a·tro

their su soo

they ellos/ellas ⓜ/ⓕ e·lyos/e·lyas
thief ladrón/ladrona ⓜ/ⓕ la·dron/ la·dro·na
thin delgado/a ⓜ/ⓕ del·ga·do/a
think pensar pen·sar
third tercio ⓜ ter·thyo
thirst sed ⓕ se
this ésto/a ⓜ/ⓕ es·te/a
this month este mes es·te mes
thread hilo ⓜ ee·lo
throat garganta ⓕ gar·gan·ta
ticket billete ⓜ bee·lye·te
ticket collector revisor/revisora ⓜ/ⓕ re·vee·sor/re·vee·so·ra
ticket machine máquina ⓕ de billetes ma·kee·na de bee·lye·tes
ticket office taquilla ⓕ ta·kee·lya
tide marea ⓕ ma·re·a
tight apretado/a ⓜ/ⓕ a·pre·ta·do/a
time (watch) hora ⓕ o·ra
time (passing) tiempo ⓜ tyem·po
time difference diferencia ⓕ de horas de·fe·ren·thya de o·ras
timetable horario ⓜ o·ra·ryo
tin hojalata ⓕ o·kha·la·ta
tin opener abrelatas ⓜ a·bre·la·tas
tiny pequeñito/a ⓜ/ⓕ pe·ke·nyee·to/a
tip propina ⓕ pro·pee·na
tired cansado/a ⓜ/ⓕ kan·sa·do/a
tissues pañuelos ⓜ pl de papel pa·nywe·los de pa·pel
toast tostada ⓕ tos·ta·da
toaster tostadora ⓕ tos·ta·do·ra
tobacco tabaco ⓜ ta·ba·ko
tobacconist estanquero ⓜ es·tan·ke·ro
tobogganing ir en tobogán eer en to·bo·gan
today hoy oy
toe dedo ⓜ del pie de·do del pye
tofu tofú ⓜ to·foo
together juntos/as ⓜ/ⓕ khoon·tos/as
toilet servicio ⓜ ser·vee·thyo
toilet paper papel ⓜ higiénico pa·pel ee·khye·nee·ko

tomato tomate ⓜ to·ma·te
tomato sauce salsa ⓕ de tomate sal·sa de to·ma·te
tomorrow mañana ma·nya·na
tomorrow afternoon mañana por la tarde ma·nya·na por la tar·de
tomorrow evening mañana por la noche ma·nya·na por la no·che
tomorrow morning mañana por la mañana ma·nya·na por la ma·nya·na
tone tono ⓜ to·no
tonight esta noche es·ta no·che
too (expensive) demasiado (caro/a) ⓜ/ⓕ de·ma·sya·do (ka·ro/a)
tooth diente ⓜ dyen·te
tooth (back) muela ⓕ mwe·la
toothache dolor ⓜ de muelas do·lor de mwe·las
toothbrush cepillo ⓜ de dientes the·pee·lyo de dyen·tes
toothpaste pasta ⓕ dentífrica pas·ta den·tee·free·ka
toothpick palillo ⓜ pa·lee·lyo
torch linterna ⓕ leen·ter·na
touch tocar to·kar
tour excursión ⓕ eks·koor·syon
tourist turista ⓜ&ⓕ too·rees·ta
tourist (slang) guiri ⓜ gee·ree
tourist office oficina ⓕ de turismo o·fee·thee·na de too·rees·mo
towards hacia a·thya
towel toalla ⓕ to·a·lya
tower torre ⓕ to·re
toxic waste residuos ⓜ pl tóxicos re·see·dwos tok·see·kos
toyshop juguetería ⓕ khoo·ge·te·ree·a
track (car racing) autódromo ⓜ ow·to·dro·mo
track (footprints) rastro ⓜ ras·tro
trade comercio ⓜ ko·mer·thyo
traffic tráfico ⓜ tra·fee·ko
traffic lights semáforos ⓜ pl se·ma·fo·ros
trail camino ⓜ ka·mee·no
train tren ⓜ tren
train station estación ⓕ de tren es·ta·thyon de tren

tram tranvía ⓜ tran·vee·a

transit lounge sala ⓕ de tránsito sa·la de tran·see·to

translate traducir tra·doo·theer

transport medios ⓜ pl de transporte me·dyos de trans·por·te

travel viajar vya·khar

travel agency agencia ⓕ de viajes a·khen·thya de vya·khes

travel books libros ⓜ pl de viajes lee·bros de vya·khes

travel sickness mareo ⓜ ma·re·o

travellers cheque cheque ⓜ de viajero che·ke de vya·khe·ro

tree árbol ⓜ ar·bol

trip viaje ⓜ vya·khe

trousers pantalones ⓜ pl pan·ta·lo·nes

truck camión ⓜ ka·myon

trust confianza ⓕ kon·fee·an·tha

trust confiar kon·fee·ar

try probar pro·bar

try (to do something) intentar (hacer algo) een·ten·tar (a·ther al·go)

T-shirt camiseta ⓕ ka·mee·se·ta

tube (tyre) cámara ⓕ de aire ka·ma·ra de ai·re

tuna atún ⓜ a·toon

tune melodía ⓕ me·lo·dee·a

turkey pavo ⓜ pa·vo

turn doblar do·blar

TV tele ⓕ te·le

TV series serie ⓕ se·rye

tweezers pinzas ⓕ pl peen·thas

twice dos veces dos ve·thes

twin beds dos camas ⓕ pl dos ka·mas

twins gemelos ⓜ pl khe·me·los

type tipo ⓜ tee·po

type escribir a máquina es·kree·beer a ma·kee·na

typical típico/a ⓜ/ⓕ tee·pee·ko/a

tyre neumático ⓜ ne·oo·ma·tee·ko

U

ultrasound ecografía ⓕ e·ko·gra·fee·a

umbrella (rain) paraguas ⓜ pa·ra·gwas

umbrella (sun) parasol ⓜ pa·ra·sol

umpire árbitro ⓜ ar·bee·tro

uncomfortable incómodo/a ⓜ/ⓕ een·ko·mo·do/a

underpants (men) calzoncillos ⓜ pl kal·thon·thee·lyos

underpants (women) bragas ⓕ pl bra·gas

understand comprender kom·pren·der

underwear ropa interior ⓕ ro·pa een·te·ryor

unemployed en el paro en el pa·ro

unfair injusto een·khoos·to

uniform uniforme ⓜ oo·nee·for·me

universe universo ⓜ oo·nee·ver·so

university universidad ⓕ oo·nee·ver·see·da

unleaded sin plomo seen plo·mo

unsafe inseguro/a ⓜ/ⓕ een·se·goo·ro/a

until (June) hasta (junio) as·ta (khoo·nyo)

unusual extraño/a ⓜ/ⓕ eks·tra·nyo/a

up arriba a·ree·ba

uphill cuesta arriba kwes·ta a·ree·ba

urgent urgente oor·khen·te

USA Estados ⓜ pl Unidos es·ta·dos oo·nee·dos

useful útil oo·teel

V

vacant vacante va·kan·te

vacation vacaciones ⓕ pl va·ka·thyo·nes

vaccination vacuna ⓕ va·koo·na

vagina vagina ⓕ va·khee·na

validate validar va·lee·dar

valley valle ⓜ va·lye

valuable valioso/a ⓜ/ⓕ va·lyo·so/a

value valor ⓜ va·lor

van caravana ⓕ ka·ra·va·na

veal ternera ⓕ ter·ne·ra

vegetable verdura ⓕ ver·doo·ra

vegetables verduras ⓕ pl ver·doo·ras

vegetarian vegetariano/a ⓜ/ⓕ
ve·khe·ta·*rya*·no/a
vein vena ⓕ *ve*·na
venereal disease enfermedad ⓕ
venérea en·fer·me·*da* ve·ne·re·a
venue local ⓜ lo·*kal*
very muy mooy
video tape cinta ⓕ de vídeo *theen*·ta
de vee·de·o
view vista ⓕ *vees*·ta
village pueblo ⓜ *pwe*·blo
vine vid ⓕ veed
vinegar vinagre ⓜ vee·*na*·gre
vineyard viñedo ⓜ vee·*nye*·do
virus virus ⓜ *vee*·roos
visa visado ⓜ vee·*sa*·do
visit visitar vee·see·*tar*
vitamins vitaminas ⓕ pl
vee·ta·*mee*·nas
vodka vodka ⓕ *vod*·ka
voice voz ⓕ voth
volume volumen ⓜ vo·*loo*·men
vote votar vo·*tar*

W

wage sueldo ⓜ *swel*·do
wait esperar es·pe·*rar*
waiter camarero/a ⓜ/ⓕ ka·ma·*re*·ro/a
waiting room sala ⓕ de espera *sa*·la
de es·*pe*·ra
walk caminar ka·mee·*nar*
wall (inside) pared ⓕ pa·*re*
wallet cartera ⓕ kar·*te*·ra
want querer ke·*rer*
war guerra ⓕ *ge*·ra
wardrobe vestuario ⓜ ves·*twa*·ryo
warm templado/a ⓜ/ⓕ tem·*pla*·do/a
warn advertir ad·ver·*teer*
wash (oneself) lavarse la·*var*·se
wash (something) lavar la·*var*
wash cloth toallita ⓕ to·a·*lyee*·ta
washing machine lavadora ⓕ
la·va·*do*·ra
watch reloj ⓜ de pulsera re·*lokh* de
pool·*se*·ra
watch mirar mee·*rar*

water agua ⓕ *a*·gwa
— tap del grifo del *gree*·fo
— bottle cantimplora ⓕ
kan·teem·*plo*·ra
waterfall cascada ⓕ kas·*ka*·da
watermelon sandía san·*dee*·a
waterproof impermeable
eem·per·me·*a*·ble
waterskiing esquí ⓜ acuático es·*kee*
a·*kwa*·tee·ko
wave ola ⓕ *o*·la
way camino ⓜ ka·*mee*·no
we nosotros/nosotras ⓜ/ⓕ
no·so·tros/no·so·tras
weak débil ⓜ&ⓕ *de* beel
wealthy rico/a ⓜ/ⓕ *ree*·ko/a
wear llevar lye·*var*
weather tiempo ⓜ *tyem*·po
wedding boda ⓕ *bo*·da
wedding cake tarta ⓕ nupcial *tar*·ta
noop·*thyal*
wedding present regalo ⓜ de bodas
re·*ga*·lo de *bo*·das
weekend fin de semana ⓜ feen de
se·*ma*·na
weigh pesar pe·*sar*
weight peso ⓜ *pe*·so
weights pesas ⓕ pl *pe*·sas
welcome bienvenida ⓕ
byen·ve·*nee*·da
welcome dar la bienvenida dar la
byen·ve·*nee*·da
welfare bienestar ⓜ byen·es·*tar*
well bien byen
well pozo ⓜ *po*·tho
west oeste ⓜ o·*es*·te
wet mojado/a ⓜ/ⓕ mo·*kha*·do/a
what lo que lo ke
wheel rueda ⓕ *rwe*·da
wheelchair silla ⓕ de ruedas *see*·lya
de *rwe*·das
when cuando *kwan*·do
where donde *don*·de
whiskey güisqui ⓜ *gwees*·kee
white blanco/a ⓜ/ⓕ *blan*·ko/a
white-water rafting rafting ⓜ
rahf·teen

Y

who quien kyen
why por qué por ke
wide ancho/a ⓜ/ⓕ an·cho/a
wife esposa ⓕ es·po·sa
win ganar ga·nar
wind viento ⓜ vyen·to
window ventana ⓕ ven·ta·na
window-shopping mirar los escaparates mee·rar los es·ka·pa·ra·tes
windscreen parabrisas ⓜ pa·ra·bree·sas
windsurfing hacer windsurf a·ther ween·soorf
wine vino ⓜ vee·no
wineglass copa ⓕ de vino ko·pa de vee·no
winery bodega ⓕ bo·de·ga
wings alas ⓕ pl a·las
winner ganador/ganadora ⓜ/ⓕ ga·na·dor/ga·na·do·ra
winter invierno ⓜ een·vyer·no
wire alambre ⓜ a·lam·bre
wish desear de·se·ar
with con kon
within (an hour) dentro de (una hora) den·tro de (oo·na o·ra)
without sin seen
woman mujer ⓕ moo·kher
wonderful maravilloso/a ⓜ/ⓕ ma·ra·vee·lyo·so/a
wood madera ⓕ ma·de·ra
wool lana ⓕ la·na
word palabra ⓕ pa·la·bra
work trabajo ⓜ tra·ba·kho
work trabajar tra·ba·khar
work experience experiencia ⓕ laboral eks·pe·ryen·thya la·bo·ral
work permit permiso ⓜ de trabajo per·mee·so de tra·ba·kho
workout entreno ⓜ en·tre·no
workshop taller ⓜ ta·lyer
world mundo ⓜ moon·do
World Cup Copa ⓕ Mundial ko·pa moon·dyal

worms lombrices ⓕ pl lom·bree·thes
worried preocupado/a ⓜ/ⓕ pre·o·koo·pa·do/a
worship adoración ⓕ a·do·ra·thyon
wrist muñeca ⓕ moo·nye·ka
write escribir es·kree·beer
writer escritor/escritora ⓜ/ⓕ es·kree·tor/es·kree·to·ra
wrong equivocado/a ⓜ/ⓕ e·kee·vo·ka·do/a

Y

yellow amarillo/a ⓜ/ⓕ a·ma·ree·lyo/a
yes sí see
(not) yet todavía (no) to·da·vee·a (no)
yesterday ayer a·yer
yoga yoga ⓜ yo·ga
yogurt yogur ⓜ yo·goor
you inf sg tú too
you ⓜ/ⓕ inf pl vosotros/as vo·so·tros/as
you pol pl Ustedes oo·ste·des
you pol sg Usted oo·ste
young joven kho·ven
your pol sg su soo
your inf sg tu too
youth hostel albergue ⓜ juvenil al·ber·ge khoo·ve·neel

Z

zodiac zodíaco ⓜ tho·dee·a·ko
zoo zoológico ⓜ zo·o·lo·khee·ko

Dictionary

SPANISH *to* ENGLISH

español–inglés

Nouns in the dictionary have their gender indicated by ⓜ or ⓕ.
If it's a plural noun, you'll also see pl. Where a word that could be
either a noun or a verb has no gender indicated, it's a verb.

A

abajo a·*ba*·kho below
abanico ⓜ a·ba·*nee*·ko fan (hand held)
abarrotado a·ba·ro *ta* do crowded
abeja ⓕ a·*be*·kha bee
abierto/a ⓜ/ⓕ a·*byer*·to/a open
abogado/a ⓜ/ⓕ a·bo·*ga*·do/a lawyer
aborto ⓜ a·*bor*·to abortion
abrazo ⓜ a·*bra*·tho hug
abrebotellas ⓜ a·bre·bo·*te*·lyas bottle opener
abrelatas ⓜ a·bre·*la*·tas can opener • tin opener
abrigo ⓜ a·*bree*·go overcoat
abrir a·*breer* open
abuela ⓕ a·*bwe*·la grandmother
abuelo ⓜ a·*bwe*·lo grandfather
aburrido/a ⓜ/ⓕ a·boo·*ree*·do/a bored • boring
acabar a·ka·*bar* end
acampar a·kam·*par* camp
acantilado ⓜ a·kan·tee·*la*·do cliff
accidente ⓜ ak·thee·*den*·te accident
aceite ⓜ a·*they*·te oil
aceptar a·thep·*tar* accept
acera ⓕ a·*the*·ra footpath

acondicionador ⓜ
a·kon·dee·thyo·na·*dor* conditioner
acoso ⓜ a·*ko*·so harassment
activista ⓜ&ⓕ ak·tee·*vees*·ta activist
actuación ⓕ ak·twa·*thyon* performance
acupuntura ⓕ a·koo·poon·*too*·ra acupuncture
adaptador ⓜ a·dap·ta·*dor* adaptor
adentro a·*den*·tro inside
adivinar a·dee·vee·*nar* guess
administración ⓕ
ad·mee·nees·tra·*thyon* administration
admitir ad·mee·*teer* admit
adoración ⓕ a·do·ra·*thyon* worship
aduana ⓕ a·*dwa*·na customs
adulto/a ⓜ/ⓕ a·*dool*·to/a adult
aeróbic ⓜ ai·ro·*beek* aerobics
aerolínea ⓕ ai·ro·*lee*·nya airline
aeropuerto ⓜ ai·ro·*pwer*·to airport
afeitadora ⓕ a·fey·ta·*do*·ra razor
afeitarse a·fey·*tar*·se shave
afortunado/a ⓜ/ⓕ a·for·too·*na*·do/a lucky
África ⓕ a·*free*·ka Africa
agencia ⓕ **de viajes** a·*khen*·thya de *vya*·khes travel agency
agenda ⓕ a·*khen*·da diary

A

agente ⓜ **inmobiliario** a·khen·te een·mo·bee·lya·ryo real estate agent

agresivo/a ⓜ/ⓕ a·gre·see·vo/a aggressive

agricultor(a) ⓜ/ⓕ a·gree·kool·tor/ a·gree·kool·to·ra farmer

agricultura ⓕ a·gree·kool·too·ra agriculture

agua ⓕ a·gwa water

— **caliente** ka·lyen·te hot water

— **mineral** mee·ne·ral mineral water

aguacate ⓜ a·gwa·ka·te avocado

aguja ⓕ a·goo·kha needle (sewing)

ahora a·o·ra now

ahorrar a·o·rar save (money)

aire ⓜ ai·re air

— **acondicionado** a·kon·dee·thyo·na·do air-conditioning

ajedrez ⓜ a·khe·dreth chess

al lado de al la·do de next to

alambre ⓜ a·lam·bre wire

alba ⓕ al·ba dawn

albaricoque ⓜ al·ba·ree·ko·ke apricot

albergue ⓜ **juvenil** al·ber·ge khoo·ve·neel youth hostel

alcachofa ⓕ al·ka·cho·fa artichoke

alcohol ⓜ al·kol alcohol

Alemania ⓕ a·le·ma·nya Germany

alérgia ⓕ a·ler·khya allergy

alérgia ⓕ **al polen** a·ler·khya al po·len hay fever

alfarería ⓕ al·fa·re·ree·a pottery

alfombra ⓕ al·fom·bra rug

algo al·go something

algodón ⓜ al·go·don cotton

alguien al·gyen someone

algún al·goon some

alguno/a ⓜ/ⓕ al·goo·no/a any

almendras ⓕ pl al·men·dras almonds

almohada ⓕ al·mwa·da pillow

almuerzo ⓜ al·mwer·tho lunch

alojamiento ⓜ a·lo·kha·myen·to accommodation

alojarse a·lo·khar·se stay (somewhere)

alpinismo ⓜ al·pee·nees·mo mountaineering

alquilar al·kee·lar hire • rent

alquiler ⓜ al·kee·ler rent

— **de coche** de ko·che car hire

altar ⓜ al·tar altar

alto/a ⓜ/ⓕ al·to/a high • tall

altura ⓕ al·too·ra altitude

ama ⓕ **de casa** a·ma de ka·sa homemaker

amable a·ma·ble kind

amanecer ⓜ a·ma·ne·ther sunrise

amante ⓜ&ⓕ a·man·te lover

amarillo/a ⓜ/ⓕ a·ma·ree·lyo/a yellow

amigo/a ⓜ/ⓕ a·mee·go/a friend

ampolla ⓕ am·po·lya blister

anacardo ⓜ a·na·kar·do cashew nut

analgésicos ⓜ pl a·nal·khe·see·kos painkillers

análisis de sangre ⓜ a·na·lee·sees de san·gre blood test

anarquista ⓜ/ⓕ a·nar·kees·ta anarchist

ancho/a ⓜ/ⓕ an·cho/a wide

andar an·dar walk

animal ⓜ a·nee·mal animal

Año Nuevo a·nyo nwe·vo New Year

antes an·tes before

antibióticos ⓜ pl an·tee·byo·tee·kos antibiotics

anticonceptivos ⓜ pl an·tee·kon·thep·tee·vos contraceptives

antigüedad ⓕ an·tee·gwe·da antique

antiguo/a ⓜ/ⓕ an·tee·gwo/a ancient

antiséptico ⓜ an·tee·sep·tee·ko antiseptic

antología ⓕ an·to·lo·khee·a anthology

anuncio ⓜ a·noon·thyo advertisement

aparcamiento ⓜ a·par·ka·myen·to carpark

apellido ⓜ a·pe·lyee·do surname

apéndice ⓜ a·*pen*·dee·the the appendix
apodo ⓜ a·*po*·do nickname
aprender a·*pren*·der learn
apretado/a ⓜ/ⓕ a·pre·*ta*·do/a tight
apuesta ⓕ a·*pwes*·ta bet
apuntar a·poon·*tar* point
aquí a·*kee* here
araña ⓕ a·ra·nya spider
árbitro ⓜ *ar*·bee·tro referee
árbol ⓜ *ar*·bol tree
arena ⓕ a·*re*·na sand
armario ⓜ ar·*ma*·ryo cupboard
arqueológico/a ⓜ/ⓕ
ar·ke·o·*lo*·khee·ko/a archaeological
arquitecto/a ⓜ/ⓕ ar·kee·*tek*·to/a
architect
arquitectura ⓕ ar·kee·tek·*too*·ra
architecture
arriba a·*ree*·ba above • up
arroyo ⓜ a·*ro*·yo stream
arroz ⓜ a·*roth* rice
arte ⓜ *ar*·te art
  gráfico *gra*·fee·ko graphic art
artes ⓕ pl **marciales** *ar*·tes
mar·*thya*·les martial arts
artesanía ⓕ ar·te·sa·*nee*·a crafts
artista ⓜ&ⓕ ar·*tees*·ta artist
ascensor ⓜ as·then·*sor* elevator
Asia ⓕ a·sya Asia
asiento ⓜ a·*syen*·to seat
  — de seguridad para bebés de
se·goo·ree·*da* pa·ra be·*bes* child seat
asma ⓜ *as*·ma asthma
aspirina ⓕ as·pee·*ree*·na aspirin
atascado/a ⓜ/ⓕ a·tas·*ka*·do/a
blocked
atletismo ⓜ at·le·*tees*·mo athletics
atmósfera ⓕ at·*mos*·fe·ra atmosphere
atún ⓜ a·*toon* tuna
audífono ⓜ ow·*dee*·fo·no hearing aid
Australia ⓕ ow·*stra*·lya Australia
autobús ⓜ ow·to·*boos* bus
autocar ⓜ ow·to·*kar* bus (intercity)
autódromo ⓜ ow·*to*·dro·mo track
(car racing)
autoservicio ⓜ ow·to·ser·*vee*·thyo
self-service
autovía ⓕ ow·to·*vee*·a motorway
avenida ⓕ a·ve·*nee*·da avenue
avergonzado/a ⓜ/ⓕ
a·ver·gon·*tha*·do/a embarrassed
avión ⓜ a·*vyon* plane
ayer a·*yer* yesterday
ayudar a·yoo·*dar* help
azúcar ⓜ a·*thoo*·kar sugar
azul a·*thool* blue

B

bailar bai·*lar* dance
bajo/a ⓜ/ⓕ *ba*·kho/a low • short
(height)
balcón ⓜ bal·*kon* balcony
ballet ⓜ ba·*le* ballet
baloncesto ⓜ ba·lon·*thes*·to
basketball
bálsamo ⓜ **de aftershave** *bal*·sa·mo
de af·ter·*sha*·eev aftershave
bálsamo ⓜ **de labios** *bal*·sa·mo de
la·byos lip balm
bañador ⓜ ba·nya·*dor* bathing suit
banco ⓜ *ban*·ko bank
bandera ⓕ ban·*de*·ra flag
bañera ⓕ ba·*nye*·ra bath
baño ⓜ *ba*·nyo bathroom
bar ⓜ bar bar
barato/a ⓜ/ⓕ ba·*ra*·to/a cheap
barco ⓜ *bar*·ko boat
barrio ⓜ *ba*·ryo suburb
basura ⓕ ba·*soo*·ra rubbish
batería ⓕ ba·te·*ree*·a battery (car) •
drums
bebé ⓜ be·*be* baby
béisbol ⓜ *beys*·bol baseball
beneficio ⓜ be·ne·*fee*·thyo profit
berenjenas ⓕ pl be·ren·*khe*·nas
aubergine • eggplant
besar be·*sar* kiss
beso ⓜ *be*·so kiss
biblia ⓕ *bee*·blya bible
biblioteca ⓕ bee·blyo·*te*·ka library

C

bicho ⓜ *bee*·cho bug

bici ⓕ *bee*·thee bike

bicicleta ⓕ bee·thee·*kle*·ta bicycle

— de carreras de ka·*re*·ras racing bike

— de montaña de mon·*ta*·nya mountain bike

bien byen well

bienestar ⓜ byen·es·*tar* welfare

bienvenida ⓕ byen·ve·*nee*·da welcome

billete ⓜ bee·*lye*·te ticket

— de ida y vuelta de *ee*·da ee *vwel*·ta return ticket

— de lista de espera de *lees*·ta de es·*pe*·ra standby ticket

billetes ⓜ pl **de banco** bee·*lye*·tes de *ban*·ko banknotes

biografía ⓕ bee·o·gra·*fee*·a biography

bistec ⓜ bees·*tek* steak (beef)

blanco y negro *blan*·ko ee *ne*·gro B&W (film)

blanco/a ⓜ/ⓕ *blan*·ko/a white

boca ⓕ *bo*·ka mouth

bocado ⓜ bo·*ka*·do bite (food)

boda ⓕ *bo*·da wedding

bodega ⓕ bo·*de*·ga winery • liquor store

bol ⓜ bol bowl

bolas ⓕ pl **de algodón** *bo*·las de al·go·*don* cotton balls

bolígrafo ⓜ bo·*lee*·gra·fo pen

bollos ⓜ pl *bo*·lyos rolls (bread)

bolo ⓜ *bo*·lo gig

bolsillo ⓜ bol·*see*·lyo pocket

bolso ⓜ *bol*·so bag • handbag

bomba ⓕ *bom*·ba bomb • pump

bombilla ⓕ bom·*bee*·lya light bulb

bondadoso/a ⓜ/ⓕ bon·da·*do*·so/a caring

bonito/a ⓜ/ⓕ bo·*nee*·to/a pretty

bordo ⓜ *bor*·do edge

a bordo a *bor*·do aboard

borracho/a ⓜ/ⓕ bo·*ra*·cho/a drunk

bosque ⓜ *bos*·ke forest

botas ⓕ pl *bo*·tas boots

— de montaña de mon·*ta*·nya hiking boots

botella ⓕ bo·*te*·lya bottle

botones ⓜ pl bo·*to*·nes buttons

boxeo ⓜ bo·*kse*·o boxing

bragas ⓕ pl *bra*·gas underpants (women)

brazo ⓜ *bra*·tho arm

broma ⓕ *bro*·ma joke

bronceador ⓜ bron·the·a·*dor* tanning lotion

bronquitis ⓜ bron·*kee*·tees bronchitis

brotes ⓜ pl **de soja** *bro*·tes de *so*·kha bean sprouts

brújula ⓕ *broo*·khoo·la compass

brumoso broo·*mo*·so foggy

buceo ⓜ boo·*the*·o snorkelling

budista ⓜ&ⓕ boo·*dees*·ta Buddhist

bueno/a ⓜ/ⓕ *bwe*·no/a good

bufanda ⓕ boo·*fan*·da scarf

buffet ⓜ boo·*fe* buffet

bulto ⓜ *bool*·to lump

burlarse de boor·*lar*·se de make fun of

burro ⓜ *boo*·ro donkey

buscar boos·*kar* look for

buzón ⓜ boo·*thon* mailbox

C

caballo ⓜ ka·*ba*·lyo horse

cabeza ⓕ ka·*be*·tha head

cabina ⓕ **telefónica** ka·*bee*·na te·le·*fo*·nee·ka phone box

cable ⓜ *ka*·ble cable

cables ⓜ pl **de arranque** *ka*·bles de a·*ran*·ke jumper leads

cabra ⓕ *ka*·bra goat

cacahuetes ⓜ pl ka·ka·*we*·tes peanuts

cacao ⓜ ka·*kow* cocoa

cachorro ⓜ ka·*cho*·ro puppy

cada *ka*·da each

cadena ⓕ **de bici** ka·*de*·na de *bee*·thee bike chain

café ⓜ ka·*fe* coffee • cafe

caída ⓕ ka·*ee*·da fall

caja ① *ka*·kha box • cashier

— fuerte *fwer*·te safe

— registradora re·khees·tra·*do*·ra cash register

cajero ⓜ **automático** ka·*khe*·ro ow·to·*ma*·tee·ko automatic teller machine

calabacín ⓜ ka·la·ba·*theen* zucchini • courgette

calabaza ① ka·la·*ba*·tha pumpkin

calcetines ⓜ pl kal·the·*tee*·nes socks

calculadora ① kal·koo·la·*do*·ra calculator

caldo ⓜ *kal*·do stock

calefacción ① **central** ka·le·tak·*thyon* then·*tral* central heating

calendario ⓜ ka·len·*da*·ryo calendar

calidad ① ka·lee·*da* quality

caliente ka·*lyen*·te hot

calle ① *ka*·lye street

calor ⓜ ka·*lor* heat

calzoncillos ⓜ pl kal·thon·*thee*·lyos underpants (men)

calzones ⓜ pl kal·*tho*·nes boxer shorts

cama ① *ka*·ma bed

— de matrimonio de ma·tree·*mo*·nyo double bed

cámara ① **(fotográfica)** *ka*·ma·ra (fo·to·*gra*·fee·ka) camera

cámara ① **de aire** *ka*·ma·ra de *ai*·re tube (tyre)

camarero/a ⓜ/① ka·ma·*re*·ro/a waiter

cambiar kam·*byar* change • exchange (money)

cambio *kam*·byo ⓜ loose change

— de dinero de dee·*ne*·ro currency exchange

caminar ka·mee·*nar* walk

camino ⓜ ka·*mee*·no trail • way

caminos ⓜ pl **rurales** ka·*mee*·nos roo·*ra*·les hiking routes

camión ⓜ ka·*myon* truck

camisa ① ka·*mee*·sa shirt

camiseta ① ka·mee·*se*·ta singlet • T-shirt

cámping ⓜ *kam*·peen campsite

campo ⓜ *kam*·po countryside • field

Canadá ⓜ ka·na·*da* Canada

canasta ① ka·*nas*·ta basket

cancelar kan·the·*lar* cancel

cáncer ⓜ *kan*·ther cancer

canción ① kan·*thyon* song

candado ⓜ kan·*da*·do padlock

cangrejo ⓜ kan·*gre*·kho crab

canguro ⓜ kan·*goo*·ro babysitter

cansado/a ⓜ/① kan·*sa*·do/a tired

cantalupo ⓜ kan·ta·*loo*·po cantaloupe

cantante ⓜ&① kan·*tan*·te singer

cantar kan·*tar* sing

cantimplora ① kan·teem·*plo*·ra water bottle

capa ① **de ozono** *ka*·pa de o·*tho*·no ozone layer

capilla ① ka·*pee*·lya shrine

capote ⓜ ka·*po*·te cloak

cara ① *ka*·ra face

caracol ⓜ ka·ra·*kol* snail

caramelos ⓜ pl ka·*ra*·me·los lollies

caravana ① ka·ra·*va*·na caravan • van • traffic jam

cárcel ① *kar*·thel prison

cardenal ⓜ kar·de·*nal* bruise

carne ① *kar*·ne meat

— de vaca de *va*·ka beef

— molida mo·*lee*·da mince meat

carnet ⓜ kar·*ne* licence

— de identidad de ee·den·tee·*da* identification card

— de conducir de kon·doo·*theer* drivers licence

carnicería ① kar·nee·the·*ree*·a butcher's shop

caro/a ⓜ/① *ka*·ro/a expensive

carpintero ⓜ kar·peen·*te*·ro carpenter

carrera ① ka·*re*·ra race (sport)

carta ① *kar*·ta letter

C

cartas ① pl *kar*·tas cards
cartón ⓜ *kar*·ton carton • cardboard
casa ① *ka*·sa house
(en) casa (en) *ka*·sa (at) home
casarse ka·*sar*·se marry
cascada ① kas·*ka*·da waterfall
casco ⓜ *kas*·ko helmet
casete ⓜ ka·*se*·te cassette
casi *ka*·see almost
casino ⓜ ka·*see*·no casino
castigar kas·tee·*gar* punish
castillo ⓜ kas·*tee*·lyo castle
catedral ① ka·te·*dral* cathedral
católico/a ⓜ/① ka·to·lee·ko/a Catholic
caza ① *ka*·tha hunting
cazuela ① ka·*thwe*·la pot (kitchen)
cebolla ① the·*bo*·lya onion
celebración ① the·le·bra·*thyon* celebration
celebrar the·le·*brar* celebrate (an event)
celoso/a ⓜ/① the·*lo*·so/a jealous
cementerio ⓜ the·men·*te*·ryo cemetery
cena ① *the*·na dinner
cenicero ⓜ the·nee·*the*·ro ashtray
centavo ⓜ then·*ta*·vo cent
centímetro ⓜ then·*tee*·me·tro centimetre
central ① **telefónica** then·*tral* te·le·fo·nee·ka telephone centre
centro ⓜ *then*·tro centre
— comercial ko·mer·*thyal* shopping centre
— de la ciudad de la thyu·*da* city centre
cepillo ⓜ the·*pee*·lyo hairbrush
— de dientes de *dyen*·tes toothbrush
cerámica ① the·*ra*·mee·ka ceramic
cerca ① *ther*·ka fence
cerca *ther*·ka near • nearby
cerdo ⓜ *ther*·do pork • pig
cereales ⓜ pl the·re·a·les cereal
cerillas ① pl las the·*ree*·lyas matches
cerrado/a ⓜ/① the·*ra*·do/a closed
— con llave kon *lya*·ve locked

cerradura ① the·ra·*doo*·ra lock (padlock)
cerrar the·*rar* close • lock • shut
certificado ⓜ ther·tee·fee·*ka*·do certificate
cerveza ① ther·*ve*·tha beer
— rubia *roo*·bya lager
cibercafé ⓜ thee·ber·ka·*fe* internet cafe
ciclismo ⓜ thee·*klees*·mo cycling
ciclista ⓜ&① thee·*klees*·ta cyclist
ciego/a ⓜ/① *thye*·go/a blind
cielo ⓜ *thye*·lo heaven • sky
ciencias ① pl *thyen*·thyas science
científico/a ⓜ/① thyen·*tee*·fee·ko/a scientist
cigarillo ⓜ thee·ga·*ree*·lyo cigarette
cigarro ⓜ thee·*ga*·ro cigarette
cine ⓜ *thee*·ne cinema
cinta ① **de vídeo** *theen*·ta de vee·de·o video tape
cinturón ⓜ **de seguridad** theen·too·*ron* de se·goo·ree·da seatbelt
circuito ⓜ **de carreras** theer·*kwee*·to de ka·re·ras racetrack (cars)
ciruela ① thee·*rwe*·la plum
— pasa *pa*·sa prune
cistitis ① thees·*tee*·tees cystitis
cita ① *thee*·ta appointment
citarse thee·*tar*·se date
citología ① thee·to·lo·*khee*·a pap smear
ciudad ① thyu·*da* city
ciudadanía ① thyu·da·da·*nee*·a citizenship
clase ① **preferente** *kla*·se pre·fe·*ren*·te business class
clase ① **turística** *kla*·se too·*rees*·tee·ka economy class
clásico/a ⓜ/① *kla*·see·ko/a classical
clienta/e ⓜ/① klee·*en*·ta/e client
clínica ① *klee*·nee·ka private hospital
cobrar (un cheque) ko·*brar* (oon *che*·ke) cash (a cheque)
coca ① *ko*·ka cocaine

cocaína ① ko·ka·ee·na cocaine

coche ⓜ ko·che car

— cama ka·ma sleeping car

cocina ① ko·thee·na kitchen • stove

cocinar ko·thee·nar cook

cocinero ⓜ ko·thee·ne·ro chef • cook

coco ⓜ ko·ko coconut

codeína ① ko·de·ee·na codeine

código ⓜ **postal** ko·dee·go pos·tal post code

cojonudo/a ⓜ/① ko·kho·noo·do/a fantastic

col ⓜ kol cabbage

cola ① ko·la queue

colchón ⓜ kol·chon mattress

colega ⓜ&① ko·le·ga colleague • mate

coles ⓜ pl **de Bruselas** ko·les de broo·se·las brussels sprouts

coliflor ⓜ ko·lee·flor cauliflower

colina ① ko·lee·na hill

collar ⓜ ko·lyar necklace

color ⓜ ko·lor colour

comedia ① ko·me·dya comedy

comenzar ko·men·thar begin • start

comer ko·mer eat

comerciante ⓜ&① ko·mer·thyan·te business person

comercio ⓜ ko·mer·thyo trade

comezón ⓜ ko·me·thon itch

comida ① ko·mee·da food

— de bebé de be·be baby food

— en el campo en el kam·po picnic

comisaría ① ko·mee·sa·ree·a police station

cómo ko·mo how

cómodo/a ⓜ/① ko·mo·do/a comfortable

compact ⓜ kom·pak CD

compañero/a ⓜ/① kom·pa·nye·ro/a companion

compañía ① kom·pa·nyee·a company

compartir kom·par·teer share (with)

comprar kom·prar buy

comprender kom·pren·der understand

compresas ① pl kom·pre·sas sanitary napkins

compromiso ⓜ kom·pro·mee·so engagement

comunión ① ko·moo·nyon communion

comunista ⓜ&① ko·moo·nees·ta communist

con kon with

coñac ⓜ ko·nyak brandy

concentración ① kon·then·tra·thyon rally

concierto ⓜ kon·thyer·to concert

condición ① **cardíaca** kon·dee·thyon kar·dee·a·ka heart condition

condones ⓜ pl kon·do·nes condoms

conducir kon·doo·theer drive

conejo ⓜ ko·ne·kho rabbit

conexión ① ko·ne·ksyon connection

confesión ① kon·fe·syon confession

confianza ① kon·fee·an·tha trust

confiar kon·fee·ar trust

confirmar kon·feer·mar confirm

conocer ko·no·ther know (someone)

conocido/a ⓜ/① ko·no·thee·do/a famous

consejo ⓜ kon·se·kho advice

conservador(a) ⓜ/① kon·ser·va·dor/ kon·ser·va·do·ra conservative

consigna ① kon·seeg·na left luggage

— automática ow·to·ma·tee·ka luggage lockers

construir kons·troo·eer build

consulado ⓜ kon·soo·la·do consulate

contaminación ① kon·ta·mee·na·thyon pollution

contar kon·tar count

contestador ⓜ **automático** kon·tes·ta·dor ow·to·ma·tee·ko answering machine

contrato ⓜ kon·tra·to contract

control ⓜ kon·trol checkpoint

convento ⓜ kon·ven·to convent

copa ① ko·pa drink

— de vino de vee·no wineglass

C

CH

Copa ① **Mundial** ko·pa moon·dyal World Cup

copos de maíz ko·pos de ma·eeth corn flakes

corazón ⓜ ko·ra·thon heart

cordero ⓜ kor·de·ro lamb

cordillera ① kor·dee·lye·ra mountain range

correcto/a ⓜ/① ko·rek·to/a right (correct)

correo ⓜ ko·re·o mail

— urgente oor·khen·te express mail

correos ko·re·os post office

correr ko·rer run

corrida ① **de toros** ko·ree·da de to·ros bullfight

corriente ① ko·ryen·te current (electricity)

corriente ko·ryen·te ordinary

corrupto/a ⓜ/① ko·roop·to/a corrupt

cortar kor·tar cut

cortauñas ⓜ pl kor·ta·oo·nyas nail clippers

corto/a ⓜ/① kor·to/a short (length)

cosecha ① ko·se·cha crop

coser ko·ser sew

costa ① kos·ta coast • seaside

costar kos·tar cost

crecer kre·ther grow

crema ① kre·ma cream

— hidratante ee·dra·tan·te moisturising cream

— solar so·lar sunblock

críquet ⓜ kree·ket cricket

cristiano/a ⓜ/① krees·tya·no/a Christian

crítica ① kree·tee·ka review

cruce ⓜ kroo·the intersection

crudo/a ⓜ/① kroo·do/a raw

cuaderno ⓜ kwa·der·no notebook • square

cualificaciones ① pl kwa·lee·fee·ka·thyo·nes qualifications

cuando kwan·do when

cuánto kwan·to how much

cuarentena ① kwa·ren·te·na quarantine

Cuaresma ① kwa·res·ma Lent

cuarto ⓜ kwar·to quarter

cubiertos ⓜ pl koo·byer·tos cutlery

cubo ⓜ koo·bo bucket

cucaracha ① koo·ka·ra·cha cockroach

cuchara ① koo·cha·ra spoon

cucharita ① koo·cha·ree·ta teaspoon

cuchillas ① pl **de afeitar** koo·chee·lyas de a·fey·tar razor blades

cuchillo ⓜ koo·chee·lyo knife

cuenta ① kwen·ta bill

— bancaria ban·ka·rya bank account

cuento ⓜ kwen·to story

cuerda ① kwer·da rope • string

— para tender la ropa pa·ra ten·der la ro·pa clothes line

cuero ⓜ kwe·ro leather

cuerpo ⓜ kwer·po body

cuesta abajo kwes·ta a·ba·kho downhill

cuesta arriba kwes·ta a·ree·ba uphill

cuestionar kwes·tyo·nar question

cuevas ① pl kwe·vas caves

cuidar kwee·dar care for • mind (an object)

cuidar de kwee·dar de care (for someone)

culo ⓜ koo·lo bum (of body)

culpable kool·pa·ble guilty

cumbre ① koom·bre peak

cumpleaños ⓜ koom·ple·a·nyos birthday

currículum ⓜ koo·ree·koo·loom resumé

curry ⓜ koo·ree curry

cus cus ⓜ koos koos cous cous

CH

chaleco ⓜ **salvavidas** cha·le·ko sal·va·vee·das lifejacket

champán ⓜ cham·pan Champagne

champiñón ⓜ cham·pee·nyon mushrooms

champú m cham·*poo* shampoo
chaqueta f cha·*ke*·ta jacket
cheque m *che*·ke check (bank)
cheques m pl **de viajero** *che*·kes de vya·*khe*·ro travellers cheque
chica f *chee*·ka girl
chicle m *chee*·kle chewing gum
chico m *chee*·ko boy
chocolate m cho·ko·*la*·te chocolate
choque m *cho*·ke crash
chorizo m cho·*ree*·tho salami (Spanish sausage)
chupete m choo·*pe*·te dummy • pacifier

D

dados m pl *da*·dos dice (die)
dañar da·*nyar* hurt
dar dar give
— de comer de ko·*mer* feed
— gracias *gra*·thyas thank
— la bienvenida la byen·ve·*nee*·da welcome
— una patada oo·na pa·*ta*·da kick
darse cuenta de *dar*·se *kwen*·ta de realise
de de from
— (cuatro) estrellas de (*kwa*·tro) es·*tre*·lyas (four)star
— izquierdas de eeth·*kyer*·das left-wing
— pena de *pe*·na terrible
— primera clase de pree·*me*·ra *kla*·se first-class
— segunda mano de se·*goon*·da *ma*·no second-hand
— vez en cuando de veth en *kwan*·do sometimes
deber de·*ver* owe
débil *de*·beel weak
decidir de·thee·*deer* decide
decir de·*theer* say • tell
dedo m *de*·do finger
— del pie del pye toe
defectuoso/a m/f de·fek·*two*·so/a faulty

deforestación f de·fo·res·ta·*thyon* deforestation
dejar de·*khar* leave • quit
delgado/a m/f del·*ga*·do/a thin
delirante de·lee·*ran*·te delirious
demasiado caro/a m/f de·ma·*sya*·do *ka*·ro/a too (expensive)
democracia f de·mo·*kra*·thya democracy
demora f de·*mo*·ra delay
dentista m&f den·*tees*·ta dentist
dentro de (una hora) *den*·tro de (*oo*·na *o*·ra) within (an hour)
deportes m pl de·*por*·tes sport
deportista m&f de·por·*tees*·ta sportsperson
depósito m de·*po*·see·to deposit
derecha f de·*re*·cha right (not left)
derechista de·re·*chees*·ta right-wing
derechos m pl **civiles** de·*re*·chos thee·*vee*·les civil rights
derechos m pl **humanos** de·re·chos oo·*ma*·nos human rights
desayuno m des·a·*yoo*·no breakfast
descansar des·kan·*sar* rest
descanso m des·*kan*·so intermission
descendiente m des·then·*dyen*·te descendant
descomponerse des·kom·po·*ner*·se decompose
descubrir des·koo·*breer* discover
descuento m des·*kwen*·to discount
desde (mayo) *des*·de (*ma*·yo) since (may)
desear de·se·*ar* wish
desierto m de·*syer*·to desert
desodorante m de·so·do·*ran*·te deodorant
desperdicios m pl **nucleares** des·per·*dee*·thyos noo·kle·*a*·res nuclear waste
despertador m des·per·ta·*dor* alarm clock
después de des·*pwes* de after

destino ⓜ des·*tee*·no destination
destruir des·troo·*eer* destroy
detallado/a ⓜ/ⓕ de·ta·*lya*·do/a itemised
detalle ⓜ de·*ta*·lye detail
detener de·te·*ner* arrest
detrás de de·*tras* de behind
devocionario ⓜ de·vo·thyo·*na*·ryo prayer book
día ⓜ *dee*·a day
— festivo fes·*tee*·vo holiday
diabetes ⓕ dee·a·*be*·tes diabetes
diafragma ⓜ dee·a·*frag*·ma diaphragm
diapositiva ⓕ dya·po·see·*tee*·va slide
diariamente dya·rya·*men*·te daily
diarrea ⓕ dee·a·*re*·a diarrhoea
dieta ⓕ dee·*e*·ta diet
dibujar dee·boo·*khar* draw
diccionario ⓜ deek·thyo·*na*·ryo dictionary
diente (de ajo) *dyen*·te (de a·kho) clove (garlic)
dientes ⓜ pl *dyen*·tes teeth
diferencia ⓕ **de horas** dee·fe·*ren*·thya de o·ras time difference
diferente dee·fe·*ren*·te different
difícil dee·*fee*·theel difficult
dinero ⓜ dee·*ne*·ro money
— en efectivo en e·fek·*tee*·vo cash
Dios dyos god
dirección ⓕ dee·rek·*thyon* address
directo/a ⓜ/ⓕ dee·*rek*·to/a direct
director(a) ⓜ/ⓕ dee·rek·*tor*/ dee·rek·*to*·ra director
disco ⓜ *dees*·ko disk
discoteca ⓕ dees·ko·*te*·ka disco
discriminación ⓕ dees·kree·mee·na·*thyon* discrimination
discutir dees·koo·*teer* argue
diseño ⓜ dee·*se*·nyo design
disparar dees·pa·*rar* shoot
DIU ⓜ de·ee·oo IUD
diversión ⓕ dee·ver·*syon* fun
divertirse dee·ver·*teer*·se enjoy (oneself)

doblar do·*blar* turn • bend
doble do·ble double
docena ⓕ do·*the*·na dozen
doctor(a) ⓜ/ⓕ dok·*tor*/dok·*to*·ra doctor
dólar ⓜ *do*·lar dollar
dolor ⓜ do·*lor* pain
— de cabeza de ka·*be*·tha headache
— de estómago de es·*to*·ma·go stomachache
— de muelas de *mwe*·las toothache
— menstrual mens·*trwal* period pain
dolorido/a ⓜ/ⓕ do·lo·*ree*·do/a sore
doloroso/a ⓜ/ⓕ do·lo·*ro*·so/a painful
donde *don*·de where
dormir dor·*meer* sleep
dos ⓜ/ⓕ pl dos two
— camas *ka*·mas twin beds
— veces *ve*·thes twice
drama ⓜ *dra*·ma drama
droga ⓕ *dro*·ga drug • dope
drogadicción ⓕ dro·ga·deek·*thyon* drug addiction
drogas ⓕ pl *dro*·gas drugs
ducha ⓕ *doo*·cha shower
dueño/a ⓜ/ⓕ *dwe*·nyo/a owner
dulce *dool*·the sweet
dulces ⓜ pl *dool*·thes sweets
duro/a ⓜ/ⓕ *doo*·ro/a hard

E

eczema ⓕ ek·*the*·ma eczema
edad ⓕ e·*da* age
edificio ⓜ e·dee·*fee*·thyo building
editor(a) ⓜ/ⓕ e·dee·*tor*/e·dee·*to*·ra editor
educación ⓕ e·doo·ka·*thyon* education
egoísta e·go·*ees*·ta selfish
ejemplo ⓜ e·*khem*·plo example
ejército ⓜ e·*kher*·thee·to military
el ⓜ el the
él ⓜ el he
elecciones ⓕ pl e·lek·*thyo*·nes elections
electricidad ⓕ e·lek·tree·thee·*da* electricity

elegir ⓜ e·le·*kheer* pick • choose

ella ⓘ e·lya she

ellos/ellas ⓜ/ⓘ e·lyos/e·lyas they

embajada ⓘ em·ba·*kha*·da embassy

embajador(a) ⓜ/ⓘ em·ba·kha·*dor*/em·ba·kha·*do*·ra ambassador

embarazada em·ba·ra·*tha*·da pregnant

embarcarse em·bar·*kar*·se board (ship etc)

embrague ⓜ em·*bra*·ge clutch

emergencia ⓘ e·mer·*khen*·thya emergency

emocional e·mo·thyo·*nal* emotional

empleado/a ⓜ/ⓘ em·ple·a·do/a employee

empujar em·poo·*khar* push

en en on

— el extranjero el eks·tran·*khe*·ro abroad

— el paro el *pa*·ro unemployed

encaje ⓜ en·*ka*·khe lace

encantador(a) ⓜ/ⓘ en·kan·ta·*dor*/en·kan·ta·*do*·ra charming

encendedor ⓜ en·then·de·*dor* lighter

encontrar en·kon·*trar* find • meet

encurtidos ⓜ pl en·koor·*tee*·dos pickles

energía ⓘ **nuclear** e·ner·*khee*·a noo·*kle·ar* nuclear energy

enfadado/a ⓜ/ⓘ en·fa·*da*·do/a angry

enfermedad ⓘ en·fer·me·*da* disease

— venérea ve·*ne*·re·a venereal disease

enfermero/a ⓜ/ⓘ en·fer·*me*·ro/a nurse

enfermo/a ⓜ/ⓘ en·*fer*·mo/a sick

enfrente de en·*fren*·te de in front of

enorme e·*nor*·me huge

ensalada en·sa·*la*·da salad

enseñar en·se·*nyar* show • teach

entrar en·*trar* enter

entre *en*·tre among • between

entregar en·tre·*gar* deliver

entrenador(a) ⓜ/ⓘ en·tre·na·*dor*/en·tre·na·*do*·ra coach

entreno ⓜ en·*tre*·no workout

entrevista ⓘ en·tre·*vees*·ta interview

enviar en·vee·*ar* send • ship off

epilepsia ⓘ e·pee·*lep*·sya epilepsy

equipaje ⓜ e·kee·pa·*khe* luggage

equipo ⓜ e·*kee*·po equipment • team

— de inmersión de een·mer·*syon* diving equipment

— de música ⓜ de *moo*·see·ka stereo

equitación ⓘ e·kee·ta·*thyon* horse riding

equivocado/a ⓜ/ⓘ e·kee·vo·*ka*·do/a wrong

error ⓜ e·*ror* mistake

escalada ⓘ es·ka·*la*·da rock climbing

escalera ⓘ es·ka·*le*·ra stairway

escaleras ⓘ pl **mecánicas** es·ka·*le*·ras me·*kan*·icas escalator

escarcha ⓘ es·*kar*·cha frost

escarpado/a ⓜ/ⓘ es·kar·*pa*·do/a steep

escasez ⓘ es·ka·*seth* shortage

escenario ⓜ es·the·*na*·ryo stage

Escocia ⓘ es·ko·*thya* Scotland

escoger es·ko·*kher* choose

escribir es·kree·*beer* write

— a máquina a ma·*kee*·na type

escritor(a) ⓜ/ⓘ es·kree·*tor*/es·kree·*to*·ra writer

escuchar es·koo·*char* listen

escuela ⓘ es·*kwe*·la school

— de párvulos de *par*·voo·los kindergarten

escultura ⓘ es·kool·*too*·ra sculpture

espacio ⓜ es·*pa*·thyo space

espalda ⓘ es·*pal*·da back (body)

España ⓘ es·*pa*·nya Spain

especial es·pe·*thyal* special

especialista ⓜ&ⓘ es·pe·thya·*lees*·ta specialist

especies ⓘ pl **en peligro de extinción** es·pe·*thyes* en pe·*lee*·gro de eks·teen·*thyon* endangered species

espectáculo ⓜ es·pek·*ta*·koo·lo show

espejo ⓜ es·*pe*·kho mirror

esperar es·pe·*rar* wait

F

espinaca ① es·pee·*na*·ka spinach
esposa ① es·*po*·sa wife
espuma ① **de afeitar** es·*poo*·ma de a·fey·*tar* shaving cream
espumoso/a ⓜ/① es·poo·*mo*·so/a sparkling • foamy
esquí ⓜ es·*kee* skiing
— acuático a·*kwa*·tee·ko waterskiing
esquiar es·kee·*ar* ski
esquina ① es·*kee*·na corner
esta noche es·ta *no*·che tonight
éste/a ⓜ/① *es*·te/a this
estación ① es·ta·*thyon* season • station
— de autobuses de ow·to·*boo*·ses bus station
— de metro de *me*·tro metro station
— de tren de tren railway station
estacionar es·ta·thyo·*nar* park (car)
estadio ⓜ es·*ta*·dyo stadium
estado ⓜ **civil** es·*ta*·do thee·*veel* marital status
estado ⓜ **del bienestar** es·*ta*·do del byen·es·*tar* social welfare • wellbeing
Estados ⓜ pl **Unidos** es·*ta*·dos oo·*nee*·dos USA
estafa ① es·*ta*·fa rip-off
estanquero ⓜ es·tan·*ke*·ro tobacconist
estante ⓜ es·*tan*·te shelf
estar es·*tar* to be
— constipado/a ⓜ/① kons·tee·*pa*·do/a have a cold
— de acuerdo de a·*kwer*·do agree
estatua ① es·*ta*·twa statue
este *es*·te east
esterilla ① es·te·*ree*·lya mat
estilo ⓜ es·*tee*·lo style
estómago ⓜ es·*to*·ma·go stomach
estrellas ① pl es·*tre*·lyas stars
estreñimiento ⓜ es·tre·nyee·*myen*·to constipation
estudiante ⓜ&① es·too·*dyan*·te student
estudio ⓜ es·*too*·dyo studio
estufa ① es·*too*·fa heater

estúpido/a ⓜ/① es·*too*·pee·do/a stupid
etiqueta ① **de equipaje** e·tee·*ke*·ta de e·kee·*pa*·khe luggage tag
euro ⓜ *e*·oo·ro euro
Europa ① e·oo·*ro*·pa Europe
eutanasia ① e·oo·ta·*na*·sya euthanasia
excelente eks·the·*len*·te excellent
excursión ① eks·koor·*syon* tour
excursionismo ⓜ eks·koor·syo·*nees*·mo hiking
experiencia ① eks·pe·*ryen*·thya experience
— laboral ① la·bo·*ral* work experience
exponer eks·po·*ner* exhibit
exposición ① eks·po·see·*thyon* exhibition
expreso eks·*pre*·so express
exterior ⓜ eks·te·*ryor* outside
extrañar eks·tra·*nyar* miss (feel sad)
extranjero/a ⓜ/① eks·tran·*khe*·ro/a foreign

F

fábrica ① *fa*·bree·ka factory
fácil *fa*·theel easy
facturación ① **de equipajes** fak·too·ra·*thyon* de e·kee·*pa*·khes check-in
falda ① *fal*·da skirt
falta ① *fal*·ta fault
familia ① fa·*mee*·lya family
fantástico/a ⓜ/① fan·*tas*·tee·ko/a great
farmacia ① far·ma·*thya* chemist (shop) • pharmacy
farmacéutico ⓜ far·ma·thee·*oo*·tee·ko chemist (person)
faros ⓜ pl *fa*·ros headlights
fecha ① *fe*·cha date (time)
— de nacimiento de na·thee·*myen*·to date of birth
feliz fe·*leeth* happy

ferretería ① fe·re·te·*ree*·a hardware store

festival ⓜ fes·tee·*val* festival

ficción ① feek·*thyon* fiction

fideos ⓜ pl fee·*de*·os noodles

fiebre ① *fye*·bre fever

— glandular glan·doo·*lar* glandular fever

fiesta ① *fyes*·ta party

filete ⓜ fee·*le*·te fillet

film ⓜ feelm film

fin ⓜ feen end

— de semana de se·*ma*·na weekend

final ⓜ fee·*nal* end

firma ① *feer*·ma signature

firmar feer·*mar* sign

flor ① flor flower

florista ⓜ&① flo·*rees*·ta florist

folleto ⓜ fo·*lye*·to brochure

footing ⓜ foo·teen jogging

forma ① *for*·ma shape

fotografía ① fo·to·gra·*fee*·a photograph

fotógrafo/a ⓜ/① fo·*to*·gra·fo/a photographer

fotómetro ⓜ fo·*to*·me·tro light meter

frágil *fra*·kheel fragile

frambuesa ① fram·*hwe*·sa raspberry

franela ① fra·*ne*·la flannel

franqueo ⓜ fran·*ke*·o postage

freír fre·*eer* fry

frenos ⓜ pl *fre*·nos brakes

frente a *fren*·te a opposite

fresa ① *fre*·sa strawberry

frío/a ⓜ/① *free*·o/a cold

frontera ① fron·*te*·ra border

fruta ① *froo*·ta fruit

fruto **seco** *froo*·to *se*·ko dried fruit

fuego ⓜ *fwe*·go fire

fuera de juego *fwe*·ra de *khwe*·go offside

fuerte *fwer*·te strong

fumar foo·*mar* smoke

funda ① **de almohada** *foon*·da de al·*mwa*·da pillowcase

funeral ⓜ foo·ne·*ral* funeral

fútbol ⓜ *foot*·bol football · soccer

— australiano ow·stra·*lya*·no Australian Rules football

futuro ⓜ foo·*too*·ro future

G

gafas ① pl *ga*·fas glasses

— de sol de sol sunglasses

— de submarinismo de soob·ma·ree·*nees*·mo goggles

galleta ① ga·*lye*·ta biscuit · cookie

galletas ① pl **saladas** ga·*lye*·tas sa·*la*·das biscuits · crackers

gambas ① pl *gam*·bas prawns

ganador(a) ⓜ/① ga·na·*dor*/ga·na·*do*·ra winner

ganar ga·*nar* earn · win

garbanzos ⓜ pl gar·*ban*·thos chickpeas

garganta ① gar·*gan*·ta throat

gasolina ① ga·so·*lee*·na petrol

gasolinera ① ga·so·lee·*ne*·ra service station

gatito/a ⓜ/① ga·*tee*·to/a kitten

gato/a ⓜ/① *ga*·to/a cat

gay gai gay

gemelos ⓜ pl khe·*me*·los twins

general khe·ne·*ral* general

gente ① *khen*·te people

gimnasia ① **rítmica** kheem·*na*·sya *reet*·mee·ka gymnastics

ginebra ① khee·*ne*·bra gin

ginecólogo ⓜ khee·ne·*ko*·lo·go gynaecologist

gobierno ⓜ go·*byer*·no government

gol ⓜ gol goal

goma ① *go*·ma condom · rubber

gordo/a ⓜ/① *gor*·do/a fat

grabación ① gra·ba·*thyon* recording

gracioso/a ⓜ/① gra·*thyo*·so/a funny

gramo ⓜ *gra*·mo gram

grande *gran*·de big · large

grande almacene ⓜ *gran*·de al·ma·*the*·ne department store

granja ① *gran*·kha farm

gratis *gra*·tees free (of charge)

grifo ⓜ *gree*·fo tap
gripe ⓕ *gree*·pe influenza
gris grees grey
gritar gree·*tar* shout
grupo ⓜ *groo*·po group
— de rock de rok rock band
— sanguíneo san·*gee*·ne·o blood group
guantes ⓜ pl *gwan*·tes gloves
guardarropa ⓜ gwar·da·*ro*·pa cloakroom
guardería ⓕ gwar·de·*ree*·a childminding service • creche
guerra ⓕ *ge*·ra war
guía ⓜ&ⓕ *gee*·a guide (person)
guía ⓕ *gee*·a guidebook
— audio *ow*·dyo audioguide
— del ocio del o·thyo entertainment guide
— telefónica te·le·*fo*·nee·ka phone book
guindilla ⓕ geen·*dee*·lya chilli
guión ⓜ gee·*on* script
guiri ⓜ *gee*·ree tourist (slang)
guisantes gee·*san*·tes peas
güisqui *gwees*·kee whiskey
guitarra ⓕ gee·*ta*·ra guitar
gustar(le) goos·*tar*(·le) like

H

habitación ⓕ a·bee·ta·*thyon* bedroom • room
— doble *do*·ble double room
— individual een·dee·vee·*dwal* single room
hablar a·*blar* speak • talk
hace sol a·the sol sunny
hacer a·*ther* do • make
— dedo *de*·do hitchhike
— surf soorf surf
— windsurf ween·soorf windsurfing
hachís ⓜ a·*chees* hash
hacia a·thya towards
— abajo a·ba·kho down
halal a·*lal* halal

hamaca ⓕ a·*ma*·ka hammock
hambriento/a ⓜ/ⓕ am·*bryen*·to/a hungry
harina ⓕ a·*ree*·na flour
hasta (junio) *as*·ta (*khoo*·nyo) until (June)
hecho/a ⓜ/ⓕ e·cho/a made
— a mano a *ma*·no handmade
— de (algodón) de (al·go·*don*) made of (cotton)
heladería ⓕ e·la·de·*ree*·a ice cream parlour
helado ⓜ e·*la*·do ice cream
helar e·*lar* freeze
hepatitis ⓕ e·pa·*tee*·tees hepatitis
herbolario ⓜ er·bo·*la*·ryo herbalist (shop)
herida ⓕ e·*ree*·da injury
hermana ⓕ er·*ma*·na sister
hermano ⓜ er·*ma*·no brother
hermoso/a ⓜ/ⓕ er·*mo*·so/a beautiful
heroína ⓕ e·ro·*ee*·na heroin
hielo ⓜ *ye*·lo ice
hierba ⓕ *yer*·ba grass
hierbas ⓕ pl *yer*·bas herbs
hígado ⓜ *ee*·ga·do liver
higos ⓜ pl *ee*·gos figs
hija ⓕ *ee*·kha daughter
hijo ⓜ *ee*·kho son
hijos ⓜ pl *ee*·khos children
hilo ⓜ thread *ee*·lo
— dental den·*tal* dental floss
hinchas ⓜ&ⓕ pl *een*·chas supporters
hindú een·*doo* Hindu
hipódromo ⓜ ee·*po*·dro·mo racetrack (horses)
historial profesional ees·to·*ryal* pro·fe·syo·*nal* CV
histórico/a ⓜ/ⓕ ees·*to*·ree·ko/a historical
hockey ⓜ *kho*·kee hockey
— sobre hielo so·bre *ye*·lo ice hockey
hoja ⓕ o·kha leaf • sheet (of paper)

hojalata ① o·kha·*la*·ta tin
Holanda ① o·*lan*·da Netherlands
hombre ⓜ *om*·bre man
hombros ⓜ pl *om*·bros shoulders
homosexual ⓜ&① o·mo·se·*kswal* homosexual
hora ① o·ra time
horario ⓜ o·ra·ryo timetable
horas ① pl **de abrir** o·ras de a·*breer* opening hours
hormiga ① or·mee·ga ant
horno ⓜ or·no oven
horóscopo ⓜ o·ros·ko·po horoscope
hospital ⓜ os·pee·*tal* hospital
hostelería ① os·te·le·*ree*·a hospitality
hotel ⓜ o·*tel* hotel
hoy oy today
hueso ⓜ we·so bone
huevo ⓜ we·vo egg
humanidades ① pl oo·ma·nee·*da*·des humanities

I

identificación ①
ee·den·tee·fee·ka·*thyon* identification
idiomas ⓜ pl ee·*dyo*·mas languages
idiota ⓜ/① ee·*dyo*·ta idiot
Iglesia ① ee·*gle*·sya church
igual ee·*gwal* same
igualdad ① ee·gwal·*da* equality
impermeable ⓜ eem·per·me·*a*·ble raincoat
impermeable eem·per·me·*a*·ble waterproof
importante eem·por·*tan*·te important
impuesto ⓜ eem·pwes·to tax
— sobre la renta so·bre la *ren*·ta income tax
incluido een·kloo·ee·do included
incómodo/a ⓜ/① een·ko·mo·do/a uncomfortable
India ① *een*·dya India
indicador ⓜ een·dee·ka·*dor* indicator
indigestión ① een·dee·khes·*tyon* indigestion

industria ① een·*doos*·trya industry
infección ① een·fek·*thyon* infection
inflamación ① een·fla·ma·*thyon* inflammation
informática ① een·for·*ma*·tee·ka IT
ingeniería ① een·khe·nye·*ree*·a engineering
ingeniero/a ⓜ/① een·khe·*nye*·ro/a engineer
Inglaterra ① een·gla·*te*·ra England
inglés ⓜ een·*gles* English • English language
ingrediente ⓜ een·gre·*dyen*·te ingredient
injusto/a ⓜ/① een·*khoos*·to/a unfair
inmigración ① een·mee·gra·*thyon* immigration
inocente ee·no·*then*·te innocent
inseguro/a ⓜ/① een·se·goo·ro/a unsafe
instituto ⓜ eens·tee·*too*·to high school
intentar (hacer algo) een·ten·*tar* (a·*thor* al·go) try (to do something)
interesante een·te·re·*san*·te interesting
internacional een·ter·na·thyo·*nal* international
Internet ⓜ een·ter·*net* Internet
intérprete ⓜ&① een·*ter*·pre·te interpreter
inundación ① ee·noon·da·*thyon* flooding
invierno ⓜ een·*vyer*·no winter
invitar een·vee·*tar* invite
inyección ① een·yek·*thyon* injection
inyectar(se) een·yek·*tar*(·se) inject (oneself)
ir eer go
— de compras de *kom*·pras go shopping
— de excursión de eks·koor·*syon* hike
— en tobogán en to·bo·*gan* tobogganing
Irlanda ① eer·*lan*·da Ireland

irritación ① ee·ree·ta·*thyon* rash
— **de pañal** de pa·*nyal* nappy rash
isla ① *ees*·la island
itinerario ⓜ ee·tee·ne·*ra*·ryo itinerary
IVA ⓜ *ee*·va sales tax
izquierda ① eeth·*kyer*·da left

J

jabón ⓜ kha·*bon* soap
jamón ⓜ kha·*mon* ham
Japón ⓜ kha·*pon* Japan
jarabe ⓜ kha·*ra*·be cough medicine
jardín botánico ⓜ khar·*deen* bo·*ta*·nee·ko botanic garden
jarra ① *kha*·ra jar
jefe/a ⓜ/① *khe*·fe/a boss • leader
— **de sección** de sek·*thyon* manager
jengibre ⓜ khen·*khee*·bre ginger
jeringa ① khe·*reen*·ga syringe
jersey ⓜ kher·*sey* jumper • sweater
jet lag ⓜ dyet lag jet lag
jockey ⓜ *dyo*·kee jockey
joven *kho*·ven young
joyería ① kho·ye·*ree*·a jeweller (shop)
jubilado/a ⓜ/① khoo·bee·*la*·do/a retired
judías ① pl khoo·*dee*·as beans
judío/a ⓜ/① khoo·*dee*·o/a Jewish
juegos de ordenador ⓜ pl *khwe*·gos de or·de·na·*dor* computer games
juegos olímpicos ⓜ pl *khwe*·gos o·*leem*·pee·kos Olympic Games
juez ⓜ&① khweth judge
jugar khoo·*gar* play (sport/games)
jugo ⓜ *khoo*·go juice
juguetería ① khoo·ge·te·*ree*·a toyshop
juntos/as ⓜ/① pl *khoon*·tos/as together

K

kilogramo ⓜ kee·lo·*gra*·mo kilogram
kilómetro ⓜ kee·*lo*·me·tro kilometre

kiwi ⓜ *kee*·wee kiwifruit
kosher *ko*·sher Kosher

L

labios ⓜ pl *la*·byos lips
lado ⓜ *la*·do side
ladrón ⓜ la·*dron* thief
lagartija ① la·gar·*tee*·kha lizard
lago ⓜ *la*·go lake
lamentar la·men·*tar* regret
lana ① *la*·na wool
lápiz ⓜ *la*·peeth pencil
— **de labios** de *la*·byos lipstick
largo/a ⓜ/① *lar*·go/a long
lata ① *la*·ta can
lavadero ⓜ la·va·*de*·ro laundry
lavadora ① la·va·*do*·ra washing machine
lavandería ① la·van·de·*ree*·a laundrette
lavar la·*var* wash (something)
lavarse la·*var*·se wash (oneself)
leche ① *le*·che milk
— **de soja** de *so*·kha soy milk
— **desnatada** des·na·*ta*·da skimmed milk
lechuga ① le·*choo*·ga lettuce
leer le·*er* read
legal le·*gal* legal
legislación ① le·khees·la·*thyon* legislation
legumbre ① le·*goom*·bre legume
lejos *le*·khos far
leña ① *le*·nya firewood
lentejas ① pl len·*te*·khas lentils
lentes de contacto ⓜ pl *len*·tes de kon·*tak*·to contact lenses
lento/a ⓜ/① *len*·to/a slow
lesbiana ① les·bee·*a*·na lesbian
leve *le*·ve light
ley ① ley law
libra ① *lee*·bra pound (money)
libre *lee*·bre free (not bound)
librería ① lee·bre·*ree*·a bookshop
libro ⓜ *lee*·bro book
— **de frases** de *fra*·ses phrasebook

libros ⓜ pl **de viajes** lee·bros de vya·khes travel books
líder ⓜ lee·der leader
ligar lee·gar pick up
lila lee·la purple
lima lee·ma lime
límite ⓜ **de equipaje** lee·mee·te de e·kee·pa·khe baggage allowance
limón ⓜ lee·mon lemon
limonada ① lee·mo·na·da lemonade
limpio/a ⓜ/① leem·pyo/a clean
línea ① lee·ne·a line
linterna ① leen·ter·na flashlight • torch
listo/a ⓜ/① lees·to/a ready
lo que lo ke what
local ⓜ lo·kal venue
local lo·kal local
loco/a ⓜ/① lo·ko/a crazy
lodo ⓜ lo·do mud
lombrices ① pl lom·bree·thes worms
los dos los dos both
lubricante ⓜ loo·bree·kan·te lubricant
luces ① pl loo·thes lights
luchar contra loo·char kon·tra fight against
lugar ⓜ loo·gar place
— de nacimiento de na·thee·myen·to place of birth
lujo ⓜ loo·kho luxury
luna ① loo·na moon
— llena lye·na full moon
— de miel de myel honeymoon
luz ① looth light

LL

llamada ① lya ma·da phone call
— a cobro revertido a ko·bro re·ver·tee·do collect call
llamar por telefono lya·mar por te·le·fo·no to make a phone call
llano/a ⓜ/① lya·no/a flat
llave ① lya·ve key
llegadas ① pl lye·ga·das arrivals

llegar lye·gar arrive
llenar lye·nar fill
lleno/a ⓜ/① lye·no/a full
llevar lye·var carry • wear
lluvia ① lyoo·vya rain

LL

M

machismo ⓜ ma·chees·mo sexism
madera ① ma·de·ra wood
madre ① ma·dre mother
madrugada ① ma·droo·ga·da early morning
mago/a ⓜ/① ma·go/a magician
maíz ⓜ ma·eeth corn
maleta ① ma·le·ta suitcase
maletín ⓜ ma·le·teen briefcase
— de primeros auxilios ⓜ de pree·me·ros ow·ksee·lyos first-aid kit
malo/a ⓜ/① ma·lo/a bad
mamá ① ma·ma mum
mamograma ⓜ ma·mo·gra·ma mammogram
mañana ① ma·nya·na tomorrow • morning (6am–1pm)
— por la mañana por la ma·nya·na tomorrow morning
— por la noche por la no·che tomorrow evening
— por la tarde por la tar·de tomorrow afternoon
mandarina ① man·da·ree·na mandarin
mandíbula ① man·dee·boo·la jaw
mando a distancia man·do a dees·tan·thya remote control
mango ⓜ man·go mango
manifestación ① ma·nee·fes·ta·thyon demonstration
manillar ⓜ ma·nee·lyar handlebar
mano ① ma·no hand
manta ① man·ta blanket
manteca ① man·te·ka lard
mantel ⓜ man·tel tablecloth
mantequilla ① man·te·kee·lya butter
manzana ① man·tha·na apple
mapa ⓜ ma·pa map

M

maquillaje ⓜ ma·kee·*lya*·khe make-up

máquina ⓕ *ma*·kee·na machine

— de billetes de bee·*lye*·tes ticket machine

— de tabaco de ta·*ba*·ko cigarette machine

mar ⓜ mar sea

marido ⓜ ma·*ree*·do husband

maravilloso/a ⓜ/ⓕ ma·ra·vee·*lyo*·so/a wonderful

marcador ⓜ mar·ka·*dor* scoreboard

marcapasos ⓜ mar·ka·*pa*·sos pacemaker

marcar mar·*kar* score

marea ⓕ ma·*re*·a tide

mareado/a ⓜ/ⓕ ma·re·a·do/a dizzy • seasick

mareo ⓜ ma·*re*·o travel sickness

margarina ⓕ mar·ga·*ree*·na margarine

marihuana ⓕ ma·ree·*wa*·na marijuana

mariposa ⓕ ma·ree·*po*·sa butterfly

marrón ma·*ron* brown

martillo ⓜ mar·*tee*·lyo hammer

más cercano/a ⓜ/ⓕ mas ther·*ka*·no/a nearest

masaje ⓜ ma·*sa*·khe massage

masajista ⓜ&ⓕ ma·sa·*khees*·ta masseur

matar ma·*tar* kill

matrícula ⓕ ma·*tree*·koo·la license plate number

matrimonio ⓜ ma·tree·*mo*·nyo marriage

mayonesa ⓕ ma·yo·*ne*·sa mayonnaise

mecánico ⓜ me·*ka*·nee·ko mechanic

mechero ⓜ me·*che*·ro lighter

medianoche ⓕ me·dya·*no*·che midnight

medias ⓕ pl *me*·dyas stockings • pantyhose

medicina ⓕ me·dee·*thee*·na medicine

medico/a ⓜ/ⓕ *me*·dee·co/a doctor

medio ⓜ **ambiente** *me*·dyo am·*byen*·te environment

medio/a ⓜ/ⓕ *me*·dyo/a half

mediodía ⓜ me·dyo·*dee*·a noon

medios ⓜ pl **de comunicación** *me*·dyos de ko·moo·nee·ka·*thyon* media

medios ⓜ pl **de transporte** *me*·dyos de trans·*por*·te means of transport

meditación ⓕ meditation me·dee·ta·*thyon*

mejillones ⓜ pl me·khee·*lyo*·nes mussels

mejor me·*khor* better • best

melocotón ⓜ me·lo·ko·*ton* peach

melodía ⓕ me·lo·*dee*·a tune

melón ⓜ me·*lon* melon

mendigo/a ⓜ/ⓕ men·*dee*·go/a beggar

menos *me*·nos less

mensaje ⓜ men·*sa*·khe message

menstruación ⓕ mens·trwa·*thyon* menstruation

mentiroso/a ⓜ/ⓕ men·tee·*ro*·so/a liar

menú ⓜ me·*noo* menu

menudo/a ⓜ/ⓕ me·*noo*·do/a little

a menudo a me·*noo*·do often

mercado ⓜ mer·*ka*·do market

mermelada ⓕ mer·me·*la*·da jam • marmalade

mes ⓜ mes month

mesa ⓕ *me*·sa table

meseta ⓕ me·*se*·ta plateau

metal ⓜ me·*tal* metal

meter (un gol) me·*ter* (oon gol) kick (a goal)

metro ⓜ *me*·tro metre

mezclar meth·*klar* mix

mezquita ⓕ meth·*kee*·ta mosque

mi mee my

microondas ⓜ mee·kro·*on*·das microwave

miel ⓕ myel honey

miembro ⓜ *myem*-bro member

migraña ⓕ mee-*gra*-nya migraine

milímetro ⓜ mee-*lee*-me-tro millimetre

millón ⓜ mee-*lyon* million

minusválido/a ⓜ/ⓕ mee-noos-*va*-lee-do/a disabled

minuto ⓜ mee-*noo*-to minute

mirador ⓜ mee-ra-*dor* lookout

mirar mee-*rar* look • watch

— los escaparates los es-ka-pa-*ra*-tes window-shopping

misa ⓕ *mee*-sa mass

mochila ⓕ mo-*chee*-la backpack

módem ⓜ *mo*-dem modem

(carne) molida (*kar*-ne) mo-*lee*-da mince (meat)

mojado/a ⓜ/ⓕ mo-*kha*-do/a wet

monasterio ⓜ mo-nas-*te*-ryo monastery

monedas ⓕ pl mo-*ne*-das coins

monja ⓕ *mon*-kha nun

monopatinaje ⓜ mo-no-pa-tee-*na*-khe skateboarding

montaña ⓕ mon-*ta*-nya mountain

montar mon-*tar* ride

— en bicicleta en bee-thee-*kle*-ta cycle

monumento ⓜ mo-noo-*men*-to monument

mordedura ⓕ mor-de-*doo*-ra bite (dog)

morir mo-*reer* die

mosquitera ⓕ mos-kee-*te*-ra mosquito net

mosquito ⓜ mos-*kee*-to mosquito

mostaza ⓕ mos-*ta*-tha mustard

mostrador ⓜ mos-tra-*dor* counter

mostrar mos-*trar* show

motocicleta ⓕ mo-to-thee-*kle*-ta motorcycle

motor ⓜ mo-*tor* engine

motora ⓕ mo-*to*-ra motorboat

muchas/os ⓜ/ⓕ pl *moo*-chas/os many

mudo/a ⓜ/ⓕ *moo*-do/a mute

muebles ⓜ pl *mwe*-bles furniture

muela ⓕ *mwe*-la tooth (back)

muelle ⓜ *mwe*-lye spring

muerto/a ⓜ/ⓕ *mwer*-to/a dead

muesli ⓜ *mwes*-lee muesli

mujer ⓕ moo-*kher* woman

multa ⓕ *mool*-ta fine

mundo ⓜ *moon*-do world

muñeca ⓕ moo-*nye*-ka doll • wrist

murallas ⓕ pl moo-*ra*-lyas city walls

músculo ⓜ *moos*-koo-lo muscle

museo ⓜ moo-*se*-o museum

— de arte de *ar*-te art gallery

música ⓕ *moo*-see-ka music

músico/a ⓜ/ⓕ *moo*-see-ko/a musician

— ambulante am-boo-*lan*-te busker

muslo ⓜ *moos*-lo drumstick (chicken)

musulmán(a) ⓜ/ⓕ moo-sool-*man*/ moo-sool-*ma*-na Muslim

muy mooy very

N

nacionalidad ⓕ na-thyo-na-lee-*da* nationality

nada *na*-da none • nothing

nadar na-*dar* swim

naranja ⓕ na-*ran*-kha orange

nariz ⓕ na-*reeth* nose

nata ⓕ *na*-ta cream

— agria *na*-ta *a*-grya sour cream

naturaleza ⓕ na-too-ra-*le*-tha nature

naturopatía ⓕ na-too-ro-pa-*tee*-a naturopathy

náusea ⓕ *now*-se-a nausea

náuseas ⓕ pl **del embarazo** *now*-se-as del em-ba-*ra*-tho morning sickness

navaja ⓕ na-*va*-kha penknife

Navidad ⓕ na-vee-*da* Christmas

necesario/a ⓜ/ⓕ ne-the-*sa*-ryo/a necessary

necesitar ne-the-see-*tar* need

negar ne-*gar* deny

negar ne·*gar* refuse
negocio ⓜ ne·*go*·thyo business
— **de artículos básicos** de ar·*tee*·koo·los ba·*see*·kos convenience store
negro/a ⓜ/ⓕ *ne*·gro/a black
neumático ne·oo·*ma*·tee·ko tyre
nevera ⓕ ne·*ve*·ra refrigerator
nieto/a ⓜ/ⓕ *nye*·to/a grandchild
nieve ⓕ *nye*·ve snow
niño/a ⓜ/ⓕ *nee*·nyo/a child
no no no
— **fumadores** foo·ma·*do*·res non-smoking
— **incluido** een·kloo·*ee*·do excluded
noche ⓕ *no*·che evening • night
Nochebuena ⓕ no·che·*bwe*·na Christmas Eve
Nochevieja ⓕ no·che·*vye*·kha New Year's Eve
nombre ⓜ *nom*·bre name
— **de pila** de *pee*·la Christian name
norte ⓜ *nor*·te north
nosotros/as ⓜ/ⓕ pl no·*so*·tros/no·*so*·tras we
noticias ⓕ pl no·*tee*·thyas news
— **de actualidad** de ak·twal·ee·*da* current affairs
novia ⓕ *no*·vya girlfriend
novio ⓜ *no*·vyo boyfriend
nube ⓕ *noo*·be cloud
nublado noo·*bla*·do cloudy
nueces *nwe*·thes nuts
— **crudas** *kroo*·das raw nuts
— **tostadas** tos·*ta*·das roasted nuts
nuestro/a ⓜ/ⓕ *nwes*·tro/a our
Nueva Zelanda ⓕ *nwe*·va the·*lan*·da New Zealand
nuevo/a ⓜ/ⓕ *nwe*·vo/a new
número ⓜ *noo*·me·ro number
— **de la habitación** de la a·bee·ta·*thyon* room number
— **de pasaporte** de pa·sa·*por*·te passport number
nunca *noon*·ka never

O

o o or
obra ⓕ *o*·bra play • building site
obrero/a ⓜ/ⓕ o·*bre*·ro/a factory worker • labourer
océano ⓜ o·*the*·a·no ocean
ocupado/a ⓜ/ⓕ o·koo·*pa*·do/a busy
ocupar o·koo·*par* live (somewhere)
oeste ⓜ o·*es*·te west
oficina ⓕ o·fee·*thee*·na office
— **de objetos perdidos** de ob·*khe*·tos per·*dee*·dos lost property office
— **de turismo** de too·*rees*·mo tourist office
oír o·*eer* hear
ojo ⓜ *o*·kho eye
ola ⓕ *o*·la wave
olor ⓜ o·*lor* smell
olvidar ol·vee·*dar* forget
ópera ⓕ *o*·pe·ra opera
operación ⓕ o·pe·ra·*thyon* operation
opinión ⓕ o·pee·*nyon* opinion
oporto ⓜ o·*por*·to port (wine)
oportunidad ⓕ o·por·too·nee·*da* chance
oración ⓕ o·ra·*thyon* prayer
orden ⓜ *or*·den order (placement)
ordenador ⓜ or·de·na·*dor* computer
— **portátil** por·ta·teel laptop
ordenar or·de·*nar* order
oreja ⓕ o·*re*·kha ear
orgasmo ⓜ or·*gas*·mo orgasm
original o·ree·khee·*nal* original
orquesta ⓕ or·*kes*·ta orchestra
oscuro/a ⓜ/ⓕ os·*koo*·ro/a dark
ostra ⓕ *os*·tra oyster
otoño ⓜ o·*to*·nyo autumn
otra vez *o*·tra veth again
otro/a ⓜ/ⓕ *o*·tro/a other • another
oveja ⓕ o·*ve*·kha sheep
oxígeno ⓜ o·*ksee*·khe·no oxygen

P

padre ⓜ *pa*·dre father
padres ⓜ pl *pa*·dres parents

pagar pa·*gar* pay
página ① pa·*khee*·na page
pago ⓜ *pa*·go payment
país ⓜ pa·*ees* country
pájaro ⓜ *pa*·kha·ro bird
palabra ① pa·*la*·bra word
palacio ⓜ pa·*la*·thyo palace
palillo ⓜ pa·*lee*·lyo toothpick
pan ⓜ pan bread
— **integral** in te·*gral* wholemeal bread
— **moreno** mo·*re*·no brown bread
panadería ① pa·na·de·*ree*·a bakery
pañal ⓜ pa·*nyal* diaper • nappy
pantalla ① pan·*ta*·lya screen
pantalones ⓜ pl pan·ta·*lo*·nes
pants • trousers
— **cortos** *kor*·tos shorts
pañuelos ⓜ pl **de papel** pa *nywe*·los
de pa·*pel* tissues
papá ⓜ pa·*pa* dad
papel ⓜ pa·*pel* paper
— **de fumar** de foo·*mar* cigarette
papers
— **higiénico** ee·*khye*·nee·ko toilet
paper
paquete ⓜ pa·*ke*·te packet • package
para llevar pa·ra lye·*var* to take away
parabrisas ⓜ pa·ra·*bree*·sas
windscreen
paracaidismo ⓜ pa·ra·kai·*dees*·mo
skydiving
parada ① pa·*ra*·da stop
— **de autobús** de ow·to·*boos* bus stop
— **de taxis** de ta·*ksees* taxi stand
paraguas ⓜ pa·*ra*·gwas umbrella
parapléjico/a ⓜ/①
pa·ra·*ple*·khee·ko/a paraplegic
parar pa·*rar* stop
pared ① pa·*re* wall (inside)
pareja ① pa·*re*·kha pair (couple)
parlamento ⓜ par·la·*men*·to
parliament
paro ⓜ *pa*·ro dole
parque ⓜ *par*·ke park
— **nacional** na·thyo·*nal* national park

parte ① *par*·te part
partida ① **de nacimiento** par·*tee*·da
de na·thee·*myen*·to birth certificate
partido ⓜ par·*tee*·do match (sport) •
(political) party
pasado ⓜ pa·*sa*·do past
pasado mañana pa·sa·do ma·*nya*·na
day after tomorrow
pasado/a ⓜ/① pa·*sa*·do/a off (food)
pasajero ⓜ pa·sa·*khe*·ro passenger
pasaporte ⓜ pa·sa·*por*·te passport
Pascua ① *pas*·kwa Easter
pase ⓜ *pa*·se pass
paseo ⓜ pa·*se*·o street
paso ⓜ *pa*·so step
— **de cebra** de the·bra pedestrian
crossing
pasta ① *pas*·ta pasta
— **dentífrica** den·*tee*·free·ka
toothpaste
pastel ⓜ pas·*tel* cake • pie
— **de cumpleaños** de
koom·ple·a·*nyos* birthday cake
pastelería ① pas te·le·*ree*·a cake
shop
pastilla ① pas·*tee*·lya pill
pastillas ① pl **de menta** pas·*tee* lyas
de *men*·ta mints
pastillas ① pl **para dormir**
pas·*tee*·lyas pa·ra dor·*meer* sleeping
pills
patata ① pa·*ta*·ta potato
paté ⓜ pa·*te* pate (food)
patinar pa·*tee*·nar rollerblading • ice
skating
pato ⓜ *pa*·to duck
pavo ⓜ *pa*·vo turkey
paz ① path peace
peatón ⓜ&① pe·a·*ton* pedestrian
pecho ⓜ *pe*·cho chest
pechuga ① pe·*choo*·ga breast
(poultry)
pedal ⓜ pe·*dal* pedal
pedazo ⓜ pe·*da*·tho piece
pedir pe·*deer* ask (for something)

peine ⓜ *pey*·ne comb
pelea ⓕ pe·*le*·a fight
película ⓕ pe·*lee*·koo·la movie • film (camera)
— en color en ko·*lor* colour film
peligroso/a ⓜ/ⓕ pe·lee·*gro*·so/a dangerous
pelo ⓜ *pe*·lo hair
pelota ⓕ pe·*lo*·ta ball
— de golf de golf golf ball
peluquero/a ⓜ/ⓕ pe·loo·*ke*·ro/a hairdresser
pendientes ⓜ pl pen·*dyen*·tes earrings
pene ⓜ *pe*·ne penis
pensar pen·*sar* think
pensión ⓕ pen·*syon* boarding house
pensionista ⓜ&ⓕ pen·syo·*nees*·ta pensioner
pepino ⓜ pe·*pee*·no cucumber
pequeñito/a ⓜ/ⓕ pe·ke·*nyee*·to/a tiny
pequeño/a ⓜ/ⓕ pe·*ke*·nyo/a small
pera ⓕ *pe*·ra pear
perder per·*der* lose
perdido/a ⓜ/ⓕ per·*dee*·do/a lost
perdonar per·do·*nar* forgive
perejil ⓜ pe·re·*kheel* parsley
perfume ⓜ per·*foo*·me perfume
periódico ⓜ pe·*ryo*·dee·ko newspaper
periodista ⓜ&ⓕ pe·ryo·*dees*·ta journalist
permiso ⓜ per·*mee*·so permission • permit
— de trabajo ⓜ de tra·*ba*·kho work permit
permitir per·mee·*teer* allow • permit
pero *pe*·ro but
perro/a ⓜ/ⓕ *pe*·ro/a dog
perro ⓜ **lazarillo** *pe*·ro la·tha·*ree*·lyo guide dog
persona ⓕ per·*so*·na person
pesado/a ⓜ/ⓕ pe·*sa*·do/a heavy
pesar pe·*sar* weigh

pesas ⓕ pl *pe*·sas weights
pesca ⓕ *pes*·ka fishing
pescadería ⓕ pes·ka·de·*ree*·a fish shop
pescado ⓜ pes·*ka*·do fish (as food)
peso ⓜ *po*·so weight
petición ⓕ pe·tee·*thyon* petition
pez ⓜ peth fish
picadura ⓕ pee·ka·*doo*·ra bite (insect)
picazón ⓜ pee·ka·*thon* itch
pie ⓜ pye foot
piedra ⓕ *pye*·dra stone
piel ⓕ pyel skin
pierna ⓕ *pyer*·na leg
pila ⓕ *pee*·la battery (small)
píldora ⓕ *peel*·do·ra the Pill
pimienta ⓕ pee·*myen*·ta pepper
pimiento ⓜ pee·*myen*·to capsicum • bell pepper
— rojo *ro*·kho red capsicum
— verde *ver*·de green capsicum
piña ⓕ *pee*·nya pineapple
pinchar peen·*char* puncture
ping pong ⓜ peeng pong table tennis
pintar peen·*tar* paint
pintor(a) ⓜ/ⓕ peen·*tor*/peen·*to*·ra painter
pintura ⓕ peen·*too*·ra painting
pinzas ⓕ pl *peen*·thas tweezers
piojos ⓜ pl *pyo*·khos lice
piqueta ⓕ pee·*ke*·ta pickaxe
piquetas ⓕ pl pee·*ke*·tas tent pegs
piscina ⓕ pees·*thee*·na swimming pool
pista ⓕ *pees*·ta court (tennis)
— de tenis de *te*·nees tennis court
pistacho ⓜ pees·*ta*·cho pistachio
plancha ⓕ *plan*·cha iron
planeta ⓜ pla·*ne*·ta planet
planta ⓕ *plan*·ta plant
plástico ⓜ *plas*·tee·ko plastic
plata ⓕ *pla*·ta silver
plataforma ⓕ pla·ta·*for*·ma platform
plátano ⓜ *pla*·ta·no banana

plateado/a ⓜ/ⓕ pla·te·a·do/a silver
plato ⓜ *pla*·to plate
playa ⓕ *pla*·ya beach
plaza ⓕ *pla*·tha square
— de toros de *to*·ros bullring
pobre *po*·bre poor
pobreza ⓕ po·*bre*·tha poverty
pocos *po*·kos few
poder po·*der* can (be able)
poder ⓜ po·*der* power
poesía ⓕ po·e·*see*·a poetry
polen ⓜ *po*·len pollen
policía ⓕ po·lee·*thee*·a police
política ⓕ po·*lee*·tee·ka policy •
politics
político ⓜ po·*lee*·tee·ko politician
póliza ⓕ *po*·lee·tha policy (insurance)
pollo ⓜ *po*·lyo chicken
pomelo ⓜ po·*me*·lo grapefruit
poner po·*ner* put
popular po·poo·*lar* popular
póquer ⓜ *po*·ker poker
por (día) por (*dee*·a) per (day)
por ciento por *thyen*·to percent
por qué por ke why
por vía aérea por vee·a a·e·re·a air
mail
por vía terrestre por vee·a te·res·tre
surface mail
porque *por*·ke because
portero/a ⓜ/ⓕ por·*te*·ro/a
goalkeeper
posible po·*see*·ble possible
postal ⓕ pos·*tal* postcard
póster ⓜ *pos*·ter poster
potro ⓜ *po*·tro foal
pozo ⓜ *po*·tho well
precio ⓜ *pre*·thyo price
— de entrada de en·*tra*·da admission
price
— del cubierto del koo·*byer*·to cover
charge
preferir pre·fe·*reer* prefer
pregunta ⓕ pre·*goon*·ta question
preguntar pre·goon·*tar* ask
(a question)

preocupado/a ⓜ/ⓕ
pre·o·koo·*pa*·do/a worried
preocuparse por pre·o·koo·*par*·se por
care (about something)
preparar pre·pa·*rar* prepare
presidente/a ⓜ/ⓕ pre·see·*den*·te/a
president
presión ⓕ pre·*syon* pressure
— arterial ar·te·*ryal* blood pressure
prevenir pre·ve·*neer* prevent
primavera ⓕ pree·ma·*ve*·ra spring
(season)
primer ministro ⓜ pree·*mer*
mee·*nees*·tro prime minister
primera ministra ⓕ pree·*me*·ra
mee·*nees*·tra prime minister
primero/a ⓜ/ⓕ pree·*me*·ro/a first
principal preen·thee·*pal* main
prisa ⓕ *pree*·sa hurry
prisionero/a ⓜ/ⓕ pree·syon·*ne*·ro/a
prisoner
privado/a ⓜ/ⓕ pree·*va*·do/a private
probar pro·*bar* try
producir pro·doo·*theer* produce
productos ⓜ pl **congelados**
pro·*dook*·tos kon·khe·*la*·dos frozen
foods
profesor(a) ⓜ/ⓕ pro·fe·*sor*/
pro·fe·so·ra lecturer • instructor •
teacher
profundo/a ⓜ/ⓕ pro·*foon*·do/a deep
programa ⓜ pro·*gra*·ma programme
prolongación ⓕ pro·lon·ga·*thyon*
extension (visa)
promesa ⓕ pro·*me*·sa promise
prometida ⓕ pro·me·*tee*·da fiancee
prometido ⓜ pro·me·*tee*·do fiance
pronto *pron*·to soon
propietaria ⓕ pro·pye·*ta*·rya landlady
propietario ⓜ pro·pye·*ta*·ryo landlord
propina ⓕ pro·*pee*·na tip
proteger pro·te·*kher* protect
protegido/a ⓜ/ⓕ pro·te·*khee*·do/a
protected
protesta ⓕ pro·*tes*·ta protest

P

Q

provisiones ⓕ pl pro·bee·syo·nes provisions

proyector ⓜ pro·yek·tor projector

prudente proo·den·te sensible

prueba ⓕ prwe·ba test

— del embarazo del em·ba·ra·tho pregnancy test kit

pruebas ⓕ pl **nucleares** prwe·bas noo·kle·a·res nuclear testing

pub ⓜ poob bar (with music) • pub

pueblo ⓜ pwe·blo village

puente ⓜ pwen·te bridge

puerro ⓜ pwe·ro leek

puerta ⓕ pwer·ta door

puerto ⓜ pwer·to port • harbour

puesta ⓕ **del sol** pwes·ta del sol sunset

pulga ⓕ pool·ga flea

pulmones ⓜ pl pool·mo·nes lungs

punto ⓜ poon·to point (tip/score)

puro ⓜ poo·ro cigar

puro/a ⓜ/ⓕ poo·ro/a pure

Q

(el mes) que viene (el mes) ke vye·ne next (month)

quedar ke·dar leave (behind)

quedarse ke·dar·se stay (remain)

quedarse sin ke·dar·se seen run out of

quejarse ke·khar·se complain

quemadura ⓕ ke·ma·doo·ra burn

— de sol de sol sunburn

querer ke·rer love • want

queso ⓜ ke·so cheese

— crema kre·ma cream cheese

— de cabra de ka·bra goat's cheese

quien kyen who

quincena ⓕ keen·the·na fortnight

quiosco ⓜ kyos·ko news stand • newsagency

quiste ⓜ **ovárico** kees·te o·va·ree·ko ovarian cyst

quizás kee·thas maybe

R

rábano ⓜ ra·ba·no radish

— picante pee·kan·te horseradish

rápido/a ⓜ/ⓕ ra·pee·do/a fast

raqueta ⓕ ra·ke·ta racquet

raro/a ⓜ/ⓕ ra·ro/a rare (item)

rastro ⓜ ras·tro track (footprints)

rata ⓕ ra·ta rat

ratón ⓜ ra·ton mouse

raza ⓕ ra·tha race (people)

razón ⓕ ra·thon reason

realista re·a·lees·ta realistic

recibir re·thee·beer receive

recibo ⓜ re·thee·bo receipt

reciclable re·thee·kla·ble recyclable

reciclar re·thee·klar recycle

recientemente re·thyen·te·men·te recently

recogida ⓕ **de equipajes** re·ko·khee·da de e·kee·pa·khes baggage claim

recolección ⓕ **de fruta** re·ko·lek·thyon de froo·ta fruit picking

recomendar re·ko·men·dar recommend

reconocer re·ko·no·ther recognise

recordar re·kor·dar remember

recorrido ⓜ **guiado** re·ko·ree·do gee·a·do guided tour

recto/a ⓜ/ⓕ rek·to/a straight

recuerdo ⓜ re·kwer·do souvenir

red ⓕ red net

redondo/a ⓜ/ⓕ re·don·do/a round

reembolsar re·em·bol·sar refund

reembolso ⓜ re·em·bol·so refund

referencias ⓕ pl re·fe·ren·thyas references

refresco ⓜ re·fres·ko soft drink

refugiado/a ⓜ/ⓕ re·foo·khya·do/a refugee

regalar re·ga·lar exchange (gifts)

regalo ⓜ re·ga·lo gift

— de bodas de bo·das wedding present

régimen ⓜ re·khee·men diet

reglas ⓕ pl re·glas rules

reina ⓕ rey·na queen

reírse re·eer·se laugh

relación ① re·la·*thyon* relationship
relajarse re·la·*khar*·se relax
religión ① re·lee·*khyon* religion
religioso/a ⓜ/① re·lee·*khyo*·so/a religious
reliquia ① re·*lee*·kya relic
reloj ⓜ re·*lokh* clock
— **de pulsera** de pool·*se*·ra watch
remo ⓜ *re*·mo rowing
remolacha ① re·mo·*la*·cha beetroot
remoto/a ⓜ/① re·*mo*·to/a remote
reparar re·pa·*rar* repair
repartir re·par·*teer* divide up (share)
repetir re·pe·*teer* repeat
república ① re·*poo*·blee·ka republic
requesón ⓜ re·ke·*son* cottage cheese
reserva ① re·*ser*·va reservation
reservar re·ser·*var* book (make a reservation)
resfriado ⓜ res·free·a·do cold
residencia ① **de estudiantes** re·see·*den*·thya de es·too·*dyan*·tes college
residuos ⓜ pl **tóxicos** re·*see*·dwos *tok*·see·kos toxic waste
respirar res·pee·*rar* breathe
respuesta ① res·*pwes*·ta answer
restaurante ⓜ res·tow·*ran*·te restaurant
revisar re·vee·*sar* check
revisor(a) ⓜ/① re·vee·*sor*/re·vee·*so*·ra ticket collector
revista ① re·*vees*·ta magazine
rey ⓜ *rey* king
rico/a ⓜ/① *ree*·ko/a rich
riesgo ⓜ *ryes*·go risk
río ⓜ *ree*·o river
ritmo ⓜ *reet*·mo rhythm
robar ro·*bar* rob • steal
roca ① *ro*·ka rock
rock ⓜ *rok* rock (music)
rodilla ① ro·*dee*·lya knee
rojo/a ⓜ/① *ro*·kho/a red
rollo ⓜ **repelente contra mosquitos** *ro*·lyo re·pe·*len*·te *kon*·tra mos·*kee*·tos mosquito coil

romántico/a ⓜ/① ro·*man*·tee·ko/a romantic
romper rom·*per* break
ron ⓜ *ron* rum
ropa ① *ro*·pa clothing
— **de cama** de *ka*·ma bedding
— **interior** een·te·*ryor* underwear
rosa *ro*·sa pink
roto/a ⓜ/① *ro*·to/a broken
rueda ① *rwe*·da wheel
rugby ⓜ *roog*·bee rugby
ruidoso/a ⓜ/① rwee·*do*·so/a loud
ruinas ① pl *rwee*·nas ruins
ruta ① *roo*·ta route

S

sábado ⓜ *sa*·ba·do Saturday
sábana ① *sa*·ba·na sheet (bed)
saber sa·*ber* know (something)
sabroso/a ⓜ/① sa·*bro*·so/a tasty
sacar sa·*kar* take out • take (photo)
sacerdote ⓜ sa·ther·*do*·te priest
saco ⓜ **de dormir** *sa*·ko de dor·*meer* sleeping bag
sal ① *sal* salt
sala ① **de espera** *sa*·la de es·*pe*·ra waiting room
sala ① **de tránsito** *sa*·la de *tran*·see·to transit lounge
salario ⓜ sa·la·*ryo* rate of pay • salary
salchicha ① sal·*chee*·cha sausage
saldo ⓜ *sal*·do balance (account)
salida ① sa·*lee*·da departure • exit
saliente ⓜ sa·*lyen*·te ledge
salir con sa·*leer* kon go out with
salir de sa·*leer* de depart
salmón ⓜ sal·*mon* salmon
salón de belleza ⓜ sa·*lon* de be·*lye*·tha beauty salon
salsa ① *sal*·sa sauce
— **de guindilla** de geen·*dee*·lya chilli sauce
— **de soja** de *so*·kha soy sauce
— **de tomate** de to·*ma*·te tomato sauce • ketchup

S

saltar sal·*tar* jump
salud ① sa·*loo* health
salvaeslips ⓜ pl sal·va·e·*sleeps* panty liners
salvar sal·*var* save
sandalias ① pl san·*da*·lyas sandals
sandía ① san·*dee*·a watermelon
sangrar san·*grar* bleed
sangre ① *san*·gre blood
santo/a ⓜ/① *san*·to/a saint
sarampión ⓜ sa·ram·*pyon* measles
sartén ① sar·*ten* frying pan
sastre ⓜ *sas*·tre tailor
sauna ① *sow*·na sauna
secar se·*kar* dry
secretario/a ⓜ/① se·kre·*ta*·ryo/a secretary
sed ① se thirst
seda ① *se*·da silk
seguir se·*geer* follow
segundo/a ⓜ/① se·*goon*·do/a second
seguro ⓜ se·*goo*·ro insurance
seguro/a ⓜ/① se·*goo*·ro/a safe
sello ⓜ *se*·lyo stamp
semáforos ⓜ pl se·*ma*·fo·ros traffic lights
Semana ① **Santa** se·*ma*·na san·ta Easter Week
sembrar sem·*brar* plant
semidirecto/a ⓜ/① se·mee·dee·*rek*·to/a non-direct
señal ① se·*nyal* sign
sencillo/a ⓜ/① sen·*thee*·lyo/a simple
(un billete) sencillo ⓜ (oon bee·*lye*·te) sen·*thee*·lyo one-way (ticket)
sendero ⓜ sen·*de*·ro mountain path • path
senos ⓜ pl *se*·nos breasts
sensibilidad ① sen·see·bee·lee·*da* sensitivity • film speed
sensual sen·*swal* sensual
sentarse sen·*tar*·se sit

sentimientos ⓜ pl sen·tee·*myen*·tos feelings
sentir sen·*teer* feel
separado/a ⓜ/① se·pa·*ra*·do/a separate
separar se·pa·*rar* separate
ser ser be
serie ① *se*·rye series
serio/a ⓜ/① *se*·ryo/a serious
seropositivo/a ⓜ/① se·ro·po·see·*tee*·vo/a HIV positive
serpiente ① ser·*pyen*·te snake
servicio ⓜ ser·*vee*·thyo service charge
— militar mee·lee·*tar* military service
— telefónico automático te·le·*fo*·nee·ko ow·to·*ma*·tee·ko direct-dial
servicios ⓜ pl ser·*vee*·thyos toilets
servilleta ① ser·vee·*lye*·ta napkin
sexo ⓜ *sek*·so sex
— seguro se·*goo*·ro safe sex
sexy *sek*·see sexy
si see if
sí see yes
SIDA ⓜ *see*·da AIDS
sidra ① *see*·dra cider
siempre *syem*·pre always
silla ① *see*·lya chair
— de ruedas de *rwe*·das wheelchair
sillín ⓜ see·*lyeen* saddle
similar see·mee·*lar* similar
simpático/a ⓜ/① seem·*pa*·tee·ko/a nice
sin seen without
— hogar o·*gar* homeless
— plomo *plo*·mo unleaded
sinagoga ① see·na·*go*·ga synagogue
Singapur ⓜ seen·ga·*poor* Singapore
sintético/a ⓜ/① seen·*te*·tee·ko/a synthetic
soborno ⓜ so·*bor*·no bribe
sobre *so*·bre about • on top of
sobre ⓜ *so*·bre envelope
sobredosis ① so·bre·*do*·sees overdose

T

sobrevivir so·bre·vee·*veer* survive

socialista ⓜ&ⓕ so·thya·*lees*·ta socialist

sol ⓜ sol sun

soldado ⓜ sol·*da*·do soldier

sólo so·lo only

solo/a ⓜ/ⓕ so·lo/a alone

soltero/a ⓜ/ⓕ sol·*te*·ro/a single

sombra ⓕ *som*·bra shadow

sombrero ⓜ som·*bre*·ro hat

soñar so·*nyar* dream

sondeos ⓜ pl son·*de*·os polls

sonreír son·re·*eer* smile

sopa ⓕ so·pa soup

sordo/a ⓜ/ⓕ sor·do/a deaf

sorpresa ⓕ sor·*pre*·sa surprise

su soo her • his • their

subir soo·*beer* climb

submarinismo ⓜ soob·ma·ree·*nees*·mo diving

subtítulos ⓜ pl soob·*tee*·too·los subtitles

sucio/a ⓜ/ⓕ soo·thyo/a dirty

sucursal ⓕ soo·koor·*sal* branch office

sudar soo·*dar* perspire

suegra ⓕ *swe*·gra mother-in-law

suegro ⓜ *swe*·gro father-in-law

sueldo ⓜ *swel*·do wage

suelo ⓜ *swe*·lo floor

suerte ⓕ *swer*·te luck

suficiente soo·fee·*thyen*·te enough

sufrir soo·*freer* suffer

sujetador ⓜ soo·khe·ta·*dor* bra

supermercado ⓜ soo·per·mer·*ka*·do supermarket

superstición ⓕ soo·pers·tee·*thyon* superstition

sur ⓜ soor south

surf ⓜ **sobre la nieve** soorf *so*·bre la *nye*·ve snowboarding

T

tabaco ⓜ ta·*ba*·ko tobacco

tabla ⓕ **de surf** *ta*·bla de soorf surfboard

tablero ⓜ **de ajedrez** ta·*ble*·ro de a·khe·*dreth* chess board

tacaño/a ⓜ/ⓕ ta·*ka*·nyo/a stingy

talco ⓜ *tal*·ko baby powder

talla ⓕ *ta*·lya size (clothes)

taller ⓜ ta·*lyer* workshop

también tam·*byen* also

tampoco tam·po·ko neither

tampones ⓜ pl tam·*po*·nes tampons

tanga ⓕ *tan*·ga g-string

tapones ⓜ pl **para los oídos** ta·*po*·nes *pa*·ra los o·ee·dos earplugs

taquilla ⓕ ta·*kee*·lya ticket office

tarde *tar*·de late

tarjeta tar·*khe*·ta card

— de crédito de *kre*·dee·to credit card

— de embarque de em·*bar*·ke boarding pass

— de teléfono de te·le·fo·no phone card

tarta ⓕ **nupcial** *tar*·ta noop·*thyal* wedding cake

tasa ⓕ **del aeropuerto** *ta*·sa del ay·ro·*pwer*·to airport tax

taxi ⓜ *ta*·ksee taxi

taza ⓕ *ta*·tha cup

té ⓜ te tea

teatro ⓜ te·*a*·tro theatre

teclado ⓜ te·*kla*·do keyboard

técnica ⓕ *tek*·nee·ka technique

tela ⓕ *te*·la fabric

tele ⓕ *te*·le TV

teleférico ⓜ te·le·*fe*·ree·ko cable car

teléfono ⓜ te·*le*·fo·no telephone

— móvil *mo*·veel mobile phone

— público poo·*blee*·ko public telephone

telegrama ⓜ te·le·*gra*·ma telegram

telenovela ⓕ te·le·no·*ve*·la soap opera

telescopio ⓜ te·les·*ko*·pyo telescope

televisión ⓕ te·le·vee·*syon* television

temperatura ⓕ tem·pe·ra·*too*·ra temperature (weather)

templado/a ⓜ/ⓕ tem·*pla*·do/a warm

templo ⓜ *tem*·plo temple
temporada ⓕ tem·po·*ra*·da season (in sport)
temprano tem·*pra*·no early
tenedor ⓜ te·ne·*dor* fork
tener te·*ner* have
— hambre *am*·bre to be hungry
— prisa *pree*·sa to be in a hurry
— sed seth to be thirsty
— sueño *swe*·nyo to be sleepy
tenis ⓜ *te*·nees tennis
tensión ⓕ **premenstrual** ten·*syon* pre·mens·*trwal* premenstrual tension
tentempié ⓜ ten·tem·*pye* snack
tercio ⓜ *ter*·thyo third
terminar ter·mee·*nar* finish
ternera ⓕ ter·*ne*·ra veal
ternero ⓜ ter·*ne*·ro calf
terremoto ⓜ te·re·*mo*·to earthquake
testarudo/a ⓜ/ⓕ tes·ta·*roo*·do/a stubborn
tía ⓕ *tee*·a aunt
tiempo ⓜ *tyem*·po time • weather
a— a *tyem*·po on time
a— completo/parcial a *tyem*·po kom·*ple*·to/par·*thyal* full-time/part-time
tienda ⓕ **(de campaña)** *tyen*·da (de kam·*pa*·nya) tent
tienda ⓕ *tyen*·da shop
— de comestibles de ko·mes·*tee*·bles grocery
— de fotografía de fo·to·gra·*fee*·a camera shop
— de eléctrodomésticos de e·*lek*·tro·do·*mes*·tee·kos electrical store
— de cámping de *kam*·peen camping store
— de recuerdos de re·*kwer*·dos souvenir shop
— de ropa de *ro*·pa clothing store
— deportiva de·por·*tee*·va sports store
Tierra ⓕ *tye*·ra Earth

tierra ⓕ *tye*·ra land
tiesto ⓜ *tyes*·to pot (plant)
tijeras ⓕ pl tee·*khe*·ras scissors
tímido/a ⓜ/ⓕ *tee*·mee·do/a shy
típico/a ⓜ/ⓕ *tee*·pee·ko/a typical
tlpo ⓜ *lee*·po type
— de cambio de kam·byo exchange rate
tirar tee·*rar* pull
tiritas ⓕ pl tee·*ree*·tas band-aids
título ⓜ *tee*·too·lo degree
toalla ⓕ to·*a*·lya towel
toallita ⓕ to·a·*lyee*·ta face cloth
tobillo ⓜ to·*bee*·lyo ankle
tocar to·*kar* touch
— la guitarra la gee·*ta*·ra play guitar
tocino ⓜ to·*thee*·no bacon
todavía (no) to·da·*vee*·a (no) (not) yet
todo *to*·do all • everything
tofú ⓜ to·*foo* tofu
tomar to·*mar* take • drink
tomate ⓜ to·*ma*·te tomato
— secado al sol se·*ka*·do al sol sun-dried tomato
tono ⓜ *to*·no tone
torcedura ⓕ tor·the·*doo*·ra sprain
tormenta ⓕ tor·*men*·ta storm
toro ⓜ *to*·ro bull
torre ⓕ *to*·re tower
tos ⓕ tos cough
tostada ⓕ tos·*ta*·da toast
tostadora ⓕ tos·ta·*do*·ra toaster
trabajar tra·ba·*khar* work
trabajo ⓜ tra·*ba*·kho job • work
— administrativo ad·mee·nees·tra·*tee*·vo paperwork
— de camarero/a ⓜ/ⓕ de ka·ma·*re*·ro/a bar work
— de casa de *ka*·sa housework
— de limpieza de leem·*pye*·tha cleaning
— eventual e·ven·*twal* casual work
traducir tra·doo·*theer* translate
traer tra·*er* bring
traficante ⓜ&ⓕ **de drogas** tra·fee·*kan*·te de *dro*·gas drug dealer

tráfico ⓜ *tra*·fee·ko traffic
tramposo/a ⓜ/ⓕ tram·po·so/a cheat
tranquilo/a ⓜ/ⓕ tran·*kee*·lo/a quiet
tranvía ⓕ tran·*vee*·a tram
a través a tra·*ves* across
tren ⓜ tren train
— de cercanías de ther·ka·*nee*·as local train
trepar tre·*par* climb • scale
tres en raya tres en *ra*·ya noughts & crosses
triste *trees*·te sad
tú inf too you
tu too your
tubo ⓜ **de escape** *too*·bo de es·*ka*·pe exhaust
tumba ⓕ *toom*·ba grave
tumbarse toom·*bar*·se lie (not stand)
turista ⓜ&ⓕ too·*rees*·ta tourist
— operador(a) ⓜ/ⓕ o·pe·ra·*dor*/o·pe·ra·*do*·ra tourist operator

U

uniforme ⓜ oo·nee·*for*·me uniform
universidad ⓕ oo·nee·ver·*see*·da university
universo ⓜ oo·nee·*ver*·so universe
urgente oor·*khen*·te urgent
Usted pol oos·*te* you
Ustedes pol pl oos·*te*·des you
útil *oo*·teel useful
uvas ⓕ pl *oo*·vas grapes
— pasas *pa*·sas raisins

V

vaca ⓕ *va*·ka cow
vacaciones ⓕ pl va·ka·*thyo*·nes holidays • vacation
vacante va·*kan*·te vacant
vacío/a ⓜ/ⓕ va·*thee*·o/a empty
vacuna ⓕ va·*koo*·na vaccination
vagina ⓕ va·*khee*·na vagina
vagón ⓜ **restaurante** va·*gon* res·tow·*ran*·te dining car

validar va·lee·*dar* validate
valiente va·*lyen*·te brave
valioso/a ⓜ/ⓕ va·*lyo*·so/a valuable
valle ⓜ *va*·lye valley
valor ⓜ va·*lor* value
vaqueros ⓜ pl va·*ke*·ros jeans
varios/as ⓜ/ⓕ pl *va*·ryos/as several
vaso ⓜ *va*·so (drinking) glass
vegetariano/a ⓜ/ⓕ ve·khe·ta·*rya*·no/a vegetarian
vela ⓕ *ve*·la candle
velocidad ⓕ ve·lo·thee·*da* speed
velocímetro ⓜ ve·lo·*thee*·me·tro speedometer
velódromo ⓜ ve·*lo*·dro·mo racetrack (bicycles)
vena ⓕ *ve*·na vein
vendaje ⓜ ven·*da*·khe bandage
vendedor(a) ⓜ/ⓕ **de flores** ven·de·*dor*/ven·de·*do*·ra de *flo*·res florist
vender ven·*der* sell
venenoso/a ⓜ/ⓕ ve·ne·*no*·so/a poisonous
venir ve·*neer* come
ventana ⓕ ven·*ta*·na window
ventilador ⓜ ven·tee·la·*dor* fan (machine)
ver ver see
verano ⓜ ve·*ra*·no summer
verde *ver*·de green
verdulería ⓕ ver·doo·le·*ree*·a greengrocery (shop)
verdulero/a ⓜ/ⓕ ver·doo·*le*·ro/a grocer (shopkeeper)
verduras ⓕ pl ver·*doo*·ras vegetables
vestíbulo ⓜ ves·*tee*·boo·lo foyer
vestido ⓜ ves·*tee*·do dress
vestuario ⓜ ves·*twa*·ryo wardrobe
vestuarios ⓜ pl ves·*twa*·ryos changing room
vez ⓕ veth once
viajar vya·*khar* travel
viaje ⓜ *vya*·khe trip
vid ⓕ veed vine

Y

vida ① *vee*·da life
vidrio ⓜ *vee*·dryo glass
viejo/a ⓜ/① *vye*·kho/a old
viento ⓜ *vyen*·to wind
vinagre ⓜ vee·*na*·gre vinegar
viñedo ⓜ vee·*nye*·do vineyard
vino ⓜ *vee*·no wine
violar vyo·*lar* rape
virus ⓜ *vee*·roos virus
visado ⓜ vee·*sa*·do visa
visitar vee·see·*tar* visit
vista ① *vees*·ta view
vitaminas ① pl vee·ta·*mee*·nas vitamins
víveres ⓜ pl *vee*·ve·res food supplies
vivir vee·*veer* live (life)
vodka ① *vod*·ka vodka
volar vo·*lar* fly
volumen ⓜ vo·*loo*·men volume
volver vol·*ver* return
vosotros/as ⓜ/① pl inf vo·*so*·tros/as you
votar vo·*tar* vote
voz ① voth voice
vuelo doméstico ⓜ *vwe*·lo do·*mes*·tee·ko domestic flight

Y

y ee and
ya ya already
yip ⓜ yeep jeep
yo yo I
yoga ⓜ *yo*·ga yoga
yogur ⓜ yo·*goor* yogurt

Z

zanahoria ① tha·na·o·rya carrot
zapatería ① tha·pa·te·*ree*·a shoe shop
zapatos ⓜ pl tha·*pa*·tos shoes
zodíaco ⓜ tho·*dee*·a·ko zodiac
zoológico ⓜ zo·o·*lo*·khee·ko zoo
zumo ⓜ *thoo*·mo juice
— de naranja de na·*ran*·kha orange juice

Index

índice

For topics that are covered in several sections of this book, we've indicated the most relevant page number in bold.

10 Ways to Start a Sentence

When's (the next flight)?	¿Cuándo sale (el próximo vuelo)?	kwan·do sa·le (el prok·see·mo vwe·lo)
Where's (the station)?	¿Dónde está (la estación)?	don·de es·ta (la es·ta·thyon)
Where can I (buy a ticket)?	¿Dónde puedo (comprar un billete)?	don·de pwe·do (kom·prar oon bee·lye·te)
How much is (a room)?	¿Cuánto cuesta (una habitación)?	kwan·to kwes·ta (oo·na a·bee·ta·thyon)
Do you have (a map)?	¿Tiene (un mapa)?	tye·ne (oon ma·pa)
Is there (a toilet)?	¿Hay (servicios)?	ai (ser·vee·thyos)
I'd like (a coffee).	Quisiera (un café).	kee·sye·ra (oon ka·fe)
Can I (enter)?	¿Se puede (entrar)?	se pwe·de (en·trar)
Could you please (help me)?	¿Puede (ayudarme), por favor?	pwe·de (a·yoo·dar·me) por fa·vor
Do I have to (get a visa)?	¿Necesito (obtener un visado)?	ne·the·see·to (ob·te·ner oon vee·sa·do)